# City of Streams

# City *of* Streams

## GALWAY FOLKLORE AND FOLKLIFE IN THE 1930S

Caitríona Hastings

The
History
Press
Ireland

First published 2017

The History Press Ireland
50 City Quay
Dublin 2
Ireland
www.thehistorypress.ie

The History Press Ireland is a member of Publishing Ireland,
the Irish book publishers' association.

British Library Cataloguing in Publication Data.
A catalogue record for this book is available from the British Library.

ISBN 978 0 7509 8315 0

Typesetting and origination by The History Press

Printed and bound by TJ International Ltd

# CONTENTS

# ABOUT THE AUTHOR

Caitríona Hastings was born in County Tyrone. Retired now and living in Galway, she lectured in Irish Studies in the University of Ulster and then in Heritage Studies in Galway-Mayo Institute of Technology.

Caitríona has published a number of children's books in the Irish language: *Dea-Scéala* (1998), *Balor* (2009), *An Gréasaí Bróg agus Na Síoga* (2010), *Mac Rí Éireann* (2011), *Ó Chrann go Crann* (2012), *Hubert* (2014), *An tÉan Órga* (2014) and *Ridire an Ghaiscidh* (2017). Many of these books have received national awards.

In 2009, The History Press published *Ag Bun na Cruaiche: Folklore and Folklife from the Foot of Croagh Patrick*. Like *City of Streams*, it presents an edited selection of the traditional materials amassed under the auspices of the Irish Folklore Commission's Schools' Scheme, in the environs of Croagh Patrick, County Mayo.

Caitríona believes that traditional material is a valuable resource, to be conserved and handed on in new and attractive ways that suit the new age. It will inspire new creativity and point out ways to sustainable living in our own time.

# ACKNOWLEDGEMENTS

This work owes acknowledgement to the input of many generous people.

Firstly, I wish to thank the wonderful staff in Galway city's libraries, in the headquarters, in St Augustine Street and in Westside, not forgetting Mary's help with the micro-reader and the very patient, knowledgeable and encouraging Petrina Mee who supplied so much information and John Fitzgibbon who helped with images – *gura fada buan sibh uilig*!

The principals of the various national schools who provided details of the schools' histories – *go raibh maith agaibh*.

*Mile buíochas leis an* Dr Ríonach Uí Ógáin, Director of the National Folklife Collection, University College Dublin, for permission to reproduce the texts from the Schools' Collection and Críostóir Mac Carthaigh for help in accessing images from the collection.

My sincere gratitude to Brian Smith, Insight Centre for Data Analysis, NUI Galway, for permission to use images from the *Beo* Irish Digital Heritage Archive, to Brendan Mc Gowan, Galway City Museum, and Tom Kenny for generously sharing their image archives and Dean Kelly for his technical expertise.

Thanks to Peadar O'Dowd who provided useful information, both in his written work and in personal communication.

The map showing the distribution of schools in Galway city and environs was provided by Barry Dalby of EastWest Mapping.

*Buíochas le m'fhear céile Gary as a chuid tacaíochta arís – sonas ort.*

Finally, I want to express my esteem for the Galway teachers and pupils who assembled this wonderful archive of memory in the late 1930s. We remember them with gratitude, as we do the many people who gave them this great body of lore.

# INTRODUCTION

> Between 300 and 400 national school teachers attended a conference held in
> the Presentation Convent School Tuam, on Saturday [13 November 1937], in
> connection with the scheme recently introduced by which pupils are encour-
> aged to collect folklore from their parents and neighbours.[1]

This announcement heralded the launch of the Schools' Folklore Collection
in Galway county in the 1930s. Two inspectors from the Department of
Education addressed the conference. They outlined the 'noble task of collecting the vestiges of our ancient culture, which fortunately are still extant
among the country folk of Ireland', in which endeavour, teachers and pupils
were to be engaged for the next year and a half. Both inspectors were keen
to highlight the virtues of the proposed project: educational in terms of
improving the pupils' listening, dictation and writing skills in both Irish and
English, social in terms of encouraging interaction between the pupils and
adults in their home circle, connecting home and school. The inspectors
ended by appealing to the teachers 'to make a determined effort to save our
great national heritage – Irish Folklore'.

This book presents a selection of the folklore and folklife traditions collected in and around Galway city in 1937–38, under the Schools' Folklore
Collection scheme. In the Irish language, folklore is known as '*béaloideas*',
oral knowledge or instruction. It is that part of our cultural heritage which
is passed on orally, aurally and by imitation. The Irish phrase '*ó ghlúin go
glúin*', literally 'from knee to knee', describes the natural process through
which traditional knowledge of every kind has been transmitted down the
generations. The terms 'memory culture' and 'unofficial culture' have also
been used to indicate the nature of folklore.

In recent times the wider term 'Intangible Cultural Heritage' has been coined. In 2003 UNESCO, adopting the Convention for the Safeguarding of Intangible Cultural Heritage, defined Intangible Cultural Heritage as:

> The practices, representations, expression, as well as the knowledge and skills, that communities, groups, and, in some cases, individuals recognize as part of their culture. It is sometimes called living cultural heritage, and is manifest inter alia in the following domains:
>
> Oral traditions and expressions including language;
> Performing arts;
> Social practices, rituals and festive events;
> Knowledge and practices concerning nature and the universe; traditional craftsmanship.[2]

UNESCO's broad definition of Intangible Heritage matches perfectly the scope of material assembled under the Schools' Folklore Collection. Under this scheme, it was neither anthropologists nor sociologists from outside who recorded the information, but the young children of the area who documented their own particular and unique local culture.

## 'OPENING THE CULTURE-HOARD …'

In the title poem of the collection *North* (1975), the late Seamus Heaney introduced the Anglo-Saxon idea of unlocking the 'word-hoard', tapping into his own particular personal lexicon, his own familiar myths, in order to find a voice, words and images to 'refract' his experience; to give his poems direction, cohesion and resonance:

> Lie down/ in the word-hoard, burrow/ the coil and gleam/ of your furrowed brain …
> Keep your eye clear/ as the bleb of the icicle,/ trust the feel of what nubbed treasure/ your hands have known.[3]

His home place, Mossbawn, was Heaney's starting and finishing point. There he would return again and again to find vision and his own authentic articulation.

Folklore is a bit like that. The 'culture-hoard' of folklore yields preserved local information, but more importantly perhaps, it gives perspective on that material. It provides a view-finder with which to see the present. The Schools' Folklore Collection is an important archive of memory. Now, after more than seventy years, it seems that enough time has elapsed to render this 'culture-hoard' of interest and value to us. Socio-economic conditions have improved so much since the 1930s that it has become easier to consider those other days when life was more difficult for everyone. Every aspect of that time is illumined by the collection which also illumines our own time, giving us a local point of reference from which to evaluate the enormous changes which have taken place in the interim.

## THE SCHOOLS' FOLKLORE SCHEME

The material here is based on the collections made by senior pupils in fourteen national schools in Galway city and its environs, under the direction and guidance of their principal teachers. For various reasons not all primary schools participated in the survey, which was known officially as the Schools' (Folklore) Scheme (*Scéim na Scol*).

These are the Galway schools represented here: *Caisleán Gearr*/Castlegar NS; *Mionloch*/ Menlo NS; *Ceathrú an Bhrúnaigh*/Carrowbrowne NS; *Scoil Naomh Séamus*/Freeport NS Barna; *Páirc na Sceach*/Bushpark NS; *Clochar na Toirbhirte*, Rahoon/Presentation Convent, Rahoon; *Clochar na Trócaire* (Newtownsmith)/Convent of Mercy NS (Newtownsmith); *Scoil San Nioclás (Buachaillí)*/St Nicholas' NS (Boys); *Scoil San Nioclás (Cailíní)*/St Nicholas' NS (Girls); *Scoil Naomh Breandán*/St Brendan's NS; *Scoil Bhaile Chláir na Gaillimhe (Cailíní)*/Claregalway NS (Girls); *Scoil Bhaile Chláir na Gaillimhe (Buachaillí)*/Claregalway NS (Boys); *Uarán Mór (Buachaillí)*/Oranmore NS (Boys); Oranmore Convent.

The Schools' Scheme was devised by Séamus Ó Duilearga and Seán Ó Súilleabháin as an important adjunct to the work of the Irish Folklore

Commission, which has been described as 'a great salvage operation financed by the young independent Irish state'.[4]

In the eighteen-month period between September 1937 and January 1939, approximately 100,000 schoolchildren, aged 11–14, in 5,000 primary schools throughout the Republic of Ireland took part in what may well have been the biggest folklore-collecting scheme ever mounted anywhere in the world. *'Scéim na Scol'* was organised with the collaboration of the Department of Education, in conjunction with the Irish National Teachers' Organisation.[5]

Using a handbook[6] provided by the Folklore Commission, under the weekly direction of their teachers, the children sought material from parents, grandparents, teachers and older members of their community and wrote it down in their school copybooks.

## ARCHIVE

Today, the results of those eighteen months' work, can be viewed, bound and paginated in 1,128 volumes (500,000 manuscript pages), preserved in what was formerly the Department of Irish Folklore (now The National Folklore Collection), University College Dublin. The rest of it is contained in a large collection of the school copybooks into which the raw material was originally written by the children.[7] The folklore collected in each county may also be accessed on microfilm in the respective county libraries. The material relating to schools in County Galway can be viewed in the county library, Galway city. In very recent times, a scheme has been initiated to digitise the National Folklore Collection of Ireland at University College Dublin, on a phased basis. Fortunately, the Galway Schools' Collection is among the first to be made available and can now be accessed at www.dúchas.ie.

## COLLECTING

The handbook distributed to schools sounded an urgent note. The senior pupils were:

invited to participate in the task of rescuing from oblivion the traditions which, in spite of the vicissitudes of the historic Irish nation, have, century in, century out, been preserved with loving care by their ancestors. The task is an urgent one for in our own time most of this important natural oral heritage will have passed away forever.

Looking back now, we realise that this project took place at a crucial time, as the world geared up for the Second World War. After the war many things would have changed, here in Ireland as well as in the rest of Europe. Spanning the years 1937 and 1938, the Schools' Scheme, could hardly have been conducted at a more fortuitous time.

## SCOPE OF THE SURVEY

This was a very well-planned operation, leaving little to chance. In thirty-seven pages of the handbook the Commission outlined the areas of tradition, which were considered worthy of investigation. A range of questions was given under each topic, to guide the young collectors. The collected material corresponds to these categories. If the children collected a good deal of information on 'Hidden Treasure' in their localities, it was as a result of that topic being highlighted in the handbook. In modern times, people are often surprised by the amount of information collected on the 'Care of the Feet', for example. But this was an important topic in the 1930s when some people were still going barefoot on occasion, and when the memory of going barefoot was still very alive.

Here is a list of the topics to be investigated:

Hidden Treasure; A Funny Story; A Collection of Riddles; Weather Lore; Local Heroes; Local Happenings; Severe Weather; Old Schools; Old Crafts; Local Marriage Customs; In Penal Times; Local Place Names; Bird Lore; Local Cures; Home-made Toys; The Lore of Certain Days; Travelling Folk; Fairy Forts; Local Poets; Famine Times; Games I Play; The Local Roads; My Home District; Our Holy Wells; Herbs; The Potato Crop; Proverbs; Festivals; The Care of Our Farm Animals; Churning; The Care of the Feet; The Local Forge; Clothes Made Locally; The Local Patron Saint; The Local Fairs; The

The market, Eyre Square, Galway.

Landlord; Food in Olden Times; Hurling and Football Matches; An Old Story; Old Irish Tales; A Song; Local Monuments; Bread; Buying and Selling; Old Houses; Stories of Giants and Warriors; The Leipreachan or Mermaid; Local Ruins; Religious Stories; The Old Graveyards; A Collection of Prayers; Emblems and Objects of Value; Historical Tradition; Strange Animals.

Instead of their usual weekly composition, fifth- and sixth-class pupils were given time to write down in their copybooks the folklore which they had collected that week. A percentage of that material was then copied into a logbook, either by the teacher or by the pupils themselves. In some schools, entries were almost entirely written into the log by the respective principal teachers, based on information collected by the pupils. In other cases, the entries are either handwritten by the children themselves, or, if written by the teacher, attributed to the child from whose copybook they are copied. The material presented here is based on the microfilm in the Galway County Library, which represents the material in the logbooks from each school. A visit to the copybooks, held in the National Folklore Collection at University College Dublin, will reveal further information; but that was outside the scope of this research.

# LANGUAGE

Information on the various topics and responses were recorded in Irish or English, depending on the district, the school, the teachers and the pupils. As this was a collection undertaken at a particularly important time in Ireland's nation-building process, some teachers may have requested students to complete their responses in Irish even if Irish was not the local vernacular.[8]

## SCHOOLS AND THE IRISH LANGUAGE

As part of the Irish-language revival policy of the new Irish State, the Irish language was made compulsory at curriculum and examination level in primary- and secondary-level schools.

At primary level, an attempt was being made to 'gaelicise' as much as possible every aspect of the curriculum and to deliver it through Irish. In 1926, the Department of Education expected infant classes to be taught entirely through Irish. Classes for older pupils could also be taught in Irish, where the teacher and pupils had sufficient competence in the language. Certain subjects, such as nature study and science, were to be removed from the curriculum in order to allow more time for the language. Teachers were incentivised to use Irish in their classrooms by increased inspectors' ratings for those who used and promoted it most effectively.

Ten years later, by the time the Schools' Folklore Collection took place, there was debate among educationalists, teachers' organisations, politicians and Irish-language advocates, about the educational efficacy of such a policy, both in terms of language acquisition and general educational attainment.[9]

The material recorded in the 1937–8 collection gives a unique insight into aspects of the early linguistic policy of the state. Many pupils and teachers, even in areas where Irish was not the vernacular, wrote their 'compositions' on traditional matters in Irish, So much so, that in the case of this material from Galway city and its environs, it is fair to say that the majority of entries in the manuscripts are in Irish. Much of it is fluent, idiomatic Connacht Irish, grammatically correct and properly spelled. If the pupils were not native speakers of Irish themselves, their entries here indicate a high level of competence in the written language, though we cannot be sure if that carried over into the spoken word.

Interestingly too, pupils sometimes indicate that the information they are recording has been obtained from a family member or friend who was born in the Gaeltacht or Irish-speaking area surrounding the city. The teachers' entries and comments in the manuscripts show that they too were highly proficient in Irish.

## RESIDUAL IRISH

There is also the question of how much 'residual' Irish was still spoken in the Galway area in the 1930s. The special linguistic census taken by Coimisiún na Gaeltachta in 1925 has been faulted for recording people's *ability* to speak Irish rather than their *usage* of the language, and hence overestimating the amount of Irish being used. After 1930, census data has also been faulted for failing to distinguish between native speaker competence and 'learned' school Irish, once the language was being introduced in the schools.[10]

That said, the information from the linguistic census in 1925, and from the general census in 1926, is the only data available on the language situation at that time. It does yield some data on language ability, comparable from area to area. In 1925, 5,375 Irish speakers were recorded in Galway Urban District (46.9 per cent Irish speakers). To look at a few areas in the environs of Galway city: Barna recorded 96.7 per cent Irish speakers,

Furbo 99.7 per cent, Spiddle 98.9 per cent, Claregalway 95.3 per cent, Oranmore 56.7 per cent, and Galway Rural DED 74.2 per cent.[11]

In the 1926 Census, Galway Urban DED recorded 37 per cent Irish speakers, undifferentiated as to ability and usage.[12]

## LANGUAGE USAGE 1937–8

The linguistic picture obtaining in Galway in 1937–8 was complicated. It appears that a fairly high percentage of older people had competence in Irish. Whatever language was being spoken at home, children of school-going age were being exposed to a lot of Irish. Even in the city, some children were using Irish at home. On 3 April 1937, the *Connacht Tribune* quoted from a letter that appeared in a New York newspaper, where a Mr P. Staunton described his recent visit to the Claddagh area in Galway city. As the old Claddagh was being demolished and new houses being built, Staunton remarked on the children he had met, and their language: 'On leaving the car we were surrounded by a group of attractive children, some of them chattering in English, more in the Gaelic.'

## RECORDING ORAL TRADITION

From the standpoint of recording oral tradition, this concentration on using Irish whenever possible in school presents some distraction from the main work in hand. But there it is and we must work with it. At its best and most fluent, it can be an enhancement and present no barrier at all. It can give a glimpse into the linguistic profile of Galway eighty years ago.

I have given my own literal translation underneath all the material referenced in Irish here, for the greater inclusivity of potential readers. I also hope that these Irish-language accounts, so recently penned in historical time, might stimulate interest in the language in Galway, where it is still heard on the streets daily and where many people come to learn it every year.

# IRELAND IN THE 1930S

The Schools' Folklore Collection took place on the eve of the Second World War, or the 'Emergency' as it was referred to in Ireland. It took place in a decade that saw great cultural and political change. These were the 'Hungry Thirties', a time of enormous economic hardship when unemployment was high and emigration was taking its toll. Despite government efforts to create employment through work schemes on road building and the like, and despite some industrial development, there was still not enough employment to enable many people to stay at home.

Between 1932 and 1939, a Fianna Fáil government, led by Éamon de Valera, began the process of dismantling the Anglo-Irish Treaty. In 1937, de Valera drafted a new constitution, *Bunreacht na hÉireann*, which declared that Ireland is a sovereign, independent, democratic state. The name 'Irish Free State' was replaced with either 'Éire' or 'Ireland' and Douglas Hyde was elected its first president in 1937.

In 1937, Fianna Fáil ordered the ending of all payment of land annuities to Britain. There followed an economic war. Britain imposed a tariff of 20 per cent on Irish goods, causing great harm to the Irish cattle trade. In turn, de Valera imposed import duties on British goods such as coal. The trade war lasted until 1938 when the Anglo-Irish Trade Agreement was signed. Ireland

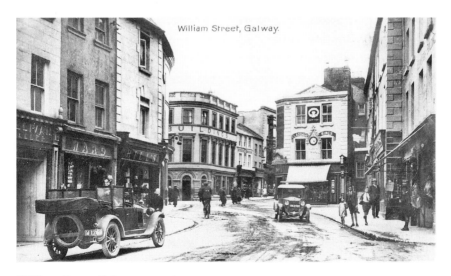

**William Street Galway,** c. **1925.**

made a one-off payment of £10 million to Britain and the Treaty ports of Berehaven, Lough Swilly and Cobh were returned to Ireland.[13]

## FARMING

Small farmers in rural Ireland had suffered greatly during the economic war. A letter from a Kilkenny farmer, quoted in an article in *The Workers' Voice* in 1936, highlights the plight of those trying to eke out a living on the land:

> The only money we could call our own was 21 shillings we got for geese in 1935. We are very lucky if we can get a bit of bad meat on a Sunday. Often I went to work on the roads with my old horse and worked a long day on a piece of flour cake and a bottle of milk.

The author of the article outlined the reasons for emigration and rural migration into urban centres at that time:

> … country people are forced to sell their produce at prices that wouldn't give them potatoes and salt and then have to buy clothes, boots, tobacco, sugar and all the needs of life at prices far above the normal market level … In other words, anything the poor farmer has to sell is dirt cheap; everything he has to buy is dirt dear.[14]

These would have been the circumstances of many of those living on the land in the environs of Galway city in 1937–38.

## ELECTRICITY

In the years 1925–29, the Irish government created the Shannon hydro-electricity scheme. By 1943 all the towns and most of the villages in Ireland had electricity. At the time of this folklore survey, many outlying rural areas were still without electricity and would remain so until the 1950s and beyond. There were no labour-saving devices in the home or on the farm and, aside from an odd household who might own a battery radio, people had to make their own entertainment.

# GALWAY IN THE 'HUNGRY THIRTIES'

In the first decades of the twentieth century, Galway's former small industrial base had declined, mostly due to rising costs. As a result the city 'was in the grip of its worst economic recession'. The situation changed to some extent in the 1930s. The Irish Metal Industries factory opened in Earl's Island in 1934. A hat factory and a chemical factory opened later that decade.[15] Local businesses and shops gave some employment too.

Some people got employment in domestic service or in labouring jobs. In the last *Connacht Tribune* of 1938, a number of 'situations vacant' were advertised, not all of them in Galway itself. A cafe in Athlone was advertising for a 'Good plain cook'. Slaney Furniture in Wexford required 'Cabinet Makers accustomed to bedroom suites'. Only first-class men needed apply for the posts and they would be offered trade union rates. In Woodquay, Galway, Miss Hurd's Registry was seeking 'Cooks, general housekeepers and maids for England' and offering £36 remuneration for same. At a box number, someone was seeking a 'Farmer's daughter [to] serve apprenticeship [3 years], grocery, hardware and boots. Help children with home lessons and assist light housework. [No fee.]'[16]

**Shop Street, Galway,** *c.* **1925.**

At the beginning of December 1938, someone was advertising for an 'Apprentice to blacksmith. Or improver. No fee. Indoor.'[17] Each day, in the Barracks at Renmore, the Irish Army was recruiting unmarried men of good character, aged 18 to 28 years, of not less than 5ft 2ins, for the Infantry Core. The recruits could expect 2 shillings pay per day. The positions would involve two years in the Army Service and ten years in the Reserve.

There was casual, unskilled employment from time to time. In spring 1938, Galway, formerly known as *Cathair na Sruthán* ('the city of the streams'), was being referred to as 'the city of the trenches'. Pipes for a new water supply were being laid throughout the city. The scheme cost £47,000 and gave temporary employment to fifty or sixty men until the end of the year.[18]

Full employment could not be hoped for in the 1930s. In October 1938, an editorial in the *Connacht Tribune* sounded a pessimistic note, warning 'country workers' of the futility of crowding into Galway in search of work. A slump had come in the building trade. Aside from Messrs Stewart, who had begun work on the new Redemptorist College at Mervue, there was no other building work available. Some 700 workers, the editorial stated, 'are at present on county relief schemes' where they could only obtain a couple of days work in the week, 'little more than kept them off the dole'.

In Galway city alone, it was stated, 'there are 200 unemployed in receipt of assistance' and that number was likely to increase. The newspaper encouraged 'citizens of every shade of politics' to consider remedies for this serious social problem. It discouraged more people from coming in to the city 'to become a burden on the taxpayer'.[19]

## FISHING

The fishing industry too was experiencing difficulties. As far back as 1925, John Connolly, a Claddagh fisherman giving evidence before Coimisiún na Gaeltachta, outlined the plight of the Claddagh fleet:

> I remember the time when there was a fleet of over 200 fishing boats sailing out of the Claddagh. In fact, the Claddagh fleet was considered the pride of Galway that time. They kept up Irish customs. They were a Gaelic-speaking people and their conversation was all in Irish. When they went out fishing

Egg and fowl market.

Fish market, Galway, *c.* 1925.

they spoke nothing but Irish at their work. Unfortunately when the fishermen brought in their takes, the fish-buyers gave them whatever price they liked, giving them under the market value of their fish. Often the fish were dumped into the sea, and now the fleet has diminished to about thirty boats. There are only thirty boats constantly fishing in Galway.[20]

This downward trend continued. On 19 November 1938, the *Connacht Tribune* stated that 'today there are in Galway little more than half a dozen boats'. The fishermen could not obtain a fair price for their catch:

Over 100,000 herring caught by about eight Claddagh boats just outside Mutton Island in Galway Bay on Tuesday night were on offer at the Galway fish market on Wednesday morning. About half this number were sold at prices in the neighbourhood of threepence per dozen and the rest had to be dumped back into the sea.

The writer goes on to criticise the Sea Fisheries' Association for being unable to find markets for excess fish not required by the local fish dealers, as the industry is 'gradually breaking up'.

# EMIGRATION

Throughout Ireland, emigration was the only cure for all these ills. The 1936 Preliminary Census Report indicated that the population of Galway city stood at 18,285, a 25.5 per cent increase since the 1926 Census. In the 1930s, rural areas were becoming depopulated and the city was experiencing growth, due to the inflow of rural people looking for work.[21]

In Britain, the steady influx of Irish immigrants did not go unnoticed. Mr Malcolm McDonald, Dominions Secretary, presented data to the British House of Commons showing a clear and steady increase in the number of Irish migrating to Great Britain: 11,000 in 1934, 14,000 in 1935 and 24,000 in 1936. Most would be employed in non-skilled and relatively poorly paid jobs.[22]

Emigrants made every effort to return home for the Christmas holidays. A London reporter of the *Connacht Sentinel* stated that a very substantial proportion of the number that left London for Ireland were 'natives of the land west of the Shannon. The majority of the reservations made on the expresses leaving London for Holyhead were made by travellers to Connacht.' In addition, there were few vacant seats on the trains and long distance services 'plying between Galway and other parts of the Free State on Christmas Eve. Galway people are scattered all over the Free State and all throughout England.'[23]

While the attachment to home was very great, the necessity to leave in order to survive was even greater.

# THE CLADDAGH VILLAGE

Just around the time of the Schools' Folklore Collection, the historic Claddagh village, situated on the west side of the city, was undergoing a transformation. A fishing community, with their own traditional customs and ways, had been living in a maze of small thatched cottages behind the Dominican church in the Claddagh for centuries. In 1934, on health grounds, Galway Corporation initiated a plan to demolish the small houses and streets and build local authority houses for the people of the Claddagh. Not everyone was delighted at this development. Some visitors bemoaned the loss of the unique fishing village with all its cultural traits.[24] The fisher folk themselves were aggrieved at the rents being demanded by the Corporation for the new houses, at a time when the income from fishing was greatly reduced.[25]

This was a period of huge change in one of the oldest traditional areas in Galway city. A new national school opened in the Claddagh in late 1933. Fortunately, the senior pupils there were able to contributed a wealth of information to the Schools' Collection.

# HEALTH

Hospitals in the Galway city area in the 1930s were under the remit of the County Council, prior to the setting-up of the Health Board in 1970. The old Infirmary on Prospect Hill closed in December 1924. Services were transferred to a new Central Hospital on Newcastle Road, the site of the old

**The traditional Claddagh houses being demolished in the 1930s.
(Courtesy of Dept of Irish Folklore, UCD)**

workhouse. The main block of the workhouse was reconstructed to provide six large wards, an operating suite, a ward for TB cases, a small casualty department and ancillary services. Funds for equipment and furniture came from a sum of £4,000 available from an Annual Bazaar. Interestingly, one pathology laboratory was used as an animal house for guinea pigs and rabbits, which were used in those days to confirm the diagnosis of tuberculosis and other infectious diseases.

The Dispensary Buildings was turned into a maternity hospital, which opened in 1924. A new dispensary for the city was constructed nearby. The Fever Hospital, which had been purpose-built in 1909/11 remained in use. Tuberculosis continued to be a big health problem right up until the 1960s. Merlin Park Regional Sanatorium was opened in 1954–5 to deal with it.[26]

Although it was possible to avail of the services of family doctors in the 1930s, people were just as likely to avail of traditional remedies and cures for human and animal complaints, particularly in respect of common everyday ailments. Doctors cost money, when money was very scarce indeed.

# RELIGION

Religious observance was very high in 1930s Ireland. In 1932, a million people thronged the centre of Dublin for the Eucharistic Congress. Religion was important in all aspects of life. In August 1937, the Dominican Fathers blessed the Claddagh fleet at the beginning of the herring-fishing season.[27] There was open-air benediction in the graveyard of the Abbey church after the annual Corpus Christi procession in June 1938.[28] Personal piety was also strong. In December 1937, the following advertisement appeared in the *Connacht Sentinel*:

> Lost – Between Jesuit Church and Nile Lodge, Child's White Scapular and Medal, enclosed in a covering. Name on one medal inside. Of no value only to owner. Would finder kindly return to Connacht Tribune or Jesuit Church.

**Castlegar first communion, 1921.**

On Sunday evening, 10 October 1937, Very Revd Michael J. Browne, DD, DCL, was consecrated Roman Catholic bishop of the united dioceses of Galway and Kilmacduagh, and of Kilfenora.[29] Bishop Browne's preachings and teachings would figure largely in the local press from that time forward.

Two weeks after his consecration, Bishop Browne, while proposing a vote of thanks to a Mrs Coyne for her lecture to the Aquinas Study Circle at Dominican Convent Taylor's Hill on 'The Convent Girl', advocated higher education for a young woman. Among other things, he said, it would 'equip her for her duties in life so that she may discharge them well and attain the true happiness that her vocation as wife and mother entitles her to'.[30]

Bishop Browne and other clergy often warned against the dangers of such pastimes as dancing and drinking. Addressing the Tuam Pioneer Association, a Revd Father Hickie warned of 'the dangers of young boys and girls contracting the habit of excessive drinking at dances', with its attendant moral consequences.[31] A letter-writer to the *Connacht Tribune*, using the pseudonym 'Pro Bono Publico', thanked Bishop Browne for a recent 'welcome, much-needed, and comprehensive address on the evils resulting from the dance craze of our day … Let us hope that many a girl, unconscious of the pitfalls surrounding her, will have her eyes opened when she reads the fatherly warning.'[32]

## ENTERTAINMENT

In a pre-electronic, pre-technological age, most people were still providing their own entertainment, either at home or on a community basis. Outside of the city, few people would have owned a radio. Music, dancing, storytelling and sport was all provided on a non-commercial basis, as had been the case for many generations. But entertainment was changing at the end of the 1930s, especially in the city. There was more commercial provision than before, in cinemas and dance venues particularly.

A 'dance craze' did indeed seem to be in full swing in Galway city, judging by the variety of accounts and advertisements in weekly papers. People came in buses and on bicycles to attend these events.

The functions of one week in February 1937 will serve to illustrate. Many of the dances were 'hops', organised by individual clubs and societies to generate funds. Blackrock Swimming Club ran their 'final hop of the term' on Tuesday, 9 February, from 8 to 12, at Bailey's Ballroom, music supplied by the Sorrento Band. Six hundred people had attended the Galway Garda (Irish-speaking Division) annual ceilidh in the Pavilion, Salthill, on 5 February, and 'everyone was sorry when the function came to an end at 4 a.m.' On Sunday, 5 February, the Sorrento Band again supplied the music for the dancers at Galway Golf Links. A great crowd also attended a 'practice dance' at Bailey's Ballroom that same weekend.[33]

Staff dinner dances were held around Christmas and the New Year. The annual staff dance for the Savoy Cinema staff was held 'at the Astaire Ballroom, on Wednesday January 4th 1939, 10-4. Bill Keaveney and his Orchestra. Special Carnival Novelties, Spot Prizes and a Running Buffet. Tickets including Taxi and Buffet-5 shillings. Dancing 10-4.'[34] In a similar vein, in February 1937, over 600 people attended the Great Southern Railway's staff dance in the Royal Hotel, where the music was supplied by the Sorrento Band No. 2.[35]

Small wonder then that the Galway guardians of public morals were becoming anxious about the new craze for dancing the night away!

Entertainment was also available in the Taibhdhearc Theatre, in the Town Hall Theatre and in the cinemas. In March 1937, the Taibhdhearc Company performed *Ag an Am Sin*, a passion play written by Séamus de Bhilmot.[36] There was an astonishing range of choice in terms of cinema, pointing to the growing popularity of that pastime. The Savoy Cinema provided entertainment on stage and screen, showing three or four different films a week. A regular feature in the Savoy was 'Question Time', a kind of quiz. A challenge quiz, between Companies 'A', 'B' and 'C' from the Renmore Army Barracks, was advertised there for 1 January 1939. That same week, patrons had a choice of four films: *Marry the Girl*, *The Bride Wore Red*, *Owd Bob* and *The Last of Mrs Cheyney*. The Town Hall Theatre offered three films that same week: *Fire Fighters*, *The Hurricaine* and *The Lilac Domino*.[37]

Christmas was a special time for celebration, involving a trip to the Galway market to buy poultry and other provisions from the local farmers. Others were working hard to provide poteen for the celebrations, though the Gardaí did their best to thwart their efforts:

At dawn on Friday a large force of Gardaí from Galway, Headford, Oughterard, Moycullen and the surrounding districts, equipped with fast motor boats, made a swoop on the Corrib islands and discovered 240 gallons of wash and other accessories used in the manufacture of poteen. This is the second raid made by them in a fortnight. On the last occasion they captured a quantity of malt and wash. The past raid is a severe blow to the illicit traffickers who were all prepared for the usual Christmas 'trade'.[38]

# SPORT

Sport played a large part in people's lives in the late 1930s. Many parishes had their own football and hurling teams. In 1938, there was much rejoicing when Galway defeated Kerry in the all-Ireland final. Interest in soccer was growing in the 1930s. Claddagh Rangers and a team called Old Claddonians were playing senior soccer. Galway Rangers won the Celtic Shield in 1933 and by 1937 they were developing a youth team.[39] The World Diving Championships took place at Blackrock, Salthill, in August 1937, as did the Galway Swimming Club's annual gala. Some people engaged in hunting and the Galway races were well attended. Golf was a pastime for some too.

# VISITORS

In the 1930s, Galway city and Salthill were becoming keenly aware of the business potential of tourism in the area. There were discussions on how to provide amenities to cater for the visitors. A heat wave in August 1938 drew huge numbers of people to the beaches 'all along the coast from Salthill to Tully'. Buses and cars brought thousands of visitors from all over the west. Two special trains from Boyle and Clonmel brought 800 'excursionists' as they were called. Four special coaches carried over one hundred visitors to Galway on Sunday, 7 August. Much of the tourism of the time seems to have involved day trippers, but the foundations were being laid for an expanded industry in the years to come.

# THE WIDER PICTURE

The people of Galway were aware of what was going on in the wider world too in the tumultuous thirties.

On 12 January 1937, great interest had been taken in one of the 'Christian Front Ambulances' which drove through Galway prior to being shipped to Spain 'to aid General Franco and his forces', a gift from the Irish Christian Front movement. The ambulance had been on display in Messrs Aylward and Donnellan's garage in Lower Salthill for a few days and was being driven around the of Ireland to 'run it in'. It cost £700 and was one of a fleet of eight being shipped to Spain that week.[40]

The *Connacht Sentinel*[41] carried a story of a plot to assassinate Stalin, by the placing of a bomb under the government box, as he watched a performance at the Little Theatre in Moscow. Apparently Stalin frequently used the box. The report concludes, 'The manager of the theatre has been arrested.'

Galwegians were also reading news of various machinations towards war on the European stage. In October 1938, Bishop Browne expressed gratitude to God for the signing of the ill-fated Munich Agreement, which he and others believed would bring peace to Europe. 'Last Sunday,' he said, 'we prayed for peace, and our first act today should be to offer up our thanksgiving that that peace has been secured.'[42]

**Shop Street, Galway,** *c.* **1940s.**

Towards the end of that year, a local editorial sounded a warning note: 'Those who hug to themselves the delusion that in a general European conflict we in this little island shall be free from its repercussions and perils are living in a fool's paradise.'[43]

# MERMAN?

On a lighter note, indicating perhaps the meeting of two very different worldviews, there was great excitement at Blackrock, Salthill, in September 1937. Crowds gathered, 'many of them armed with cameras', to get a glimpse of a strange dark figure that had been sighted in the bay – a 'merman', as it was thought to be. When the creature came in under the diving board at Blackrock, people were 'dismayed' to realise it was a 15ft-long tiger shark. A member of the Garda Síochána shot the shark in the skull with a .22 rifle.[44]

# CONCLUSION

You could say that this collection of folklore marks the beginning of the end of pre-technological, pre-industrial Ireland. By the end of the Second World War, where change had previously come exceedingly slowly, a new world order would prevail, in respect of material and popular culture. It would take some decades for twentieth-century modernity to really take hold, but the impetus was already well established. The folklore collected by the pupils indicates what had gone before and also the beginnings of that change in various aspects of people's lives. Born in the 1920s, these young people would live their lives in a very different world to their forebears.

Sometimes, it comes as a shock to realise that it is less than eighty years since these traditions were collected. The pace of change has been so great in the interim. In the foreword to an excellent book on the history of Castlegar parish, Professor Gearóid Ó Tuathaigh says, 'Knowing the history, the folklore and the "seanchas" of a local community is a powerful asset in deepening a sense of place and belonging for native and newcomer alike.'[45] This Schools' Folklore Collection is of value today, to help us, as Ó

Tuathaigh says, 'take the pulse' of this area of Galway almost eighty years ago. It is made up of *'les petites histoires'*, not the grand official history of a community, their big important dates and events, but the small intimate details of unofficial history, that which hardly ever finds its way into books and official documents.

It affords us a way of apprehending the warp and weft of a community's everyday lives, their resourcefulness, their imagination, their strengths and vulnerability over time, before modernity and globalisation became the norm. In another place, I have referred to this kind of material as a blueprint for living, a template for survival, in a particular place.[46] So it is with the sample of Galway traditions presented here.

In the City of the Streams, as Galway was called, all these streams of living tradition, refined by time, sustained the community and held them together. The teachers and pupils who recorded them for us at the end of the 1930s have done us a great service. They have left a wonderful memorial behind them.

# EDITING

The collected material reproduced here is a selection from the material held on Reels 9 and 10 of the Schools' Folklore Collection, accessed in Galway County Library Headquarters, Island House, Cathedral Square, Galway city. These reels contain a microfilmed copy of the manuscript pages that are bound in a number of volumes in the Schools' Collection in the National Folklore Collection at University College Dublin. Volumes NFC S30, NFC S31 and NFC S32 contain the Galway material referred to here. The material is collated as follows:

*Caisleán Gearr*/Castlegar NS – S30: 1–75
Teacher: Liam Ó Maolmhuidhe

*Mionloch*/Menlo NS – S30: 74–161
Teacher: Riocard Ó Tiernaigh, Claí Bán, Gaillimh

*Ceathrú an Bhrúnaigh*/Carrowbrowne NS – S30: 162–239
Teacher: Micheál Ó Reachtabhra

*Scoil Naomh Séamus*/Freeport NS Barna – S30: 240–408
Teacher: Seán Ó Maolruanaí, Bearna, Co. na Gaillimhe

*Páirc na Sceach*/Bushpark NS – S30: 409–27
Teacher: Seán Mac Suibhne, Páirc na Sceach, Gaillimh

*Clochar na Toirbhirte*, Rahoon/Presentation Convent, Rahoon – S30: 428–80
Teacher: Teacher's name is not given.

*Clochar na Trócaire* (Newtownsmith)/Convent of Mercy NS (Newtownsmith)
– S31: 1–21
Teacher: Sr M. Colmán, Clochar na Trócaire, Gaillimh

*Scoil San Nioclás (Buachaillí)*/St Nicholas' NS (Boys) – S31: 22–149
Teacher: P.S. Ó Neachtain, Carraig Mórna, Seantalamh, Gaillimh

*Scoil San Nioclás (Cailíní)*/St Nicholas' NS (Girls) – S31: 150–71
Teacher: Eibhlín Bean Uí Mhóráin, Cathair na Gaillimhe

*Scoil Naomh Breandán*/St Brendan's NS – S31: 172–267
Teacher: T. Mac Eochaidh

*Scoil Bhaile Chláir na Gaillimhe (Cailíní)*/Claregalway NS (Girls) – S32: 1–118
Teacher: Eibhlín Bean Mhic Suibhne

*Scoil Bhaile Chláir na Gaillimhe (Buachaillí)*/Claregalway NS (Boys) – S32:
119–336
Teacher: Tomás Ó Conchubhair

*Uarán Mór (Buachaillí)*/Oranmore NS (Boys) – S32: 337–500
Teachers: Micheál Ó Súilleabháin agus Máire Bean Uí Shúilleabháin

*An Clochar Uarán Mór*/Oranmore Convent – S32: 501–46
Teachers: Eibhlín Ní Gheallaigh agus An tSr M. Columba

The handwritten material from each school was read and much of it transcribed. Each item was classified under sub-headings in the six chapters presented here. Very few spelling or grammatical changes were made to the material as they were not necessary. Material in the Irish language is accompanied by my own literal translation.

Each entry's exact location in the manuscript is given below it, e.g. '(NFC) S32: 462–63'. The name of the pupil who collected the information, or the name of the teacher who transferred it into the logbook, if it is available, follows. These names are given just as they appear in the manuscript. Where an item is left blank or is illegible in the original that too is indicated in this transcription.

At the top of each entry, beside the title, the name of the school from which it came is indicated by a letter or letters, in brackets. For convenience, the name of each school has been given a shorthand designation, thus:

*Caisleán Gearr*/Castlegar NS – (C'g)

*Mionloch*/Menlo NS – (M)

*Ceathrú an Bhrúnaigh*/Carrowbrowne NS – (C'b)

*Scoil Naomh Séamus*/Freeport NS Barna – (F)

*Páirc na Sceach*/Bushpark NS – (B'p)

*Clochar na Toirbhirte*, Rahoon/Presentation Convent, Rahoon – (P)

*Clochar na Trócaire* (Newtownsmith)/Convent of Mercy NS (Newtownsmith) – (N's)

*Scoil San Nioclás (Buachaillí)*/St Nicholas' NS (Boys) – (NB)

*Scoil San Nioclás (Cailíní)*/St Nicholas' NS (Girls) – (NC)

*Scoil Naomh Breandán*/St Brendan's NS – (B)

*Scoil Bhaile Chláir na Gaillimhe (Cailíní)*/Claregalway NS (Girls) – (CGC)

*Scoil Bhaile Chláir na Gaillimhe (Buachaillí)*/Claregalway NS (Boys) – (CGB)

*Uarán Mór (Buachaillí)*/Oranmore NS (Boys) – (O'm B)

*An Clochar Uarán Mór*/Oranmore Convent – (O'm C)

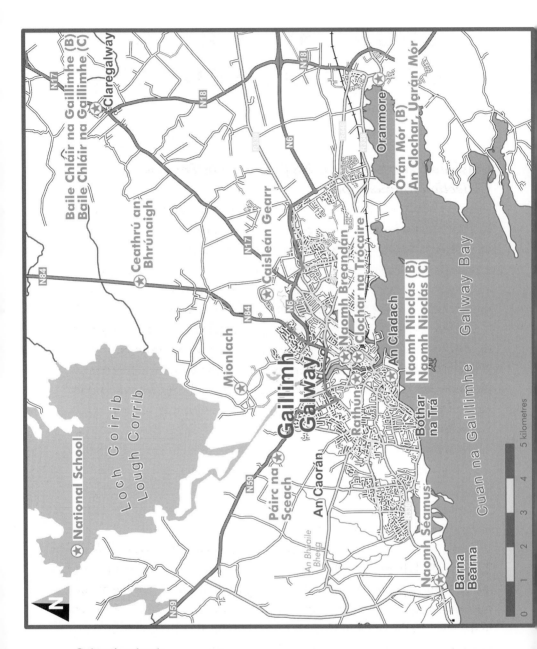

Galway's schools.

# SHORT HISTORY OF
# THE GALWAY SCHOOLS

### *Caisleán Gearr/Castlegar NS (S30: 1–75 in The Schools'*
### *Collection manuscripts)*

*Teacher: Liam Ó Maolmhuidhe*

In 1826, the Education Commissioners' report listed two hedge schools in Castlegar parish. One school built in Merlin Park, by the landlord Blake, was a free school with space for sixty pupils: forty boys and twenty girls. In addition to the usual subjects, pupils were also required to undertake scripture reading. The second school was a pay school, a thatched house which doubled as a chapel on Sundays, situated in Ballygurrane. The pupils paid one shilling and eight pence a quarter. This latter was destroyed by fire in 1827, when the school was transferred to a stable in Castlegar. This school remained until 1865 when a new national school was built beside the Tuam Road. In 1941, the new school, *Scoil Cholmcille Naofa*, was opened by the Department of Education.

(*Ó Laoi, Padraic,* History of Castlegar Parish, *Galway, 1998.*)

### *Mionloch/Menlo NS (S30: 74–161)*

*Teacher: Riocard Ó Tiernaigh, Claí Bán, Gaillimh*

Two so-called charter schools, supported by the state, were set up in the area in the 1850s. One was built by the Blakes in Mionloch, on the site of the present national school. This and the other charter school, which was built in Ballynew by the landlord Hodgson, were boycotted by the people because of their aim of proselytisation. The school in Mionloch was handed over to the Board of Education in 1863. *Scoil Bhríde* national school was established in the late 1930s. The original school had two classrooms and two more were added in the late 1970s. In 2013, the school had seven teachers and was awaiting the move into a new school building.

*(Ó Laoi, Padraic,* History of Castlegar Parish, *Galway, 1998, school website.)*

## Ceathrú an Bhrúnaigh/Carrowbrowne NS (S30: 162–239)

*Teacher: Micheál Ó Reachtabhra*

There is no tradition of a hedge school in Carrowbrowne, but it is indicated by the fact that the parish built a national school there in 1881. The school was for boys and girls and two teachers' residences were also built, on land rented from the Marquis of Clanrickarde initially, and then gifted by his successor Lord Lascelles. When the new parish school was opened in Castlegar in 1941, the Carrowbrowne school closed down and the teachers and pupils transferred to the newly constructed St Colmcille's National School which is also known as Castlegar National School.

*(Ó Laoi, Padraic,* History of Castlegar Parish, *Galway, 1998.)*

## Scoil Naomh Séamus/Freeport NS Barna (S30: 240–408)

*Teacher: Seán Ó Maolruanaí, Bearna, Co. na Gaillimhe*

The school was originally built in 1856, as an all-girls school with one classroom. A one-classroom boys' school was built in 1864, opposite Barna church. These two schools were amalgamated in 1937, on the site of the present school. There were two classrooms, cloakrooms, and outdoor toilets. Heating was provided by a turf fire and each child was expected to bring two sods of turf to school each day.

To accommodate the increased population of Barna, the school was extended on different occasions in the 1970s. The current two-storey building was erected in 1982. In the summers of 2010 and 2013, *Scoil Shéamais Naofa* was further extended with newly built classrooms. A newly designed school garden has been added.

*(School website.)*

## *Páirc na Sceach/Bushpark NS (S30: 409–427)*

*Teacher: Seán Mac Suibhne, Páirc na Sceach, Gaillimh*

In 1838, a new national school opened beside the newly consecrated Bushypark church on the main Galway–Moycullen Road. Bushypark School, dedicated to St James, was built at a cost of £129. The old school was rebuilt in 1890, and a new school was built in 1972 on a new site on the Circular Road. This building had three classrooms and forty-eight pupils in attendance. Numbers rose continually over the coming years. By 1982, there were nine teachers with an enrolment figure of 239 pupils. A larger school was required and so in 1982 an extension was built, resulting in an eight-classroom school.

Since then the school has grown steadily as new estates were built and Galway city extended out as far as Bushypark. By 1990, a further two classrooms and a new hall were needed. In 2005 St James' NS was mostly demolished and rebuilt into a modern thirteen-classroom structure. There was further development in 2011 and there are now seventeen mainstream classrooms, catering for 409 pupils and a teaching staff of twenty-two.

*(Personal communication from Mr Joe Carney, principal,*
*St Joseph's NS Bushypark, Galway. 24 February 2014.)*

## *Clochar na Toirbhirte, Rahoon/Presentation Convent, Rahoon (S30: 428–80)*

*Teacher: Teacher's name is not given in manuscript*

The Rahoon Presentation Primary School, erected in 1820 on the right bank of the river flowing by the convent grounds, was the first Presentation school in the west of Ireland. The work was undertaken by Sr Mary John Power from Kilkenny, in order to provide instruction for local children who came in large numbers. Later on, when the National Board of Education was established in 1831, the Presentation Sisters adjusted their school programme to bring it into line with the department's rules and regulations. As time went on, the original school building was extended and remodelled.

A separate Infants' School was built in 1931 and later extended in 1963. It still remains standing. The Daily Attendance Record for the year 1937 shows that there were an average of 70 boys and 140 girls attending the infant and first classes, and an average of 450 girls attending classes 2 to 8. In 1937, the pupils came from a wide area of Galway: all the way east to Bohermore, all the way west to Salthill and Barna, and locally to Canal Rd, Henry St, Grattan Rd, St Mary's Rd, Newcastle and Shantalla. The pupils belonged to every walk of life.

In 1965, the school moved to the area that had been the convent farm and to a brand new school, the present *Scoil Chroí Íosa* on Newcastle Rd. The historic, century-and-a-half-year-old school building was demolished. A new school Presentation Secondary was built on the site and opened its doors in 1968.

*(Personal communication from Sr Anne Fox, Presentation Convent, Galway. 1 March 2014)*

### Clochar na Trócaire (Newtownsmith)/Convent of Mercy NS (Newtownsmith) (S31: 1–21)

*Teacher: Sr M. Colmán, Clochar na Trócaire, Gaillimh*

In 1840, three Sisters of Mercy came to Galway on the invitation of the bishop. They set up in a house in Lombard Street, moving to St Vincent's in Newtownsmith in 1842. They were caring for the poor and sick, visiting the jail, teaching adults in Sunday school and setting up schools. In August 1845, their National School at Newtownsmith was placed under the jurisdiction of the Commissioners of National Education. Many of the children who came to the school seeking instruction were extremely poor, and often it was necessary to clothe and feed them first before any formal education took place.

In 1845, the school had 160 pupils on the roll, boys and girls. In 1875, it was an all-girls school with some 1,174 children attending. By 1889, that figure had dropped to 874, one third boys and two thirds girls. *Scoil an Linbh Íosa*, or the Mercy Primary School, was opened in January 1960. By 1969, more than 900 pupils were attending. In July of that year, *Scoil na Tríonóide Naofa* was opened in Mervue, taking a sizeable number of Renmore and Mervue pupils from *Scoil an Linbh Íosa*. Further reductions in numbers took place due to the building of primary schools in Renmore and Ballinfoile.

In 1975, *Scoil an Linbh Íosa* accepted the first class of children from the traveller community. Thus began a new phase of outreach and integration for the school which was catering for 'new Irish' pupils from some seventy-eight countries by 2010. Since 2008, one room has been dedicated to pre-school children. Like the other national schools in Galway, *Scoil an Linbh Íosa* is now making every effort to keep up with the many educational needs of a very diverse school community.

*(Sr Catherine Coffey, Scoil an Linbh Íosa, Francis St, Galway, Galway 2012.*
*Accessed in Sisters of Mercy Archive, Forster Street, Galway. Sr M.C. Scully,*
A Study of the Emergence and Growth of the Provision of Education
for Children in Galway City Since 1800, *unpublished PhD thesis, 1976.)*

## Scoil San Nioclás (Buachailli)/St Nicholas' NS (Boys) (S31: 22–149)

*Teacher: P.S. Ó Neachtain, Carraig Mórna, Seantalamh, Gaillimh*

## Scoil San Nioclás (Cailíní)/St Nicholas' NS (Girls) (S31: 150–171)

*Teacher: Eibhlín Bean Uí Mhóráin, Cathair na Gaillimhe*
The first school which opened in Galway's Claddagh in 1827 was situated roughly where the Fr Tom Burke statue is today and comprised both a boys' and a girls' school.

In 1846, during the Great Famine, the Dominicans started work on the Piscatorial School to give the young men of the village a good nautical education. In 1848, there was an average daily attendance of about 400 pupils at the school. By 1887, it had become an ordinary elementary school and its management had been handed over to the parish. Colloquially, it was referred to as Daddy Quoile's school, after the headmaster.

A new school was provided for the children of the Claddagh in the 1930s, as the cottages of the old Claddagh were being replaced, and Fr Griffin Road was opened to Salthill. It opened in 1933 and was originally divided into a boys' school and a girls' school, which later amalgamated to become co-educational.

In recent years, the school has seen extensive development of its facilities where a teaching staff of over forty caters for the needs of a diverse community of over 360 pupils.

(*'Calling all Claddagh School Past Pupils'*, Galway Advertiser, *31 January 2013.*
Seán Leonard, Claddagh NS – 80 Years of Words and Pictures, *Galway 2013.*)

### Scoil Naomh Breandán/St Brendan's NS Galway (S31: 172–267)

*Teacher: T. Mac Eochaidh*

St Brendan's National School opened on St Brendan's Road, Woodquay, in 1916. It was an all-male school which initially catered for boys from Woodquay, Sickeen, and Bohermore. After the Second World War the school began to attract pupils from Shantalla and Newcastle also. It closed down in the 1960s with most of the boys transferring to St Patrick's National School in the centre of Galway city.

St Brendan's school building was hidden behind a high wall, and it was later demolished. Part of the boundary wall is still visible at the back of the office blocks that have replaced it.

(Galway Advertiser, *29 October 2009.*)

### Scoil Bhaile Chláir na Gaillimhe (Cailíní)/Claregalway NS (Girls) (S32: 1–118)

*Teacher: Eibhlín Bean Mhic Suibhne*

### Scoil Bhaile Chláir na Gaillimhe (Buachaillí)/Claregalway NS (Boys) (S32: 119–336)

*Teacher: Tomás Ó Conchubhair*

In 1826, the Second Report of the Irish Educational Inquiry referred to a pay school held in the parish chapel in Claregalway. Fifty boys and thirty girls were attending the school at the time and the chapel was situated just off the main road, a short distance south of the river. In 1835, another report described two schools in the parish of Claregalway. Local folklore also tells of two hedge schools in the area. In 1851, the Commissioners' Report on National Education recorded a boys' school, with seventy-eight boys, and a girls' school, with fifty-four girls.

On 6 October 1930, a new school was opened, at a reputed cost of £3,000. Boys and girls were still taught separately up until 1970 when the two schools amalgamated. At the time of the amalgamation, sixty-nine boys and fifty-four girls were enrolled in the school. These numbers increased greatly as the population in Claregalway increased and the school was extended in the 1980s and again in the 1990s.

*(Claregalway Cultural and Historical Society, 1999,* Claregalway Parish History: 750 Years)

## Uarán Mór (Buachaillí)/Oranmore NS (Boys) (S32: 337–500)

*Teachers: Micheál Ó Súilleabháin agus Máire Bean Uí Shúilleabháin*

In Oranmore, boys and girls used to attend the Presentation Convent School until they made their First Holy Communion in first class. After that, the boys transferred to the Boys' National School which was situated at the junction of the old Clarenbridge and Maree roads. This was a two-teacher school with classes upstairs and down. It was a fine cut-stone building which is now a picturesque private residence. The school has school registers dating back to the 1900s. In May 1925, the register shows there were fifty-eight pupils on the roll, including two boys who were over 15 years of age.

The present school building goes back to 1971 and the modern school has been developing since then. Currently there are ten classes, an enrolment of 260 and fifteen teachers.

*(Personal communication from school principal, and the school web site.)*

## An Clochar, Uarán Mór ( Cailíní)/Oranmore Convent NS (Girls) (S32: 501–46)

*Teachers: Eibhlín Ní Ghealaigh agus An tSr. M. Columba*

In 1861, Councillor John Blake bequeathed £2,000 which was used to purchase the former hotel in the village of Oranmore for the first Presentation Convent there.

Children from a wide area around Oranmore, and beyond, flocked eagerly to the Presentation school. The first school, known today as 'The Old National School', was built in 1886. There were 350 pupils in 1874 though this number decreased in later years following famine and fever in the area in the spring of 1880. Many children who walked long distances to school were given a meal. Clothing too was given and charitable ladies of the area held a bazaar each year to support the work of the Sisters.

During 1916 a spacious hall was built with a residence attached, to provide for instruction in Domestic Economy. In 1973, a new primary school was built to accommodate the increasing numbers of pupils due to development in the Galway area. This was further extended in the late 1980s when pupil numbers continued to grow.

At present Scoil Mhuire, as the school is now known, caters for over 400 pupils, many of them new Irish, and there are twenty-four teachers.

*(School website.)*

# 1

# MY HOME PLACE

Thugtaí Cathair na Sruthán ar an gcathair seo uair amháin,
mar gheall ar go raibh a lán sruthán ag sníomh a mbealach tríd.

*[This city was once called the City of Streams, because there used
to be a lot of streams winding their way through it.]*

The pupils, and everyone they spoke to, had an intimate knowledge of their home place. The accounts furnish us with the myriad small, local details that are woven together to make up the fabric of a familiar landscape, a place called home.

We see the common surnames of the families living in the area, how their place names have evolved, the kind of houses they lived in, their graveyards, churches and holy wells, their castles and forts and raths, and how they have named their roadways.

The story of the home place is bound up with various personages, happenings and places: the giant Fiachail (who was supposed to have jumped from Loch a' tSaile to Renmore), the dreaded Cromwell, Thomas Murray the weaver, Daniel O'Connell (who spoke from a large rock in Shantalla), a lane where the tinkers used to live and another where the pooka would be sighted. Each place, however small, had a name, and each name involved a story. Indeed, sometimes we see that fanciful beliefs were firmly held about the origins and sources of such matters.

The extracts reveal that unbaptised children were buried seperately in a *lisín*, though that custom was changing. Along the coast, people earned their

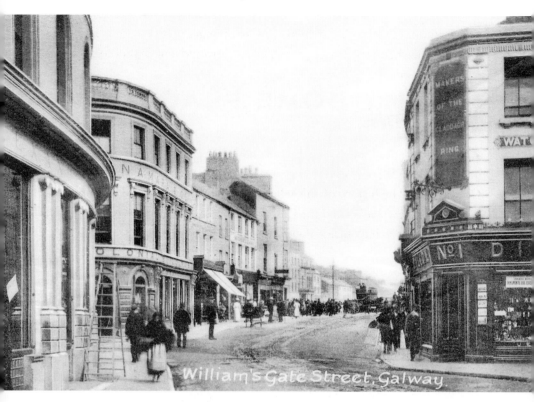

**William's Gate Street in Galway, c. 1925.**

livelihood by fishing and by picking winkles on the shore. Glenascaul folk were still referring to the two parts of their village as '*baile thoir*' and '*baile thiar*' and neighbours used to gather into each others' houses for country dances and 'raffles'. They still had great veneration for their holy wells, going there on pilgrimage on the specially appointed feast days. While the vast majority of houses had thatched roofs in former times, some were now being slated. Not long before this, many villages could boast a full range of skilled craftspeople, making them self-sufficient to a large degree. However, by this time, a lot of houses were empty or in ruins, due to many migrating and emigrating in search of employment.

Life was beginning to change in the late 1930s. Collecting this folklore gave the pupils a wonderful opportunity to become aware of the small complexities of their own place, just before the emergence of a modern, technological, rational and global culture. Born in the late 1920s, the world they faithfully document here would have changed out of all ken by the time they reached maturity, never mind how it would look in their old age.

# MY HOME

### *The Claddagh (NB)*

The Claddagh fishing village is situated to the west of Galway overlooking Galway Bay. The history of this village may be traced back for centuries. It is only in recent years that the Claddagh people practised the habits and dress of people living outside their own circle.

*(S31: 27. Martin Browne. I got this information from Mrs Browne, Fair Hill, Galway.)*

Fishermen's cottages in Claddagh, a fishing suburb of Galway, *c.* 1901.

## *Lochatalia (NB)*

A giant was once supposed to live near Loughatalia. He was able to throw large rocks about half a mile away. One time another giant wanted to fight him and he was called Fiachail. They met and they had a great fight. The first giant put the second one, Fiachail, to flight and he was supposed to jump from Loughatalia to Renmore. That was known afterwards as the Giant's Leap. This lake is so called because the seawater comes into the sea lake, Loughatalia, sometimes.

*(S31: 137. Patrick Doyle, from Mrs Doyle, 39, New Docks, Galway, 25 April 1938.)*

## *An Cladach [The Claddagh] (NB)*

Tá mé i mo chónaí ins an gCladach. Is é an t-ainm atá ar an bparóiste seo ná paróiste Naomh Nioclás. Fadó bhí a lán seantithe ins an gCladach ach tá siad leagtha anois agus tá tithe nua ann. Seo iad na hainmneacha is coitianta ins an gCladach: Ó Maordha, Ó Flaitheartaigh, Ó hÁirt agus Ó Cuirrín. Tá cúigear ins an gCladach atá os cionn 70 bliain. Tá a lán Gaeilge ag gach duine acu agus tá siad in ann scéalta a insint freisin. Chuaigh a lán daoine ón gCladach go hAimeiriceá fadó.

**TRANSLATION:**

I live in the Claddagh. This parish is called St Nicholas'. Long ago there were many old houses in the Claddagh but they are demolished now and new ones built. The most common names in the Claddagh are: Moore, O'Flaherty, Harte and Curran. Five residents are over 70. Each of them has plenty of Irish and they can tell stories too. Many people from the Claddagh went to America long ago.

*(S31: 104–5. Máirtín Mac Coitigh.)*

## *Naomhphátrún an Cheantair [The Local Patron Saint] (NB)*

Is é Naomh Nioclás an t-ainm atá ar naomhphátrún an cheantair seo. Ní raibh mainistir nó cill nó teampall ag an naomh nó ag a chuid manach. Tá scéalta deasa ar an naomh sin againn. Tugtar Santa Claus mar ainm eile ar

Naomh Nioclás. Bhí croí maith ag an naomh agus bhí sé go han-mhaith do na daoine bochta. Théadh sé ó theach go teach, bia agus féiríní aige le cur faoi na doirse. Creidtear ann ón lá sin go dtí an lá atá inniu ann.

Tá áiteanna ann agus tá siad ainmnithe as an naomh: Sráidbhaile Naomh Nioclás, Sráid Naomh Nioclás, Séipéal Paróisteach Naomh Nioclás, Teampall Naomh Nioclás (Protastúnach). Níl aon tobar beannaithe tiomnaithe don naomh.

**TRANSLATION:**

The local patron saint is Saint Nicholas. The saint did not have a monastery or a church here, and neither did his monks. We have nice stories about him. Another name for Saint Nicholas is Santa Claus. He had a kind heart and was very good to the poor people. He'd go from house to house putting food and presents under the doors. People believe in him from that time to this.

Some places are called after the saint: St Nicholas' village, St Nicholas' Street, St Nicholas' parish chapel, St Nicholas' church (Protestant). No holy well is dedicated to him.

*(S31: 122–3. Pádraig Ó Dubhghaill. Fuaireas seo ó Bhean Uí Dhubhghaill, 39, Na Duganna, Gaillimh.)*

## An Cladach [The Claddagh] (NC)

Insan gCladach fadó bhí rí agus banríon ina gcónaí. Chuala mé seanbhean ag rá lá amháin go raibh ór le fáil insan gCladach agus is é an áit a bhfuil sé le fáil ná i gCeann Láimhrighe.

Nuair a bhí Cromail ag teacht isteach ar an trá chuir na daoine an t-ór insan áit sin. Shíolraigh muintir an Chladaigh ó na Spáinnigh agus mar gheall air sin bíonn fáinne speisialta acu. Sé an t-ainm atá ar an bhfáinne sin 'Croí agus Lámh'. Tá dealbh i dteampall Naomh Muire agus chuir na daoine an dealbh sin freisin insan talamh nuair a bhí Cromail ag teacht isteach.

**TRANSLATION:**

Long ago a king and queen used to live in the Claddagh. I heard an old woman saying one day there was gold in the Claddagh. *Ceann Láimhrighe* is the name of the place.

When Cromwell was coming ashore the people buried gold there. Claddagh people are descended from Spaniards and so they have a special ring. It is called the 'heart and hand'. There's a statue in St Mary's church and they buried that too when Cromwell was coming.

*(S31: 167. Máire Ní Iarnáin a fuair ó Stofán Ó Siúrtáin, An Cladach, Gaillimh.)*

### Glenscaul (O'm B)

The name 'Glenascaul' means the 'valley of the shadows'. There are twenty-one houses in the village now. Long ago there were fifty houses there. There were two weavers in the village, Seamus Coirc and Patch Coirc. There was one carpenter. His name was Lackey Cuniff. The ruins of their houses are still to be seen. There was a tailor in the village named Brian Ruane and his wife's name was Cáit Ireland. They all had thatched houses and the thatch was tied with straw ropes. The most common surname is Mc Grath.

There are two graveyards in the village where the unbaptised children were buried. There are three wells in the village. One of the wells is called Tobar Bun an Stábla. The farmers in Glenscaul bought their farms under the Ardilaun Act.

*(S32: 363. Written by Seán de Búrca, Gleann na Scáil, Uarán Mór.)*

### Ceantar Cheathrú an Bhrúnaigh [Carrowbrown District] (C'b)

Sé an t-ainm atá ar mo cheantar Ceathrú an Bhrúnaigh. Sé an chiall atá le 'ceathrú' píosa mór talaimh. Bhain an píosa talaimh seo le sliocht de na Brúnaigh fadó. Chónaigh siad sa seanchaisleán atá in aice na scoile.

Sé an t-ainm atá ar mo bhaile ná Baile Dubhlaoich. Tá seanchaisleán sa mbaile agus deireann na seandaoine go raibh dream ann fadó agus sé an t-ainm a bhí orthu ná Dubhlaoich. An Casileán Gearr an t-ainm atá ar mo pharóiste. Tá go leor tithe agus daoine i mo bhaile. Bhí seacht dteach fichead ann fadó. Níl ann anois ach aon teach fichead.

Tá mise i mo chónaí i gCoill Uachtair agus i bparóiste an Chaisleáin Ghearr. Bhí cnoc mór ann agus bhí go leor crann ag fás ann. Tá teach is

48

Castlegar National School, 1925.

fiche i gCoill Uachtair. Ta dhá theach cheann slinne ann agus naoi déag de thithe cheann tuí.

**TRANSLATION:**

My district is called Carrowbrown. 'Carrow' means a big piece of land. The Browns owned this land a long time ago. They lived in the old castle beside the school.

My townland is called Ballindooly. There's an old castle and the old people say that people called Dooley used to live there. My parish is called Castlegar. There are plenty of people here. There used to be twenty-seven houses and now there are only twenty-one.

I live in Killoughter, in the parish of Castlegar. There was a big hill there and many trees growing on it. There are twenty-one houses in Killoughter. Two houses have slate roofs and nineteen are thatched.

*(S30: 192–3. Stiofán Ó Briain, 62, Ceathrú an Bhrúnaigh,*
*Gaillimh. Feilméara, 30 Márta 1938.)*

### Roscahill (P)

When we came from America first we went to live for a year in Roscahill near Uachtar Ard. We lived very near the castle of the great O'Flahertys, kings of Connaught. And strange to say, the house in which we lived had recently been owned by a Miss O'Flaherty, a direct descendant of the family of O'Flaherty.

Of course, we heard some interesting stories from the people in the neighbourhood, one of which I remember very well. In the reign of Queen Elizabeth, the O'Flaherty clan were most ambitious and one lady of the family sent word to the queen that she would govern the district on condition that Elizabeth should make her a captain. The queen, unaware that the personage was a lady, granted the request.

The castle is a lovely sight with its towers and ramparts and beside it flows a little river, which wends its way gently into the Corrib. But strange to say, beneath that smooth surface, on the sandy bottom, lie the countless bones of the enemy who were let drop through a trapdoor at the bottom of the castle into the river.

At the mouth of this river, there are a number of little islands and as the legend goes, since the O'Flahertys died, every year amidst these islands appears another island.

*(S30: 440–1. Imelda Donagh, Grattan Terrace, Galway. 11 years.*
*I got this story from my father who heard it from the villagers.)*

### Oranmore [Fuarán Mór na Féinne] (O'm B)

The village of Oranmore is situated about six miles to the east of Galway city. It is named after the great cold spring called *Tobar na Caillighe*, from which the people got their supply of water. It's said that the Fianna often drank from this well, hence the name.

The story concerning the well runs as follows. Long ago there was a small house situated where the well is now. There were two old women living in the house and one night, as they were sitting by the fire, the water began to come up through the floor and they were compelled to leave their home and seek shelter elsewhere. Another story says that the older women of the village congregated here every evening and spent the evening, chatting and gossiping. Hence the name.

Now, there are some fifty houses in the village of Oranmore. Judging from the ruins of houses, there must have been some seventy houses here formerly. Formerly, the village had its own boat maker, tailor, saddler, hatter, and weavers and carpenter. There are the ruins of an old mill which was occupied up to fifty years ago.

The people from the various villages within a distance of two or three miles used to gather into the houses at night and amuse themselves by raffling some animal, usually a donkey. They then travelled from village to village for the raffle. As a rule there was a dance in the houses where they congregated. More often than not, when the winner of the raffle went to look for the donkey, there was none to be found.

Years ago in Oranmore village, several people living there derived a living from the sea. Many families spent the day picking winkles. Those winkles were taken, by donkey and cart, to the market in Loughrea (some 18 miles away) and to Tuam (about 18 miles from Oranmore).

*(S32: 369–71. Taken down by Caomhghin Ó Treabhair, Rinn Mhíl, from his mother.)*

**Oranmore Boys' National School, n.d.**

**Oranmore Convent School, 1938.**

### *Frenchfort (O'm B)*

The fort in Frenchfort, Oranmore, is a circular fort. There are bushes growing beside the fort. Once a man living in Frenchfort started to dig the fort in order to level the land. He got a very bad pain in his finger. The finger became bent and he never could straighten it.

*(S32: 467. Written by the teacher.)*

### *A Fairy Pig (O'm C)*

About 300 years ago a fairy pig lived in Antrim. She was a little bigger than every other pig and was very black. The Antrim people were afraid of her. She lived in a glen in Co. Antrim called *'Gleann na Muice'*. She used travel great distances around the glen. About eight o'clock every evening she used appear.

One evening, no one in the place saw her and soon after she was seen in Oranmore. About 200 yards below Oranmore is a place called Glenascaul.

She was rooting for two hours there until she had a big deep glen rooted. The people of the village were very much afraid of her. No one in the village went to bed that night on account of her appearance. The glen is there yet and a horse and cart of hay would fit down into it.

*(S32: 537–8. No name given.)*

## Rinnville (O'm C)

There was a ledge of rock jutting out at Mine Hill, down at the back of the wood near the sea at Rinville. Long ago a witch lived there. She began to make a quay across the tide to Rosshill. When she had it half made a Connemara man passed one day in his turf boat. He said, 'God bless the work'. The witch was carrying a stone several tons weight. As the words

The Quay, Galway, *c.* 1940s.

were spoken, the strings of her apron broke and she went into a cloud of smoke into the air. There the stone lay from that day to this.

In the year 1839 came a big storm which was followed by a big tide. This tide came up to Rinville and up to Oranhill on the other side. It stayed for a week and people were picking fish for a week.

*(S32: 538–3. No name given.)*

# PLACE NAMES

### Glenascaul (O'm B)

There is a hill in Glenascaul called '*cnocán*'. It is situated in the middle of the village. Beside it is a stream called '*lochán*', supposed to be rooted [up] by the wild boar that was in the village long ago. This stream hardly ever dries up and it supplies the houses and cattle of the village with water. Sometimes the main road is flooded with its overflowing. On the hill there are many heavy big rocks stuck in the ground. Under one of these rocks it is said the wild boar was buried.

There are many names on the fields, such as '*páirc cill*' meaning deer park [?], where a lot of deer were reared long ago. '*Leacán*' got its name from the number of big stones that were in it. '*Gort Buí*' gets its name from the yellow furze covering the field long ago.

The people of the village call the eastern side of the village '*baile thoir*' and the western side '*baile thiar*'.

*(S32: 394–9. Written down by Micheál Ó Seachnasaigh, Gleann an Scáil,*
*Uarán Mór, Co. na Gaillimhe.)*

### Galway City (NB)

Fair Hill got its name because of the important fairs that were held there long ago. The Battery got its name because sailors were trained there. A battery is a place where guns are kept so that is how it got its name. Grattan Road was called the 'tenpenny road'. It got that name because that was the wages the men got per day. The Spanish Arch got its name because the

Spaniards always occupied that place when they were in town. Gentian Hill got its name because the old people thought that the fairies lived there. The fairies are always called the gentry. Taylor's Hill got its name because of the amount of tailors that lived there long ago.

*(S31: 62–3. Martin Browne. I got this information from Mrs Raftery whose age is about 78 years. She lives in Fair Hill, 24 January 1938.)*

### O'Connell's Rock and the Drummer's Well (NB)

There is a rock up in Shantalla and it is called O'Connell's Rock. That rock is very big and it is said that Daniel O'Connell gave a speech on Catholic Emancipation there. The little place where Daniel O'Connell gave the speech is situated in a village outside the town of Galway.

In another old place in Galway, they say there was a very big band of soldiers and one night, this drummer was walking in a field and there were a lot of wells running under the Grattan Road out to Galway Bay. This drummer was a stranger and he knew very little about the town. He saw a little village, about a quarter of a mile from where he stood. He took a short cut along the fields. He did not go far when he walked into the well. He got so excited that he drowned himself. From that day till this, the well is called the Drummer's Well.

*(S31: 64–5. Michael Cooke. I got this information from Mrs Cooke, age 36, Fairhill Road, Galway, 24 January 1938.)*

### Lynch's Folly (NB)

Once upon a time there was a man called Andrew Lynch Fitzstephens, Mayor of Galway about the year 1498. During his period of office, the Corporation of Galway started much useful work in the City of the Tribes. Amongst these was an important waterway from Loughatalia to Boulavorline. This would open up an easy passage from Lough Corrib to the sea. This work was never completed and local people called it 'Lynch's Folly'.

*(S31: 66. Martin Browne.)*

### *Cloch na Mallacht (O'm B)*

When there is a low tide there is a passage across Oranmore Bay. In the passage, which can be walked on at low tide, there is a stone called *Cloch na Mallacht*. The following story is told about it. A priest was answering a sick call and was hurrying across this passage. He stumbled on the rock and fell. He cursed the rock and since then it has been called *Cloch na Mallacht* [The Stone of the Curses].

*(S32: 364. Taken down by Caomhghin Ó Treabhair, Rinn Mhíl, from his mother.)*

### *An Chaoi a bhFuair an Caisleán Gearr an tAinm Sin [How Castlegar Got its Name] (P)*

Bhíodh na Flaitheartaigh i gcónaí ag troid in aghaidh dream Normannach darbh ainm de Búrca i nGaillimh fadó. Uair amháin nuair a bhí na Búrcaigh láidir, b'éigean do na Flaitheartaigh cíos a íoc dóibh. Ach de réir a chéile, d'éirigh na Flaitheartaigh láidir agus nuair a chuir an Búrcach a mhac go dtí an Flaitheartach leis an cháin seo a bhailiú, séard a rinne an Flaitheartach ná an ceann a bhaint de agus é a chur i mála.

Ansin, dúirt sé lena mhac féin an mála seo a thabhairt chuig an Búrcach agus a rá leis gurbh é sin an sórt cánach a d'íocfaidís dó uaidh sin amach. Rinne an mac amhlaidh. D'fhág sé an mála ag an mBúrcach agus ansin thug sé do na bonnaibh é. D'éirigh leis an bhFlaitheartach óg a cheann a thabhairt leis ach bhí cath fuilteach idir iad agus na Búrcaigh agus fuair na Búrcaigh an bua. Ansin, b'éigean do na Flaitheartaigh teitheadh go dtí áit darbh ainm Caisleán Gearr agus tógadh caisleán ansin. Bhí an caisleán seo an-ghearr agus mar gheall air sin tugadh an Caisleán Gearr ar an áit sin ó shin i leith.

**TRANSLATION:**

Long ago, the O'Flahertys were always fighting the Norman Bourkes in Galway. Once, when the Bourkes were strong, the O'Flahertys had to pay them rent. But gradually, the O'Flahertys got strong and when Bourke sent his son to O'Flaherty to collect the rent, O'Flaherty cut off his head and put it in a bag.

**Presentation (Rang a dó).**

Then he told his son to take this bag to Bourke and tell him that was the kind of rent they'd pay him in future. The son did that. He left the bag with Bourke and then he fled. He got away safely. But there was a bloody battle between them after that and the Bourkes won. Then the O'Flahertys had to flee to a place called Castlegar and a castle was built there. This castle was very short (*gearr*) and because of that, the place has been called Castlegar ever since.

*(S30: 464–5. Lil Ní Nuanáin, Bóthar na hOllscoile, Gaillimh, 13 bliana. Fuair mé an scéal seo i mBéarla ó mo sheanmháthair Bean Uí Chléirigh, Luimneach. Bhí sí ina cónaí san gCaisleán Gearr uair amháin.)*

## *Páirc Bhucháin/Cathair na Sruthán [Buchan's Field/City of Streams] (NB)*

Páirc Bhucháin: Bhí fear ina chónaí i bpáirc agus is é an t-ainm a bhí air ná Buchán. Dódh a theachsa go talamh agus ó shin amach tugtar Páirc Bhucháin ar an áit. Tá sé suite in aice na nduganna i nGaillimh.

Cathair na Sruthán: Thugtaí Cathair na Sruthán ar an gcathair seo uair amháin mar gheall ar go raibh a lán sruthán ag sníomh a mbealach tríd. Níl aon sruthán anois ann is dócha.

**TRANSLATION:**

There was a man who lived in a field and his name was Buchan. His house was burned to the ground and from that time the place is called Buchan's Field/Park. It is beside the docks in Galway.

This city was once called the City of Streams, because many streams used to wind their way through it. There are probably no streams now.

*(S31: 60–1. Pádraig Ó Dubhghaill. Fuair mé an t-eolas seo ó Bhean Uí Dhubhghaill, Na Duganna, Gaillimh.)*

## *Leacht Seoirse [Laghtgeorge] (N's)*

Fadó, bhíodh caiple draíochta á síolrú i Loch an Phlúirín i bparóiste an chuain. Bhí fear saibhir san áit agus bhíodh sé i gcónaí ag iarraidh breith ar cheann de na caiple sin.

Lá amháin rug sé ar cheann acu agus thug sé abhaile é. Chuir sé sa stábla é agus cheangail sé leis an adhastar é. Dúradh leis dá bhfágfadh sé ansin é ar feadh seacht mbliana go n-imeodh an draíocht de agus go mbeadh ceann de na caiple ab fhearr sa domhan aige.

Bhí go maith. D'fhan an fear go mífhoighdeach. Bhí sé ag comhaireamh na mblianta go dtí gur tháinig an lá roimh an seachtú bliain bheith caite. Leis an mhífhoighid a bhí air, tharraing an fear amach an capall. Shíl sé nach ndéanfadh lá amháin aon difríocht. Chuaigh sé fá dhéin Chnoc Thuaidh agus é ag marcaíocht go huaibhreach ar a chapall breá.

Ara! Níorbh fhada gur thug an capall cúpla léim. Rith sé amach ó thóin an fhir agus thit an fear ar an talamh. Maraíodh an fear agus rith an capall roimhe ach bhí a fhios aige cá raibh sé ag dul mar d'imigh sé go Baile Loch Riabhach, áit a raibh caiple dá chineál ag síolrú.

Mar gheall ar gur fear saibhir a bhí sa bhfear, tógadh leacht cuimhneacháin dó. Seoirse an t-ainm a bhí ar an bhfear agus sin an fáth gur tugadh Leacht Seoirse ar an áit, idir paróiste an chuain agus Cnoc Thuaidh, mar a maraíodh an fear saibhir sin.

**TRANSLATION:**

Long ago, enchanted horses were being born in *Loch an Phlúirín* in the harbour parish. There was a rich man and he always wanted to get one of these horses.

One day, he caught one and brought it home. He put it in the stable and tied it with a tether. He was told that if he left it there for seven years, the enchantment would leave it and he'd have one of the best horses in the world.

Very good. The man waited impatiently. He was counting the years until the day would come and the seven years would be up. He was so impatient that he pulled the horse out, just one day before the seven years were over. He thought one day would make no difference. He rode off proudly to Knock North on his fine horse.

Ara! It wasn't long till the enchanted horse gave a couple of jumps. He ran out from under the man's backside and the man fell to the ground. He was killed and the horse ran on because it knew where it was going. It headed for Loughrea where its own kind were breeding.

Because the man who was killed was a rich man, a memorial stone was erected to him. The man's name was George and that's why that place was called Laghtgeorge, between the harbour parish and Knock North, because the rich man was killed there.

*(S31: 12–3. An tSr. M. Colmán. Stiofán Ó Briain, 62,*
*Ceathrú an Bhrúnaigh, do thug an t-eolas seo uaidh.)*

## Gort Ghleann an Airgid (O'm B)

*Gort Ghleann an Airgid*: A field on the road to Galway and about midway between Oranmore and Galway. In the days of the stagecoach, highwaymen lay in wait in the trees nearby and waylaid travellers and robbed them. It is said many of them buried the money in this field. The field is also said to have been frequently used for duelling. In the days of Galway's former greatness, many duels are said to have been fought there. This field is said to have been the meeting place of the Fenians and many of the older people in the district say that a large quantity of Fenian arms is buried here.

*Ballynageeha*: The town of the fairy winds. A battle was fought here and the people believe that the fairy winds bring bad luck.

*Turloughnafolah*: The turlough of the blood, so named because of the battle that was fought here. This is a heathery field and people say that the grass grows in a peculiar manner and that it has a reddish colour.

*Glennacoule*: The glen of the wild boar, according to the people who live in the village. Behind the village there is a deep valley which is said to have been rooted out by the boar.

*Cloch na Muice*: A large rock situated in the townland of *Gurrain* and adjoining Glenascaul. This stone forms part of a wall in Roger Kelly's land. There is a shape somewhat similar to the shape of a pig (the wild boar that is supposed to have rooted out the hollow in the village of Glenascaul) on the stone. The boar, a black boar according to the people of the district, is said to have rested here after his efforts in rooting out the glen in Glenascaul. It is a large boulder and may possibly have been some kind of ceremonial stone in olden times.

*(S32: 413–4. Written down by Caomghin Ó Treabhair.*
*Retold by his mother who heard it from her father.)*


# LOCAL GRAVEYARDS

## *Rahoon Graveyard (P)*

It was first the parish church and burial ground of the Rahoon parish. There was a big monument with steps up to it, in memory of the dead, which the Maunsells built. But Bishop O'Dea gave it away, to be made into sand for the Clifden railway, and built a small one instead of it. It is now a green field with the headstone in it in honour of the dead. Maunsells Road is so called because a family named Maunsell lived there.

# My Home Place

*(S30: 458–9. Written by Mary Reilly, St Bridget's, Shantalla, Galway, 11 years.*
*I got this story from Mr Ryan. He is about 80 years of age.)*

## Galway City Graveyards (NB)

There are four graveyards in this district: Forthill, New Cemetery, Dominican and Rahoon. The dead people are put in three of these but not in the Dominican, which is only for priests. The Dominican graveyard is round; New Cemetery is square; Forthill is circular and Rahoon is square.

There are the ruins of an ancient chapel in Forthill and people are not usually buried in this place. There are trees growing in the graveyards; yew trees and weeping willows. There is a large cross which is very old in the graveyard at Forthill. There is a large tree growing through one of the tombs in the Dominican graveyard.

*(S30: 146. Pat Barrett. I got this story from Mrs Barrett,*
*33 St Dominic's Terrace, Galway. 8 June 1938.)*

## Sé Reilig [Six Graveyards] (N's)

Tá tuairim is sé reilig sa bparóiste againn. Tá ceann i gCeathrú an Bhrúnaigh agus Lisín Dáite a thugtar air. Tá ceann i gCillín agus Reilig Chillín a thugtar air. Tugtar Reilig Bhaile an Treasna ar cheann eile. Teampall Shiubháin Ní Laighín, Múr-Ros Cam agus Reilig Mionlaigh a thugtar ar chinn eile. Cuirtear daoine i ngach ceann acu fós ach amháin i dTeampall Shiubháin Ní Laighin. Tá cuma dhronuilleogach orthu ar fad.

Tá seanreilig i gCoill Uachtair nár cuireadh aoinne ann le tuairim is céad bliain anuas. Tá sé chomh fada ó shin ó cuireadh aoinne ann nach cuimhneach leis na daoine cé hé an duine deiridh a cuireadh ann.

Chuirtí na páistí nár baisteadh ariamh i reilig dóibh féin. Lisín a thugtar ar an áit sin. In áiteacha, cuirtear i reilig dóibh féin iad, ach cuirtear na daoine in aice leo in áiteacha eile. Cuirtear na daoine in aice leo sa mbaile s'againne anois.

Cuirtear cuid de na daoine anois i reilig iasachta. Amannta, tugtar bean phósta abhaile go dtí a háit dúchais lena cur tar éis a báis, mar ba mhaith léi bheith curtha in aice lena gaolta féin.

61

**Carrowbrowne pioneers, 1940s.**

Deirtear go bhfuil leaba Phádraig i reilig Mhúr-Ros Cam. Deirtear go raibh cathaoir Phádraig ann freisin ach gur tugadh easonóir dó agus d'éirigh sé san aer agus chuaigh sé trasna thar an uisce go Condae an Chláir agus tá sé in áit éigin ann fós ach ní fios do na daoine cén áit é.

**TRANSLATION:**

There are about six graveyards in our parish. There is one in Carrowbrowne and it is called *Lisín Dáite*. There is one in Killeen, called Killeen graveyard. Another is called Ballytrasna graveyard. The others are called *Teampall Shiúbháin Ní Laighín*, *Múr-Ros Cam* and Menlo. People are still buried in each one of them except for *Teampall Shiúbháin Ní Laighín*. The garveyards are all rectangular in shape.

There is an old graveyard in Killoughter where no one has been buried for about a hundred years. It is so long since anyone was buried there that people don't remember who was the last person to be buried in it.

Children who were never baptised used to be buried in a graveyard by themselves. It was called a *'lisín'*. In some places, children are buried in their own graveyard and in others they are buried beside everyone else. They are all buried together in our town land now.

Sometimes a married woman is taken home to her native place after death to be buried, because she wishes to be with her relatives.

It is said that Patrick's bed is in *Múr-Ros Cam* graveyard. They say that Patrick's chair was there too but that it was dishonoured and rose up in the air and went across the water to County Clare where it is still in some place, but the people don't know where that is.

(S31: 9–10. An tSr M. Colmán. Stiofán Ó Briain, 62,
Ceathrú an Bhrúnaigh, do thug an t-eolas seo uaidh.)


## Forthill (P)

Forthill, which is situated on the south side of Galway, within a few minutes' walk of the Dock, ranks amongst the most ancient and historic cemeteries in Ireland. Though the date on the tablet over the entrance of the old mortuary chapel is A.D. 500, there is every reason for believing that it was in existence for some centuries previous to that date. An ecclesiastical writer [Allemande] states that an Augustinian church existed on the spot now known as Forthill, early in the thirteenth century. If such is the case, it is more than probable that the cemetery also existed, as a cemetery almost immediately sprang up round each old Irish abbey. We know for certain that the old cemetery was the site of the beautiful church erected for the Augustinian friars by Margaret Athy, wife of Stephen Lynch FitzDominic, for many years Mayor of Galway.

Thirty years later, 1538, the church, monastery and adjoining lands, including the cemetery, were confiscated but the Augustinians, backed up by the townspeople, managed to retain the church and small portions of ground which constituted the cemetery. Later on, in 1596, the Irish chieftain Red Hugh O'Donnell gathered his forces on Forthill (then called the Abbey Hill) for the purpose of attacking Galway, which was then, as far as its inhabitants were concerned, an English city. An armed party sallied forth from the town and the two forces met on the hill [Forthill] and, many being wounded and slain, Red Hugh was compelled to retreat.

Four years later, 1600, by order of the Supreme Council, a Fort, one of the most formidable in the King's [realm] was erected on the site of the cemetery. From this fort it takes its present name, Forthill. For forty-three years the fort remained in the hands of the military, but finally the towns-

**Presentation girls.**

people rose in rebellion, surrounding it, cut off all supplies from the garrison and compelled them to surrender. Once again it was handed back to the Augustinian Fathers and has since remained in their possession.

When Cromwell was approaching the town in 1652, it was feared that, like Red Hugh O'Donnell, he might take advantage of Forthill as a vantage ground from which to attack the town, and so the Augustinians consented to allow their church to be pulled down, the Corporation guaranteeing to build a similar one for them within the city.

In 1811, Robert Hedges Eyre, a Protestant, out of respect for his fellow citizens, erected a handsome wall round the cemetery. In 1852, a portion of the old abbey lands was added and a still more substantial wall built. Nothing more was done until 1914 when the citizens, on the invitation and under the chairmanship of Mr M. McDonagh JP, chairman of the Urban Council, co-operated with the Augustinian Fathers in taking effective steps for the preservation and renovation of such an historic and holy spot. Already, a great many improvements have been carried out and it is hoped that as a result of the bazaar to be held in August of this year [1915] sufficient funds will be obtained to give a permanent character to the good work.

*(S30: 461–3, Written by Carmel Kavanagh, 25 Henry St, Galway, 10 years.*
*I got this story from Mrs Monaghan, Quay St, Galway.)*

*(Editor's note: This account is obviously taken from a written source dating back to 1915. No reference is given to the actual source. I have included it here in order to preserve the information it contains.)*

## Roscam Church (O'm B)

The town land of Roscam is about three and a half miles from the village of Oranmore, and about midway between Galway and Oranmore. There are the ruins of a church in the town land of Roscam, situated on a hill close to the bay. There is a holed stone in the graveyard of the church. About forty yards from this holed stone there is another holed stone. One of these stones is always said to hold water and it is said St Patrick washed his hands here. The other holes are said to be the prints of his feet and head. The people in the district believe that anyone suffering from headaches may be cured by putting his head in the hole said to be the print of St Patrick's head.

*(S32: 352. Oranmore Boys. No name, written by teacher.)*

## Cloch na Liagann (O'm B)

This is a large stone about seven feet high standing on a heap of smaller stones about a quarter of a mile from the ruins of the Roscam church. It is said that this stone was created by a local saint, St Hugh of Roscam, over the grave of the great king Brian who was the older brother of Niall of the Nine Hostages and who was ancestor of all the Kings of Connnaught of the O'Brien race.

65

The O'Connors, O'Rourkes and Flahertys all take their names from him. His sons were baptised by St Patrick.

*(S32: 393-4. No name, written by teacher.)*

# HOLY WELLS

### Toibreacha Beannaithe [Holy Wells] (NB)

… Bhí creideamh na ndaoine chomh mór sin go dtéadh siad go dtí na toibreacha beannaithe chun leigheas a fháil. Seo cuid de na toibreacha sin: Tobar an Mhaighdean Mhuire i mBaile Átha an Rí, Mainistir Chnoc an Mháigh, agus bhí ceann in aice le Baile Loch Riabhach. Nuair a théadh duine chuig ceann de na toibreacha seo b'iondúil dó píosa éadaigh a cheangal ar sceach, os cionn an tobair agus rinne sé paidreacha leis an naomh speisialta a raibh an tobar sin tiomnaithe dó.

**TRANSLATION:**

… People's faith was so strong that they used to go to the holy wells to get a cure. These are some of the holy wells: the Virgin Mary's well at Athenry, Abbeyknockmoy, and there was one beside Loughrea. Usually when some-one went to a well, he'd tie a piece of cloth on a bush above the well and say a prayer to the special saint to whom the well was dedicated.

*(S31: 71–2. Pádraig Ó Dubhghaill. Fuair mé an t-eolas seo ó Bhean Uí Dhubhghaill, 39 bl., Na Duganna, Gaillimh.)*

### Toibreacha Beannaithe [Holy Wells] (NB)

Tá dhá thobar beannaithe i gcathair na Gaillimhe, agus dhá cheann eile mórthimpeall uirthi. Tá an chéad cheann ar an dtrá atá ag dul ó Chnoc a' Rátha go dtí bóthar na farraige. Tá an ceann eile suite in aice le stáisiún na nGardaí i Sráid Eglinton. Tá ceann eile suite in aice le hÓrán Mór agus an ceann eile taobh le Béal Átha an Rí.

Seo iad na hainmneacha atá orthu: Tobar Naomh Aibhistín, Tobar Naomh Proinsias, Tobar Naomh Pádraig agus Tobar na Maighdine Muire.

Tugann daoine cuairt ar an gcéad tobar ar an lá deiridh d'Iúil. Tugtar cuairt ar an gceann eile nuair a bhíonn cead acu. Tugtar cuairt ar an gceann eile ar Lá Fhéile Pádraig, agus ar an gceann eile ar an gcúigiú lá déag de Lúnasa.

Téann na daoine mórthimpeall an tobair agus bíonn siad ag paidreoireacht an t-am go léir. Ólann siad an t-uisce ann chun leigheas a fháil ó am go ham. Is iad na paidreacha a deir siad ná trí 'Ave Maria' in ainm an naoimh speisialta.

Seo an scéal atá ag baint le tobar Naomh Aibhistín: beannaíonn cúpla sagart an t-uisce ann ar lá áirithe gach bliain agus ní bhíonn uisce an tsáile ag cur isteach air. Téann daoine cosnochtaithe chuig Tobar na Maighdine Muire chun beannacht a fháil. Ceaptar go raibh uisce ag teacht as an dtalamh ansin ar dtús agus cuireadh balla beag ann agus rinneadh an tobar ansin le cumhacht Dé.

Bhíodh daoine ag dul go dtí Tobar Naomh Aibhistín go minic, ach níor chualathas aon iomrá ar leigheas ann. Leigheas ar dhaille is mó a bhíonn daoine ag iarraidh.

Ólann daoine uisce amach as an tobar agus uaireanta cuireann siad uisce i mbuidéal ann. Chuala mé go bhfágtaí a lán rudaí mar pháipéar, fáinní nó píosaí adhmaid faoi chloch ins an tobar uisce. Níl aon iasc ar bith sa tobar sin mar uisce beannaithe atá ann agus ní féidir le hiasc maireachtáil ann. Téann na daoine 14 uaire mórthimpeall an tobair in onóir 'Íosa Críost ag glacadh na croise'. Bíonn creideamh láidir ag daoine mar gheall air sin agus is iomaí scéal atá ag fás i dtaobh an tobair.

Chuala mé scéal beag ó mo mháthair faoin mí-ádh a bhaineann le bheith ag déanamh dochair ar thobar. Bhí fear ann aon uair amháin agus bhí suim aige bheith ag tabhairt uisce beannaithe abhaile leis i mbuidéal ón dtobar. Bhí salachar istigh san mbuidéal agus nuair a cuireadh an t-uisce isteach sa mbuidéal, bhris sé díreach ag an am sin agus gearradh lámh an fhir le fórsa an bhrisidh.

**TRANSLATION:**
There are two holy wells in Galway city and two more around about it. The first one is on the beach that goes from Knockaraha to the sea road. The other one is beside the Garda station in Eglinton Street. Another one is situated beside Oranmore and the other is near Athenry.

These are their names: St Augustine's well, St Francis' well, St Patrick's well and the Virgin Mary's well. People visit the first well on the last day of July. The second is visited when they have permission. The other one is visited on St Patrick's Day and the last one on 15 August.

People go around the well and pray all the time. From time to time, they drink the well water to obtain a cure. They say three Ave Marias in the name of the special saint [to whom the well is dedicated].

This is the story about St Augustine's well: a couple of priests bless the water in it on a certain day every year and the seawater doesn't come near it. People go barefoot to the Virgin Mary's well to obtain a blessing. It is believed that water rose out of the ground there originally and a little wall was built. The well was made then, by the power of God.

People used to go often to St Augustin's well, but I never heard anything about a cure there. People are mostly looking for a cure for blindness.

They drink water out of the well and sometimes they put the water in a bottle. I heard that a lot of things like paper, rings, or pieces of wood used to be left under a stone in the well. There's no fish in that well because it's holy water and fish can't live in it. The people go round the well fourteen times in honour of Christ carrying the cross. They believe sincerely in that and there are many stories about the well.

I heard a little story from my mother about the bad luck that comes from doing harm to the well. Once there was a man and he wanted to take holy water home in a bottle from the well. There was dirt in the bottle and when the water was put into it, it broke just at that moment and the man's hand was cut by the force of the break.

*(S31: 105–7. Pádraig Ó Dubhghaill. Fuair mé an t-eolas seo*
*ó Bhean Uí Dhubhghaill, 39, Na Duganna, Gaillimh. 21 January 1938)*

### Tobair Bheannaithe [Holy Wells] (C'b)

Tá cuid mhaith toibreacha naofa thart anseo ach tá siad fada go maith óna chéile. Tá ainmneach éagsúla orthu. Tá Tobar Mhic Duaich i gClaí an Dá Mhíle. Deirtear gur leigheasadh daoine ann fadó. Tá ceann eile i gCnoc Maoil Dris. Níl aon chaint gur leigheasadh aon duine ann.

Théadh na daoine fadó ag baint feamainne Aoine an Chéasta. Nuair a thagadh siad abhaile ní itheadh siad aon rud go ndéanadh siad turas ag Tobar Mhic Duaich.

Tá tobar beannaithe i Loch an tSáile. Téann na daoine ann ar an Domhnach deiridh de Lúnasa. Nuair a théann siad ann fágann siad pingin nó biorán. Nuair a bhíonn siad ag déanamh an turais, fágann siad cúig chloch déag agus téann siad cúig uair dhéag thart air nuair a bíos an turas déanta acu. Tá Loch an tSáile taobh thoir de Ghaillimh.

Tá tobar eile i mo thalamh féin, Tobar Labhráis. Bráthair a bhí ann. Bíonn uisce ann sa ngeimhreadh. Níl aon leigheas ar an uisce. Tá ceann eile i nGort an Chalaidh. Níl aon uisce ann anois. Nuair a bhí sé ann, deirtear go raibh leigheas ann le haghaidh an bhruinne dhearg(?). Tá Tobar Labhráis trí mhíle ó Ghaillimh i gCoill Uachtair.

Tá Tobar an Choilear i Mionloch tuairim cheithre mhíle ó Ghaillimh ar an taobh thíos.

**TRANSLATION:**

There are a good few holy wells around here and they're far enough apart. They have different names. Mac Duach's well is in Two Mile Ditch. It is said that people were cured there long ago. There's another well in Knockmeeldrish. There's no talk of anyone being cured there.

Long ago the people used to go gathering seaweed on Good Friday. When they came home, they wouldn't eat anything until they did the round at Mac Duach's well.

There's a holy well in Loughatalia. People go there on the last Sunday of August. When they go, they leave a penny or a pin. When they are making the round, they leave fifteen stones and they go round fifteen times to make the round. Loughatalia is on the east side of Galway.

There's another well in my own ground, Labhras' well. He was a Brother. It has water in winter. There's no cure in the water. There's another one in Gortachalla. It has no water now. When it was there, they said it had a cure for red murrain. Labhras' well is three miles from Galway in Killoughter.

*Tobar an Choilear* is in Menlo, about four miles from Galway, on the lower side.

*(S30: 194-5. Máire Bean Uí Ógáin, 80 bliain, Baile Dubhlaoich, Gaillimh. Bean fheilméara. 6 Aibréan 1938)*

## Tobar Chnoc na Roise [Cnoc na Roise Well] (O'm C)

Fadó, nuair a bhí Naomh Pádraig ag craobhscaoileadh an chreidimh, thóg sé a lán teampall agus séipéal ar fud na tíre. Thóg sé ceann acu i gCnoc na Roise. An áit ina raibh Naomh Pádraig ag guí, tá carraig mhór ann. Tá comhartha a dhá ghlúin agus a chinn ann ó shin. Tá leac in aice leis agus cuma bháisín air. Bíonn uisce salach sa mbáisín sin i gcónaí. Sin an áit a nigheadh Naomh Pádraig a lámha agus níor thriomaigh an t-uisce ann riamh ó shin.

Tagann daoine ann an chéad Luan de gach mí ar feadh trí huaire agus fágann siad airgead nó rud éigin ar an leac ina ndiaidh.

**TRANSLATION:**

Long ago, when St Patrick was teaching the faith, he built many churches throughout the country. He built one in *Cnoc na Roise*. Where St Patrick was praying, there's a big rock. The mark of his two knees and his head are in it since that time. There's a stone beside it shaped like a basin. There's always dirty water in that basin. That's where St Patrick used to wash his hands and the water has never dried up since.

People come there on the first Monday of each month, three times, and they leave money or something else behind them on the stone.

*(S32: 502. No name given.)*

## Tobarnakornane (O'm C)

Cornane's Well: This well is situated close to Renville Castle on the north and is said to belong to St Cornane. Local tradition says this saint had three holy brothers and a sister. Each had a holy well of a different virtue.

The brothers were 'Blickhaun', whose well is Toberbracken, 'Bernaine', whose well is at Abbey near Athenry, and 'Rhushaun', whose well is near Kilcolgan Castle. The sister, whose name was St Sornia, has her well near Ballynacourty.

A station or visit had to be paid to each of the five wells on certain days before the prayer was granted. In a field west of Toberkornane is a rath of the same name. This was used as a burying place and up to about thirty years ago, children were buried there.

It was the custom after the corpse was buried for all the people to go to the well and to wash three corners of the sheet that had been round the coffin in the well and say prayers for the dead person's soul. Mrs Lynch who lived in the castle, and whose property the well was, objected to the custom and so built four strong walls about it, roofed it in and put a door with a lock and key in the wall. In the morning after the first night after the building was finished and the well locked, it was found that the water had burst the wall and had made a fresh hole for itself outside the building.

*(S32: 545–6. No name given.)*

# OLD CASTLES AND FORTS

### *Old Castles (NB)*

There are two castles in this district. One belongs to Lynch and the other to Blake. These two are believed to be built since the fifteenth century. Blake's Castle was supposed to be burned, but Lynch's Castle stands yet. This is situated in the middle of the city and Blake's is situated near Loch Corrib.

No one ever attacked these two castles, but an interesting story is told about Lynch's Castle. There are many carvings of stone on its walls, many like a monkey's head. One day a nurse had a child in her arms when a fire broke out in the room used by her. This made her afraid and she dropped the child. A monkey lifted up the child and it swarmed [*sic*] down the front wall with it. Not until he reached the ground safely did he let it go. After this, many heads made of stone were put up, in mind that this monkey was a brave animal. The Munster and Leinster Bank is now in its place, but the figures remain.

*(S31: 140–1. Patrick Doyle, from Mrs Doyle, 39 years, New Docks, Galway. 2 June 1938.)*

### Lios [A Lios] (O'm C)

Tá lios mór in aice le mo theachsa, beagnach leath-mhíle uaim. Tá an lios sin suite istigh ins an gcoill agus tá a lán lán seomraí ann mar tá sé an-mhór ar fad.

Tá scéal aisteach ag na seandaoine faoi. Seo é:

Bhí scata fear ag dul tré'n gcoill i ndeire tráthnóna amháin. Do chaill siad duine acu. Shiúil an fear seo tré'n lios agus chuaigh sé isteach go bhfeicfeadh sé na seomraí. Nuair a chuaigh sé isteach píosa, chonaic sé bóithrín beag ag dul tré'n lios. Chuaigh sé isteach ann agus níor stad sé go dtáinig sé amach i bpáirc míle go leith ón lios.

Deirtear go bhfuil an scéal seo fíor agus go raibh an-ádh ar an bhfear sin ar feadh an chuid eile dá shaol ach ní dheachaigh aoinne tré'n lios sin ariamh ó shin.

**TRANSLATION:**

There's a big *lios* near my house, about a half mile away. The *lios* is situated in the wood and there are many rooms in it because it is very, very big.

The old folk have a strange story about it. Here it is:

A group of men were going through the wood late one evening. One man went missing. He walked through the *lios* and went in to look at the rooms. When he went in some way, he saw a small road going through the *lios*. In he went and never stopped until he emerged in a field about a mile and a half from the *lios*.

They say that this is a true story and that the man was very lucky for the rest of his life. But no one else ever went through the *lios* after that.

*(S32: 508–9. No name given.)*

# ROADS

### Bóithre an Cheantair [Roads in This Area] (C'b)

Bóithrín an Chóiste: Fadó, bhíodh an cóiste bodhar ag dul siar an bóithrín sin agus suas Bóithrín an Phúca.

Bóithrín an tSeanChnoic: Bhí áit ansin fadó le daoine a chrochadh.

Bóithrín Mhuireadhaigh: Bhí seanfhíodóir ansin fadó agus Tomás Ó Muireadhaigh an t-ainm a bhí air.

Bóithrín na dTincéirí: Bhíodh na tincéirí ina gcónaí ann.

Bóithrín an Phúca: Shíleadh na daoine fadó go mbíodh púcaí ar an mbóithrín sin.

Geata Geal: Deirtear go raibh geata geal ann, bhí an dá pillar chomh bán le sneachta.

**TRANSLATION:**

The Coach Road: Long ago, there used to be a Death Coach going along that little road and up the Pooka Road.

Old Hill Road: There was a place there long ago where people were hanged.

Murray's Road: An old weaver lived there and his name was Thomas Murray.

The Tinkers' Lane: The tinkers used to live there.

The Pooka's Lane: Long ago people used to think there were pookas on that road.

White Gate: They say there was a white gate there. The two pillars were as white as snow.

*(S30: 190–1. Máirtín Ó Ruaidhín, Coill Uachtair, Gaillimh. Feilméara. 63 bliain.*
*23 Márta 1938.)*

**Carrowbrowne, 1938.**

# 2

# HEARTH AND HOME

Is deas iad na fataí nuair a théann an lón orthu,/ Is deise ná sin iad nuair
a bhíonn an bláth bán orthu,/ Ach is deise arís iad nuair a bhíonn
an bolg lán acu.

*[The potatoes are nice when the fertiliser goes on them,/ Nicer again when they have
the white flower,/ But even nicer still when the belly is full of them.]*

In 1930s Galway, the changes in housing, in areas such as the Claddagh
village, were the outward indication of a new way of life which was coming
fast, beckoned or unbeckoned. Soon, there would be fewer vernacular
houses built and roofed from local organic materials. A fire in the middle
of the floor, chimneys made of wicker, a '*cailleach*' or bed outshot in the
corner of the kitchen – these and much more would soon only be a memory.

People's dress, while still fairly simple and unflamboyant, was changing
too. Some folk now had clothes 'for Sunday and Monday'. Women were
still wearing shawls and knitted socks and stockings were the order of the
day for many. While the local newspapers were full of advertisements for
lovely modern clothes, entirely *à la mode*, in the local drapery shops, it seems
most people could not afford such luxuries. Though for the young people,
and for the town dwellers, these fashions would certainly have been in their
deepest aspirations.

From these accounts it appears that the daily diet was still simple and
unvaried, heavily reliant on potatoes and oatmeal, supplemented by fish
and the shore harvest in coastal areas. Most food was home-produced and
there was a great deal of highly refined knowledge about bread making,

churning, growing and cooking potatoes, and detailed information as to which potato varieties best suited local soil and weather conditions. This knowledge did not come under the classification of 'quaint local traditions' as it might nowadays; it was vital information for sustainable living in a cash-strapped economy. Butter churning was surrounded by a complex web of 'dos' and 'don'ts', in respect of its physical manufacture, and in respect of guarding the 'luck' of the churn, which could be stolen by someone with jealous intent. The butter, so hard won, was a source of protein, provided added taste to bland foods such as bread and potatoes and it could be sold or bartered for goods such as tea and sugar. It was as precious as gold. Town dwellers too knew how to produce their own food, and did so on whatever land was available to them. The traditional city market by St Nicholas' collegiate church provided an opportunity to buy locally produced food every Saturday and was particularly popular around Christmas time.

Farm animals were vitally important to the rural economy. They were very highly prized and cared for. An interesting adjunct to the factual information given about the farm animals in the Schools' Collection is the account of the various ways used to call each animal, an inter-language between humans and animals, another language and dialect to put beside the Irish and Hiberno-English of the time. It is a rare, intimate detail from this community's past, a precious insight into their lived experience. To a contemporary reader, one of these accounts concerning the breaking of a horse may be shocking in its harshness. We see that animal husbandry was more to do with human survival then, lacking our modern empathy for our fellow creatures.

This community was self-sufficient in many ways. As well as their food, they could provide their own candles, baskets, iron and metal goods, wool for carding and spinning and turning into yarn, to be woven into cloth or knitted. The forge had been an important centre for the community and the smith played a vital role in agriculture, transport and the carriage of goods. But the forges were becoming less common and henceforth people would have to travel farther and farther to avail of the smith's services.

The Schools' Collection asked the pupils to do research on how people cared for their feet and if they were wearing shoes at the time of the survey. It may appear a strange question now but it was a very basic matter back then, when not everyone wore shoes and when youngsters often went barefoot in summer. Bare feet had to be washed and cared for if they were not to cause a lot of trouble. Even the water in which they were washed had to be disposed of carefully, for fear of incurring the wrath of the fairies. Nothing in this society could be left to chance, it seems.

This chapter ends with some information on the playthings made by children, who probably had as much fun making balls, rabbit snares, hurleys, marbles, buzzers, pipes, tops, catapults, fifes, bird cradles, 'blasts' and whistles, as they did in playing with them. One is struck by the fact that many of the boys' toys were children's versions of adult methods of trapping and catching animals such as hares for food. The play activity was in the nature of a practice for the real thing. And which modern-day child would not love access to a cocoa tin, water and carbide, lighting a match and causing the carbide to explode 'with a loud bang' to blow the lid off the tin? Health and safety considerations did not loom large in the boys' play activities in the 1930s judging by these accounts, but the children probably did have lots of fun!

# HOUSES

### The Old Houses (NB)

Long ago the old houses had no roof but a roof of sedge. Others had straw but the sedge was best. There was no such thing as a slate at that time. They had a bed in the kitchen and the father would sleep in it, in case anyone would come in during the night.

Some used to have the fire in the middle of the floor and a hole in the middle of the roof. There is a man in the Claddagh who has the fire in the middle of the floor at this present day.

Long ago they had two doors in each house – a back door and a front door. They had neither a lock nor a key at all and they never had a second window. There was no glass in the windows at all but they had shutters outside which they used to shut at night and leave them open during the day.

*(S31: 135. Martin Finnerty. I got this from my mother, Mrs Finnerty, 52, Claddagh, Galway.)*

Thatched house, Barna, *c.* 1920.

### *Tithe na Seanaimsire [The Old Houses] (F)*

Fadó, bhíodh na tithe déanta de chlocha agus ní bhíodh fuinneog ar bith orthu agus is é an sórt dorais a bhíodh orthu cliabhána. Ní bhíodh beanna cloiche ar bith orthu fadó ach iad déanta de fhraoch agus de luachair. Tithe an-bheaga a bhí iontu agus ní bhíodh seomra ar bith iontu ach i gcorrtheach. Istigh ins an teach a bhíodh na muca acu agus ins an ngeimhreadh bhíodh cuid de na beithígh istigh acu freisin. Fraoch agus luachair agus iad ceangailte le rópaí in ionad scolb an ceann a bhíodh ar na seantithe. Gheibhidís an fraoch ar na portaigh agus an luachair i dtalamh bog.

77

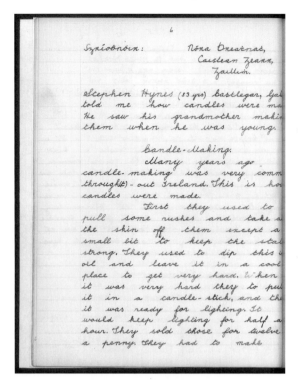

A description of candle-making recalled by Stephen Hynes and written down by Nóra Breathnach of Castlegar, Co. Galway. The Schools' Collection, Volume 0030, Page 006.

Bhíodh leaba sa chistin ins na tithe fadó, ins an teach nach raibh aon seomra ann. Istigh sa gclúid a bhíodh an leaba, in aice leis an tine. 'Cailleach' an t-ainm a thugtaí uirthi. Simléir chaolach a bhíodh orthu agus iad déanta go han-ard, agus cuid eile acu déanta de chláracha. Ní bhíodh fuinneoga ar bith ar na tithe ach ceann nó péire. An teach a mbíodh an fhuinneog ann, ní fhéadfadh na daoine feiceáil amach tríd. Leacanna, agus moirtéal dá choinneáil le chéile a bhíodh san urlár. Ní bhíodh leath-dhoras i ngach teach. Coinnle a bhíodh mar sholas acu. Dhéanadh na daoine coinnle iad féin as luachair agus ola agus gréas agus píosa de róipín dá gcoinneáil le chéile.

**TRANSLATION:**

Long ago, the houses were made of stones and no window in them. They'd have a wicker door. They wouldn't have stone gables long ago but heather and rushes. They were very small houses and only a very odd one had any separate rooms. The pigs would be inside the house and in winter the cattle would be inside too. The roofs of the old houses were made of heather and rushes tied with ropes instead of briars. They'd get the heather in the bogs and the rushes in soft ground.

There'd be a bed in the kitchen, in the corner beside the fire. It was called a 'hag'. They'd have a very high wicker-work chimney, and sometimes wooden. There'd only be one or two windows in the house. When there was a window the people couldn't see through it. The floor was made of flags, mortar holding them together. Not every house had a half-door. They had candles for light. They used to make candles themselves out of rushes and oil and grease, and a bit of cord holding them together.

*(S30: 278–81. Fuarthas an t-eolas seo ó Mháire Ní Iarnáin, 50, Foramoile, Bearna, Gaillimh. Feilméara. 9 Feabhra 1938.)*

### Old Houses (NB)

… The houses long ago had only two doors … They had a hole in the wall and a stick inside it. When they wanted to lock the door, they pulled the stick

The Claddagh, 1925.

across. … The floor was made from sand and lime; some had flagstones. The lamp they had was a rush lamp; a candle would show more light. They used to make candles long ago. They used to make them where the Munster and Leinster Bank is now.

*(S31: 136. Martin Browne. I got this story from Mrs Raftery, 78, Fair Hill, Galway. 16 May 1938.)*

# CLOTHES

## *Éadaí [Clothes] (N's)*

Insan bparóiste ina bhfuil mé i mo chónaí, níl ach beirt táilliúirí. Tá ceann acu in aice baile agus tá ceann eile insan taobh eile den pharóiste. Oibríonn siad ina dtithe féin anois, ach fadó bhíodh siad ag dul thart timpeall ó theach go teach.

Uaireanta, chaithidís seachtain nó mí in áiteacha agus bhíodh siad ag codladh ins an teach ina raibh siad ag obair. Fadó, bhíodh roinnt éadaigh istigh ag an táilliúir agus bhíodh sé ag déanamh cultacha a d'fheilfeadh do na fir óga. Dhíoladh sé ansin iad agus dhéanadh sé an oiread airgid díobh is go mbeadh roinnt bheag sochair astu, ach anois tugann na daoine an t-ábhar chuige agus déanann sé an chulaith dóibh.

Caitheann na daoine an t-éadach a cheannaítear sna siopaí anois, ach amháin an mhuintir a dhéanas an t-éadach sa mbaile, 'siad sin muintir Árainn agus muintir Chonamara. Ní chaitheann na daoine an bréidín anois mar tá siad róghalánta lena chaitheamh. Tuairim is ceathracha bliain ó shin, bhíodh léinteacha dá ndéanamh as línéadach an bhaile, ach ó shin i leith níl siad á ndéanamh mar cuireadh deireadh leis an lín san áit. Ach déantar roinnt léinteacha fir as éadach láidir a cheannaítear ins na siopaí ar a dtugtar calico agus cuirtear brollaigh línéadaigh iontu. 'An thraid' a thugtar ar an línéadach sin, is seasann na léinteacha sin an-fhada dóibh.

Déantar an-chuid stocaí a chniotáil sa mbaile sa bparóiste. Déantar stocaí le haghaidh na bhfear, stocaí le haghaidh na seanmhná agus stocaí le haghaidh na bpáistí scoile. Déanann siad an snáth a shníomhachán sa mbaile i gcuid de na tithe agus ceannaíonn daoine nach bhfuil tuirní acu sa mhuileann é. Tá go leor tuirní sa bparóiste ach tá cúig cinn ar an mbaile againn.

Bíonn dhá chulaith ag na daoine anois, 'culaith le haghaidh an Domhnaigh agus culaith le haghaidh an Luain' mar a deirtear. Caitheann na daoine éadaí speisialta ar ócáidí speisialta. Dá mbeadh beirt ag dul a phósadh, chaithfeadh siad éadaí speisialta. Bhíodh sciortaí dúghorma ar chuid de na mná, cinn donna ar chuid eile acu, de réir mar a thaitneodh leo. Bíonn cultacha dubha, cinn donna, cinn ghorma agus dathanna mar iad ar na fir. Bíonn hataí ar chuid de na fir, caipíní ar chuid eile acu agus bíonn seálanna ar na mná.

Fadó, nuair a bhíodh beirt ag dul a phósadh, chaitheadh an fear bríste glúnach, casóg-sciorta agus hata ard. Chaitheadh an bhean sciorta dúghorm agus seál breac. Má bhíonn féasta ann i ndiaidh na bainise, caitheann gach duine an t-éadach is fearr a bios acu. Bíonn áthas an domhain ar chuile dhuine agus maidir leis an lánúin féin, ceapann siad nach mbeadh lá eile le maireachtáil acu, ach ní milleán orthu é, mar ní bhíonn mórán eile laethanta mar an lá sin acu.

Ach bíonn a mhalairt de scéal acu lá sochraide. Bíonn seálta dubha ar na mná agus ar chuid de na fir bíonn cultacha dubha. Caitheann siad iad sin le comhbhrón a dhéanamh le gaolta an duine mhairbh.

Bíonn culaith le haghaidh an Domhnaigh agus culaith le haghaidh an Luain ag na daoine anois. Gach Domhnach caitheann na fir cultacha dubha, cinn donna nó cinn ghorma. Caitheann na seanfhir bríste 'cird' agus cótaí de bhréidín. Caitheann na seanmhná sciortaí dúghorma agus seálta dubha agus breaca. Caitheann na cailíní óga cótaí móra den uile shórt agus bíonn gúnaí deasa orthu freisin. Gach lá eile den tseachtain, bíonn seanghiobail d'éadaí ar gach duine. Bíonn seanchótaí dearga ar na seanmhná agus cuid acu dá dtarraingt ina ndiaidh sna lathaí. Bíonn na fir is na buachaillí is na cailíní ar an gcaoi chéanna ach caithfidh siad a gcuid oibre a dhéanamh is cuma cén chaoi a bheas siad.

**TRANSLATION:**

In this parish where I live there are only two tailors, one near here and the other at the other end of the parish. They work in their own houses now, but long ago they used to go around from house to house.

Sometimes, they would spend a week or a month in one place and they would sleep where they would be working. Long ago, the tailor would have some material in stock and he would make suits that would fit the young men. Then he'd sell them and make enough money to make a bit of profit, but now the people bring him the material and he makes the suits for them.

People wear shop-bought clothes now, except for those people who make cloth at home, in Aran and Connemara. No one wears homespun tweed now because they are too 'grand' to wear it. About forty years ago, shirts were made from homespun linen, but not now because there's no flax grown here. But some men's shirts are made of rough Calico cloth they buy in the shops and they put a linen front in them. '*An thraid*' they call that linen, and those shirts wear very well.

In this parish, many stockings are knitted at home. They make stockings for the men, for the old women and for the school children. They spin the wool at home in some of the houses and the people who don't have spinning wheels buy it in the mill. There are plenty of spinning wheels in the parish and five in our town land.

People have two sets of clothes now, 'a suit for Sunday and a suit for Monday', as they say. They wear special clothes on special occasions. If a couple were getting married they'd wear special clothes. Some of the women used to wear navy skirts and some brown, as they preferred. The men wear black suits, or brown or blue or colours like that. Some men wear hats, some wear caps and the women wear shawls.

Long ago, when a couple were going to marry, the man would wear knee britches, a frock coat and a high hat. The woman would wear a navy skirt and a patterned shawl. If there's a celebration after the wedding, everyone wears their best clothes. All are very happy, and as for the newly-wed couple, they think they'll never have another hard day, but you can't blame them, because they don't have many days like that.

And it's the opposite on a funeral day. The women wear black shawls and some of the men wear black suits. They dress like that to show sympathy with the bereaved.

Nowadays, people have clothes for Sunday and Monday. Every Sunday, the men wear black suits, or brown or blue. The old men wear cord trousers and homespun jackets. The old women wear navy skirts and black or plaid shawls. The young girls wear overcoats of every kind and nice dresses too. Every other day of the week, they all wear old rags. The old women wear old red skirts, some of them pulling them after them in the mud. The men and boys and girls are the same; but they have to do their work no matter how they are dressed.

*(S31: 1–4. An tSr. M. Colmán. Stiofán Ó Briain, 62, Ceathrú an Bhrúnaigh, do thug an t-eolas seo uaidh.)*

# FARM ANIMALS

## *Ainmhithe na Feirme [The Farm Animals] (C'b)*

Beathaítear an bhó le féar glas agus uisce sa samhradh agus le féar tirim, tornapaí, mangalaí agus deochanna bran sa ngeimhreadh. Ceanglaítear le rópa í thart ar a muineál nó le slabhra. Glaoitear uirthi mar seo: 'Prú, Prú.'

Bíonn lao aici uair sa naoi mí. Tugann sí bainne agus im dúinn ansin. Fadó nuair a bheireadh an bhó, cheanglaíodh na daoine píosa flainnín dearg thart ar a drioball le faitíos go ndéanfadh duine ar bith drochshúil dithe. Thugtaí amach an choinneal bheanaithe dá beannú. Bhíodh droch-mhná san am sin ag dul amach lá Bealtaine, iad ag sacadh cipín i ngach salachar bó, iad ag rá, 'Im na bó seo in mo chuinneog.' Bhí fear ag faire orthu dá dhéanamh. Deir sé gach uair, 'Cac na bó sin ar do chuinneog.' Nuair a chuaigh an bhean abhaile ag déanamh an maistreadh, bhí sin aici, lán chuinneog de chac bó. D'éirigh siad as a gcuid obair mhallaithe ó shin. Cuirtear leaba tuí faoi chuile bó.

Glaoitear ar na muca mar seo 'Furaish, Furaish, Furaish.' Cró na muc an t-ainm atá ar a mbothán. Cuirtear leaba tuí fúthu.

Glaoitear ar na capaill mar seo, 'Pre, Pre, Pre.' Cuirtear leaba luifearnach nó tuí agus uaireanta móin bhán bhog fúthu.

Sé an chaoi a nglaoitear ar na gamhna, 'Prín, Prín, Prín.'

Sé an chaoi a nglaoitear ar na turcaithe, 'Biadh, Biadh, Biadh.' Ar na géanna, 'Beadaí, Beadaí, Beadaí.' Ar na cearca, 'Tioc, Tioc, Tioc.' Ar na lachain, 'Píorac, Píorac, Píorac.'

Sé an t-ainm atá ar an gcapall againn ná 'Ruairí an Chnoic'; ar na ba 'An Bhó Bhreac' agus 'An Bhó Bhuí'.

**TRANSLATION:**

The cow is fed on green grass and water in the summer and hay, turnips, mangolds and bran drinks in the winter. She is tied with a rope or a chain around her neck. They call her like this, '*Prú, Prú.*'

The cow has a calf every nine months. Then she gives us milk and butter. Long ago, when the cow would calve, they'd put a piece of red flannel around her tail for fear anyone would 'blink' her. The blessed candle would be taken out to bless her. There would be evil women that time going out on May Day, shoving a stick into cow dung and saying 'The butter of this cow in my churn.' A man was watching them doing it. Every time he would say, 'That cow's dung in your churn.' When one of the women went home to churn, she had the churn full of cow manure. They stopped their cursed work since then. A bed of straw is put under every cow.

They call the pigs like this, '*Furaish, Furaish.*' Their little house is called the pigsty (*cró*). They're given a bed of straw.

They call the horses like this '*Pre, Pre.*' They're given a bed of weeds or straw or sometimes soft white turf.

They call the calves, '*Prín, Prín, Prín.*'

They call the turkeys, '*Biadh, Biadh, Biadh.*' The geese are called, '*Beadaí, Beadaí, Beadaí*', and the hens, '*Tioc, Tioc, Tioc.*' The ducks are called, '*Píorac, Píorac, Píorac.*'

Our horse is called Rory of the Hill and the cows are called the Speckled Cow and the Yellow Cow.

*(S30: 208–9. Máire Bean Uí Ógáin, 80 bl., Baile Dubhlaoich, Gaillimh. Bean fheilméara. 27 Bealtaine 1938.)*

### Ceansú Capall [Breaking Horses] (N's)

Is contúirteach an rud capall a cheansú. Nuair a bios muintir na tuaithe ag ceansú capaill, faigheann siad béalmhách agus cuireann siad ar an gcapall é. Ceanglaíonn siad faoin gcarr é. Líonann siad an carr le clocha nó le haoileach. Téann duine amháin á chinnireacht agus corruair beirt. Téann duine eile taobh thiar den charr agus beireann sé ar an srian. Bíonn greim daingean aige air ionas go bhfanfadh an capall socair.

Bíonn faitíos ar na daoine go rithfeadh an capall agus sin an fáth a gcuirtear ualaigh orthu. Tar éis seachtaine nó mar sin, cuireann siad an chéacht air agus bíonn duine dá chinnireacht i gcónaí. Bíonn siad ag obair leis mar sin chuile lá go mbíonn sé chomh tuirseach is nach mbeidh sé in ann rith. Tar éis míosa nó mar sin, bíonn cleachtadh maith aige ar an obair agus fanann sé go socair faoin gcarr nó an gcéacht nó an chliath, agus bíonn muinín ag an bhfeilméara as. Cuireann sé isteach sa stábla é gach oíche sa ngeimhreadh. Ceanglaíonn sé le hadhastar don rata é agus tugann sé féar dó le n-ithe ar feadh na hoíche. Sa samhradh, fágann sé amuigh sa pháirc é, agus bíonn súil le Dia aige go mairfeadh sé go buan chun cuidiú leis féin agus a chlann.

**TRANSLATION:**

Taming a horse is a dangerous business. When the country people break a horse, they put a bit on the horse. They tie the horse under a cart. They fill the cart with stones or manure. One person leads the horse, or maybe two. Another goes behind the cart and takes the rein. He keeps a good grip on it to hold the horse firm.

People fear that the horse will run away and that's why they put a load on it. After a week or so, they yoke it to the plough and still someone leads it. They work away like that every day until the horse is so tired it can't run. After a month or so, the horse is well used to the work and stays peacefully under the cart or plough or harrow, and the farmer trusts it. He puts it into the stable every night in winter. He ties it with a tether to the rafter and gives it hay to eat during the night. In summer, he leaves it out in the field, and hopes to goodness he will have it for a long time to help him and his family.

*(S30: 11–2. An tSr M. Colmán. Stiofán Ó Briain, 62,*
*Ceathrú an Bhrúnaigh, do thug an t-eolas seo uaidh.)*

# POTATOES

## *Potatoes (NB)*

There are a lot of potato gardens in the district in which I am situated. Every year the people get to work at their own potato gardens. The potato crop failed but once; that is when the Famine arose.

The people get the seed potatoes. Then they get a knife and cut the potatoes in the centre. They make a hole in the ground and cover the potatoes in a long ridge. Some of the people out in the country get a wooden plough to turn the clay.

Some of the names of the potatoes planted are: Champions, Kerry [*sic*] Pinks, Irish Queens, Arran Chiefs, Flounders and Epicures. The favourite potato for planting in this district is the Champion.

More potatoes are grown in our district than any other thing. The people peel the skin off the potato and mash it up and make starch.

*(S31: 107-8. Michael Cooke. I got this from Mrs Cooke, 37, Claddagh, Galway. 1 April 1938.)*

### The Potato Diggers' Meal (P)

At the time of digging the potatoes, the men used to come together in what was a *meitheal* (a number of men) and their meals consisted of roast potatoes. A fire was made in the field where they were digging and the potatoes roasted. This meal was known as a 'caste of potatoes'.

In the former times the people who could afford it bought Indian meal which was the principal food in those days. Those who could not afford to purchase this luxury dug up what was known as '*bleskcans*' (roots of weeds), [*blaoscán* – skull, eggshell] and boiled them. This was the food that the poor people had to exist on.

*(S30: 452. Written by Bea Mangan, Upper Salthill, Galway, 12 years.*
*I got this story from my uncle who heard it from his grandparents.)*

### Na Fataí [The Potatoes] (CGC)

Cuireann muid fataí gach bliain. Treabhann m'athair an talamh ar dtús le céachta agus ansin déanann sé na druileanna. Scarann sé aoileach orthu agus leasú freisin. Gearrtar na fataí ina sciolláin agus cuireann sé iad ins na druileanna. Tagann fear eile ina dhiaidh agus cuireann sé cré orthu le láighe. Tugann na comharsana cúnamh dá chéile ag cur na bhfataí.

Caitheann siad aire mhaith a thabhairt do na fataí an fhaid is a bíos siad ag fás. Cuireann siad cré leo ar dtús. Tamall ina dhiaidh sin cuireann siad

86

aithchré orthu. Bíonn siad mór go maith nuair a chuireann siad spray orthu chun iad a chosaint ar an dubhachán.

Baintear na fataí sa bhfómhar. Cuirtear isteach i bpoill iad. Cuirtear tuí agus cré orthu. Fágtar ansin iad go dtí an t-earrach.

Seo iad na fataí is mó a fhásann siad san áit seo: Kerr Pink, Arran Banner, Arran Chief, Champions, May Queen agus Epicure.

**TRANSLATION:**

We plant potatoes every year. First, my father turns the ground with a plough and then he makes drills. He spreads manure on them and fertiliser too. The potatoes are cut into 'splits' and then he plants them in the ground. Another man comes after him and uses a loy to cover them with clay. The neighbours help each other to plant the potatoes.

They must look after the potatoes well while they are growing. First they put clay on them. After a while they put on more clay. The potatoes are quite big when they spray them, to protect them from blight.

Potatoes are harvested in the autumn. They are put in pits. Thatch and clay are put on the pits.

These are the kinds of potatoes grown here: Kerr Pink, Arran Banner, Arran Chief, Champions, May Queen and Epicure.

*(S32: 70–1. Micheál Ó [illegible], Creig Buí, Baile Chláir na Gaillimhe.)*

### Rann i dtaobh na bhFataí [Rhyme about the Potatoes] (CGC)

Is deas iad na fataí nuair a théann an lón orthu,
Is deise ná sin iad nuair a bhíonn an bláth bán orthu,
Ach is deise ná sin iad nuair a bhíonn an bolg lán acu.

**TRANSLATION:**

The potatoes are nice when the fertiliser goes on them,
Nicer again when they have the white flower,
But even nicer still when the belly is full of them.

*(S32: 73. Máirtín Mac Giollarnath, 60, Cathair Gabhann,*
*Baile Chláir na Gaillimhe.)*

# CHURNING

## *An Chuigeann [The Churn] (N's)*

Tá cuigeann againn sa mbaile. Soitheach adhmaid is ea í a bhfuil cúig fonsaí thart timpeall uirthi, trí cinn sa leath-thíos agus dhá cheann sa leath-thuas. Nuair a bhíonn maistreadh dá dhéanamh bíonn na rudaí seo in úsáid, clár na cuigne, claibín agus an lointhe.

Blítear an bhó dhá uair sa ló, ar maidin agus sa tráthnóna, agus má bhlítear níos minice í imíonn an bainne uaithi. Nuair a bhíonn bean an tí ag dul amach le bó a bhleaghan, tugann sí stóilín i láimh amháin agus canna sa láimh eile. De ghnáth beireann sí léi chomh maith sauspan le haghaidh climirtí na bó, sé sin an chuid is fearr den bhainne. Coinníonn sí í seo i gcóir an tae.

Muna mbíonn sí in ann dul go héasca ag na sineachaí, tugann sí bosóg bheag don bhó chun a chos deiridh a chur siar. Ansin suíonn sí síos go compordach ar an stóilín ag bleaghan ar a mine géire agus ag gabháil foinn de ghnáth san am céanna.

Ar bheith críochnaithe di, cuireann sí crosóg leis an mbainne ar dhroim na bó chun í a bheannú. Tugann sí an bainne go teach an bhainne agus séalaíonn sí é trí shíothlán, ar fhaitíos go mbeadh deannach nó ribeacha fionnaidh na bó ann. Leamhnacht a thugtar ar an mbainne úr sin. Ansin, cuireann sí an leamhnacht i gcíléaraí móra leathana. Fágann sí ansin é ar feadh dhá uair dhéag an chloig. Ansin baineann sí an t-uachtar de le sgamín agus cuireann sí i gcroca nó i bhfeircín é. Má bhíonn lao ann, tugann sí cuid den leamhnacht dó, agus má bhíonn gamhain ann téighean sí roinnt den bhainne sciomtha, meascann sí min bhuí nó min choirce tríd agus tugann sí dó é. Meascann sí an bainne sciomtha chomh maith trí bhia na muc.

Nuair a bhíonn an croca lán d'uachtar, déanann bean an tí an maistreadh. Ar dtús scólann sí an chuigeann, an claibín, clár na cuigne agus an lointhe le huisce friuchta agus cuireann sí amach faoin aer iad len iad a fhuaradh. Tógann sí isteach ansin iad agus doirteann sí an t-uachtar isteach sa gcuigeann. Cuireann sí cos na lointhe trí pholl ar chlár na cuigne agus leagann sí ar bhéal na cuigne é. Fágann sí an claibín anuas air ansin. Cuireann sí marc i bhfoirm croise ar chliathán na cuigne ionas go mbeidh an t-ádh ar an maistreadh. Cuireann sí splanc tine faoi thóin na cuigne freisin ionas go mbeadh an t-ádh ar an im agus go gcruinneoidh sé go tapa.

Beireann sí ar chois na lointhe ansin agus buaileann sí an t-uachtar go tréan go bhfeiceann sí cnaipíní ime ag éirí aníos ar bharr an bhainne. Ansin cuireann sí fód mónadh faoi thóin na cuigne. Croitheann sí an chuigeann ón dtaobh deiseal go dtí an taobh clé go mbíonn an t-im in aon chnap mór amháin. Doirteann sí isteach fíoruisce ar chlár na cuigne, ar chois na lointhe agus ar chliathán na cuigne chun na cnaipíní ime a bhaint díobh. Tógann sí an t-im amach ansin agus cuireann sí i bhfeircín é ina mbíonn fíoruisce.

Níonn sí trí huaire é go mbíonn rian an bhainne imithe as. Ansin déanann sí priontaí de agus má bhíonn an iomarca ann déanann sí aon chnap mór amháin de agus tugann sí chuig an mhargadh é. Déanann sí cácaí leis an mbláthach agus tugann sí cuid de do na leanaí.

Má thagann strainséir chuig an teach le linn do bhean an tí bheith ag déanamh maistreadh, beireann sé ar chois na lointhe ionas nach dtabharfadh sé an t-im leis. Deirtear nach ádhúil bainne a thabhairt d'aoinne Lá Bealtaine ar fhaitíos go dtabharfadh sé an t-ádh leis agus nach mbeadh uachtar ar an mbainne.

**TRANSLATION:**

We have a churn at home. It's a wooden vessel with five hoops round it, three on the lower half and two on the upper. When the butter is being made these are the things that are used: the lid of the churn, cap of churn lid, churn dash.

The cow is milked twice a day, in the morning and evening and if she is milked more often, the milk leaves her. When the woman of the house is going out to milk the cow, she takes a little stool in one hand and a can in the other. She usually takes a saucepan too, for the strippings; that's the best part of the milk. She keeps that for the tea.

If she can't get at the teats easily, she gives the cow a little slap to make the hind legs go back. Then she sits down comfortably on the stool, milking as hard as she can and usually singing at the same time.

When she finishes, she makes a cross with the milk on the cow's back, to bless her. She takes the milk to the milk house and strains it through a sieve, for fear there'd be dust or some of the cow's hairs in it. That fresh milk is

**A woman making bread. (Courtesy of Dept of Irish Folklore, UCD)**

called new milk (*leamhnacht*). Then she puts the new milk in big wide keelers/tubs. She leaves it there for twelve hours. Then she takes off the cream with a skimmer and puts it in a crock or a firkin. If there's a new calf she gives it some of the colostrum. If there are older calves, she heats some of the skimmed milk and mixes yellow meal or corn meal through it and gives it to them. She mixes the skimmed milk with the pigs' food as well.

When the crock is full of cream, the woman of the house does the churning. First of all she scalds the churn, the cap, the churn lid and the dash with boiling water and puts them out in the air to cool. She brings them in and pours the cream into the churn. She puts the dash through the churn lid and places the lid on the churn. Then she puts the cap down on it. She makes a mark in the form of a cross on the side of the churn so that the churning will be lucky. She puts a burning ember under the bottom of the churn too, so that the butter will be lucky and that it will form quickly.

She takes hold of the handle of the dash and pounds the milk strongly until she sees little lumps of butter rising on top. Then she puts a sod of turf under the churn. She shakes the churn from the right side to the left side so that the butter comes together in a big lump. She pours spring water on the churn lid, on the dash handle and on the sides of the churn to take off the pieces of butter. She lifts out the butter then and places it in firkins, which have spring water in them.

She washes it three times until every trace of milk is gone. Then she makes it up into prints and if there's too much she makes it into a large lump and takes it to market. She makes cakes of bread with the buttermilk and gives some to the children.

If a stranger comes into the house while the woman is making butter he takes a turn with the dash, so he won't bring the butter with him. They say that it isn't lucky to give anyone butter on May Day for fear he would take the luck with him and there would be no cream on the milk.

*(S30: 6–8. An tSr M. Colmán. Stiofán Ó Briain, 62, Ceathrú an Bhrúnaigh, do thug an t-eolas seo uaidh.)*

# TRADITIONAL FOOD

## *Bia na Sean [Food in the Olden Days] (NB)*

Ins an tseanaimsir, d'itheadh na daoine ceithre bhéile sa ló. Ba gnách le daoine obair a dhéanamh roimh an gcéad bhéile ar maidin. Théadh feirmeoirí amach gach maidin ar a seacht a chlog agus théadh siad abhaile ar a naoi a chlog agus d'itheadh siad a gcuid bricfeasta.

Le haghaidh an dinnéir bhíodh fataí agus cabáiste acu agus uaireanta bhíodh 'winkles' agus iasc agus fataí freisin. D'óladh siad bainne le fataí, bainne gabhair a bhíodh acu gach lá. Bhíodh bord acu i lár an urláir. Ní ithtí feoil ins an tseanaimsir ná ní raibh aon airgead acu le feoil a cheannach. Ithtí iasc ins an gCladach.

Bhíodh bia ag na daoine ar laethanta áirithe. Ar Aoine an Chéasta agus ar Dhomhnach Cásca, nuair a bhíonn mionnán ag gabhar agus nuair a bhíonn sé ceithre seachtaine d'aois, maraítear é agus bíonn mionnán acu an uair sin.

Ins an tseanam, nuair nach mbíodh aon tae acu, chuireadh na daoine uisce agus spúnóg plúir agus gráinnín salainn agus bhruith siad é ar feadh cúpla nóiméad. Chuireadh siad i gcupán é agus d'óladh siad é agus an t-ainm a bhí air 'brothchán'.

**TRANSLATION:**

Long ago, people used to eat four meals a day. Usually, they worked before their first meal in the morning. Farmers would go out at seven o'clock every morning and go home at nine for their breakfast.

For dinner they'd have potatoes and cabbage, sometimes 'winkles', and fish and potatoes too. They'd drink milk with the potatoes; they'd have goat's milk every day. Their table was placed in the middle of the floor. They didn't eat meat in the olden times because they had no money to buy it. In the Claddagh they ate fish.

People had special food on certain days. On Good Friday and Easter Sunday, if a goat had a kid and if it was four weeks old, it'd be killed and they'd have kid for that occasion.

Long ago, when people had no tea, they'd mix water and a spoonful of flour and a grain of salt and boil it for a couple of minutes. Then they'd put it in a cup and drink it and it was called '*brothchán*'.

*(S31: 127–8. Pádraig Ó Dochartaigh. Fuair mé an scéal seo ó*
*Mháire Ní Shiurtáin, 60, An Cladach, Gaillimh. 23 Márta 1938.)*

## Bread (NB)

The people long ago used to make bread at home. They made wholemeal cakes and oaten meal and potato cakes also. These people used to grind the grain at home. They made a straddle-bread which had oaten meal and a little flour in it. Griddle cakes were also made. They put some cakes to bake in pots and they used the griddle for others. They had nothing like a rolling pin, but they used a bottle instead.

*(S31: 131–2. Patrick Doyle. From Mrs Doyle, 39, New Docks, Galway. 4 April 1938.)*

## Bread (C'g)

Bread was made of wheaten meal long ago. The people ground the wheat by means of a quern. The quern was made up of two round flat-sided stones. There was a hole in the middle of one of them. The stone without the hole was stuck in the ground so that it could not be moved. Then the other stone was placed on top of it. One person caught hold of the top stone and spun it round while another person dropped corn into the hole. In this way, the corn was crushed. John Ryan of Castlegar has one of these quern stones but he never uses it. It was last used fifty years ago. The bread was usually baked on a griddle. There were two ears on a griddle and by means of these ears it was raised above the fire on a pothook.

It was the custom long ago to break an oatmeal cake, baked on the hearth, on the bride's head when she entered the house on her wedding day. This cake was supposed to be the wedding cake and was broken on the bride's head to bring her good luck. It was then distributed among the people present.

Another sort of cake that used to be baked was the potato cake or *cáca fataí*. This cake was made of mashed potatoes, new milk, a little salt and butter kneaded together and baked on a griddle.

*(S30: 61–2. Nóra Bhreathnach ó Neilí Ní Ghriallais, Caisleán Gearr, Gaillimh. 35 bliain.)*

# TRADES AND CRAFTS

### Old Trades (NB)

Long ago there lived in the Claddagh an old woman who used to make tallow candles. These candles were used at wakes. The old woman lived in the Claddagh for some years.

A couple of women out of Claddagh village used to work in a house for a certain number of years making their own soap. They used no other soap but their own, because the soap would wash their clothes and their faces very clean.

In Connemara, the people out of the villages used to make their own baskets. These baskets were made out of scallops (*scolb*s), which they got in the wood nearby. The baskets were very useful to the people for carrying in the messages, for carrying the turf and taking the fish out of the boat. I think you will see these baskets at the present day, if you go out to Connemara.

In the corner of Raven's Terrace, there was a great blacksmith. Now this blacksmith used to do a great trading with the country people and the town's people. In the time of the great frost, he had to work very hard putting nails on the horses and in their shoes and making plenty of horseshoes.

*(S31: 52–3. Martin Cox. I got this information from Mr Patrick Cubbard, No. 3 Claddagh, Galway.)*

### An Chaoi a nDéantaí Coinnle [How They Made Candles] (B'p)

Tuairim is céad bliain ó shin ní raibh aon lampa sa tír seo. Bhíodh coinnle acu mar sholas ach bhí go leor feilméaraí bochta nár fhéad coinnle a cheannach agus dhéanaidís féin cineál coinnle. Dhéanadh cuid acu cineál ar a dtugtaí 'páideoga' agus dhéanadh tuilleadh acu cineál ar a dtugtaí 'trilseáin'. Gach bliain mharaídís cúpla gabhar agus an gheir a bhíodh iontu shábháilídís í. Bhí slige i mbeagnach gach teach agus leagaidís cuid den gheir ann. Ansin gheibhidís striopa canbháis agus tharraingídís tríd an gheir leáite é nó go mbíodh riar mhaith de súite aige. Nuair a bhíodh sin déanta, leagaidís thart é go reofadh sé agus tharraingídís tríd an gheir arís é agus leanaidís orthu mar sin go mbíodh sé chomh ramhar le coinneal pingine agus seo é an sórt coinnle ar a dtugaidís 'páideog'.

Nuair a bhídís ag dul ag déanamh trilseán d'fhaighidís dhá cheann déag de bhreibh agus bhainidís an craiceann díbh. Thumaidís sa ngeir iad agus ansin bhídís réidh.

Bhíodh coinnle eile acu freisin a ghnítí as giúis. Sé an chaoi a ndéanaidís iad seo ná stumpa giúsaí a fháil agus é a scoilteadh ina mheithcheáin. Thumaidís na meithcheáin sa ngeir agus chuiridís le chéile iad. Bhíodh solas breá ar an gcoinneal seo. Bhíodh ceann de na seanchoinnleoirí acu nuair a bhídís ag lasadh na gcoinneal. Bhí áit le haghaidh na dtrí choinneal ar an gcoinnleoir seo.

**TRANSLATION:**

About a hundred years ago there weren't any lamps here. They had candles for light. There were plenty of poor farmers who couldn't afford to buy candles and they'd make their own. Some would make a kind they called '*páideoga*' [wick and tallow] and some would make '*trilseáin*' [rush lights]. Every year they'd kill a couple of goats and save the fat that'd be in them. There'd be a shell/melting pot in almost every house and they'd put some fat in that. Then they'd get a piece of canvas and draw it through the melted fat till it'd soak it up well. When that was done, they'd set it aside till it had hardened, till it was as thick as a penny candle and this is the kind of candle they'd call a '*páideog*'.

When they'd be making '*trilseáin*' they'd get twelve rushes and peel them. They'd dip them in the tallow and then they'd be ready.

There was another kind of candle too, made out of fir. They'd get a fir stump and split it up in matches. They'd dip the splinters in the tallow and put them together. There'd be a great light from those candles. They'd have an old candlestick when they were lighting the candles and it had a place for three candles.

*(S30: 417. Máire Ní Nuadháin a scríobh síos óna hathair Éamonn Ó Nuadháin, feilméara, Pollach, Maigh Cuilinn. Aibreán 1938.)*

### Rush Candles (C'g)

First they used to pull some rushes and take the skin off them, except a small bit to keep the stalk strong. They used to dip this in oil and leave it in a cool place to get very hard. They used to put it in a candlestick and then it was ready for lighting. It would keep lighting for half an hour. They sold those for twelve a penny. They had to make them for there were no shops to buy candles in, in those days. Everyone in our village long ago used to make them.

*(S30: 96. Nóra Bhreathnach, Caisleán Gearr, Gaillimh. Stephen Hynes, 53, Castlegar, Galway told me how candles were made. He saw his grandmother making them when he was young.)*

### Basket-Making (C'g)

First the sally rods are cut and pared with a pocketknife. Then they are left near the fire for about three weeks to season. Then three rods are placed at each corner. Four rods doubled are placed on every side. Then forty rods are woven through them and the sides of the basket are made. The rods are woven at the bottom. Loops are put at the bottom for an ass or a horse to carry. Skibs are made in much the same way.

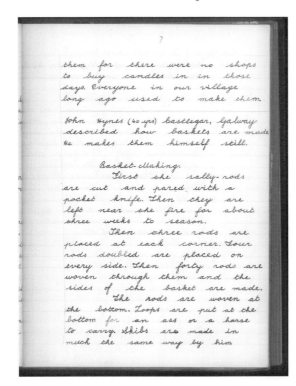

them for there were no shops
to buy candles in in those
days. Everyone in our village
long ago used to make them.

John Hynes (40 yrs) Castlegar, Galway
described how baskets are made
He makes them himself still.

Basket-Making.
First the sally-rods
are cut and pared with a
pocket knife. Then they are
left near the fire for about
three weeks to season.
Then three rods are
placed at each corner. Four
rods doubled are placed on
every side. Then forty rods are
woven through them and the
sides of the basket are made.
The rods are woven at
the bottom. Loops are put at the
bottom for an ass or a horse
to carry. Skibs are made in
much the same way by him.

A description of
basket-making recalled
by John Hynes and
written down by Nóra
Breathnach of Castlegar,
Co. Galway. The Schools'
Collection, Volume 0030,
Page 007.

*(S30: 7–8. John Hynes, 40, Castlegar, Galway, described how baskets are made.*
*He makes them himself still.)*

## *Ceárta [A Forge] (C'b)*

Níl ach aon cheárta amháin sa bparóiste seo ag Micheál Ó Truagháil, Cnoc Mhaoil Dris. Cuireann sé crúiteacha ar chaiple; deisíonn sé céachta agus déanann sé céachta. Níl ach aon teallach amháin sa gceárta. Sé an cineál boilg a bíos ag lasadh na tine ná bladar mór agus é lán gaoithe, maide mór as agus é ag ardú suas agus anuas agus séideann sé an tine go breá ansin.

**TRANSLATION:**

There's only one forge in this parish. It's owned by Micheál Ó Truagháil, Knockweeldrish. He shoes horses and repairs and makes ploughs. There's just one fire in the forge. The bellows to light the fire are made from a big bladder full of wind with a big stick out of it, which is pushed up and down to blow up the fire.

*(S30: 214. Peaits Ó Fáthaigh, Baile an Dubhlaoich, Gaillimh.*
*Feilméara, 65 bliain. 14 Meitheamh 1938.)*

# CARE OF THE FEET

## *Cúram na gCos [Care of the Feet] (N's)*

Ní bhíodh bróga ar bith ar na daoine fadó. Bhíodh píosaí de chraicne ainmhithe casta thart timpeall a gcos acu, nó ag cuid eile bhíodh píosaí adhmaid faoina gcosa acu agus iad ceangailte orthu le 'fongannaí'.

Ní chaitheann na daoine óga bróga sa samhradh anois, ach fadó ní chaitheadh na daoine beaga ná móra bróga sa samhradh. Ní chaitheadh siad bróga ach amháin sa ngeimhreadh agus bhíodh siad cosnocht ar feadh an chuid eile den bhliain. Bhíodh siad ag scaradh móna, ag sábháil féir, ag piocadh fataí agus chuile obair mar iad agus bhíodh siad cosnocht. Is iomaí uair a bhíodh siad ag caoineadh le 'oigheareacha'.

Deirtear gur maith an rud do dhuine a mbeadh 'oighearacha' air a chosa a ní in uisce na bhfataí tar éis iad a bhruith. Deirtear freisin gur cheart uisce na gcos a chaitheamh amach roimh dhul a chodladh. Níor cheart é a chaitheamh amach tar éis a dó dhéag a chlog san oíche, ar fhaitíos go mbuailfí na síógaí leis agus má fhágtar istigh é deirtear gur cheart splanc tine a chaitheamh síos ann. Ach is pisreoga iad seo faoi uisce na gcos a chaitheamh amach.

Ní dhéantar aon bhróga anois in san bparóiste ach deasaítear roinnt bheag. Tugtar taoibhín ar an bpaiste a chuirtear ar thaobh na bróige. Tugtar bairbín ar an bpíosa a chuirtear ar thosach na bróige. Tugtar bonnacha agus leathbhonnacha ar na píosaí a chuirtear faoi bhonna na mbróg ach is é an gréasaí a ghníos an obair seo anois, mar ní bhíonn aon am ag na feilméaraí len é a dhéanamh.

Bhí fear ar an mbaile ar ar tugadh 'gréasaí' mar leasainm, ach cailleadh é tamall ó shin. Tugtar 'gréasaí' ar an bhfear atá sa teach sin freisin anois ach ní raibh ceachtar acu in ann bróga a dheisiú. Níl ag rith leo ach an t-ainm.

Fadó, bhíodh na daoine ar fad ag caitheamh bróga bonn-adhmaid agus 'clogs' a thugtar mar ainm orthu. Caitheann na spailpíní agus na daoine bochta anois iad mar tá siad le fáil dhá uair níos saoire ná na bróga eile,

Haystack completed.

mar ní chaitheann aoinne iad, mar tá siad róthrom. Bíonn siad déanta d'adhmad agus bíonn píosa crua thart timpeall air. Seasann siad chomh fada is nach féidir iad a chaitheamh.

Níor leasaíodh aon leathar sa bparóiste ariamh. Chaitheadh siad píosaí de chraicne na n-ainmhithe in áit bróga agus caitheann muintir Árainn fós iad, agus is deas an rud iad a fheiceáil. Bíonn siad ar na haontaí móra i nGaillimh agus d'aithneofá ar an bpointe cén sort beithíoch ar a raibh an craiceann.

Bhíodh na gréasaithe i bfad níos flúirsí fadó, mar ní bhíodh aon mhonarcha ann le bróga a dhéanamh agus bhíodh orthusan iad a dhéanamh.

**TRANSLATION:**
People had no shoes long ago. They'd have a piece of animal skin wrapped around their feet, tied with thongs.

Young people don't wear any shoes in summer now. They only wear them in winter and they go barefoot for the rest of the year. They used to spread turf, save hay, gather potatoes and every kind of work like that, with no shoes on. They often used to cry with hacks.

It is said to be a good thing for someone who has hacks to wash his feet in the water in which potatoes have been boiled. They say also that the water in which feet are washed should be thrown out before going to bed. It shouldn't be thrown out after twelve o'clock at night, for fear it might hit the fairies. If it is left indoors, they say a lighted ember should be thrown into it but that's all superstition.

No shoes are made now in the parish but some are mended. The patch that's put on the side of a shoe is called a side-patch (*taoibhín*). The patch on front of a shoe is called a toe-patch (*bairbín*). Soles and half-soles are put on the bottom of shoes. It's the shoemaker who does all this work now because the farmers don't have time to do it.

There was a man here whose nickname was '*gréasaí*' (shoemaker), but he died a while ago. The man who lives in that house now is also called '*gréasaí*' but neither of them was able to mend a shoe. They only had the name.

Long ago, all the people wore wooden-soled shoes called clogs. The labourers and poor people wear them still, because they are twice as cheap as the other shoes, but they are too heavy. They're made of wood and have a hard rim around them. They last so long that they can't be worn out.

No leather was ever tanned in this parish. They'd wear pieces of animal skin instead of shoes and the people of Aran still do, and it's nice to see them. They go to the big fairs in Galway and you'd recognise immediately which animal the skin came from.

The shoemakers used to be more plentiful long ago, because there was no factory to make shoes and they had to make themselves.

Claregalway girls, *c.* 1923.

*(S30: 14–6. An tSr M. Colmán. Stiofán Ó Briain, 62,*
*Ceathrú an Bhrúnaigh, do thug an t-eolas seo uaidh.)*

## Cúram na gCos [Care of the Feet] (CGC)

… Sa tseanaimsir, bhíodh malraigh suas le cúig bliana déag sula chaithidís aon bhróg. Bhíodh na bacaigh ag dul thart cosnochtaithe. Sula dtéann daoine a chodladh, níonn siad a gcosa. Nuair a bhíonn tú ag cur ort do bhróga, deirtear nár cheart ceann acu a dhúnadh gan an péire a bheith ort.

**TRANSLATION:**

… In the old days, young people were up to 15 years of age before they'd wear shoes. The beggars went around barefoot. Before people go to sleep, they wash their feet. When you're putting on your shoes, they say you shouldn't tie one of them before you put them both on.

*(S32: 98. No name.)*

# CHILDREN'S LORE

## Playthings Made by the Boys of the Parish (C'g)

The boys of this parish make many playthings: balls, rabbit snares, hurleys, marbles, buzzers, pipes, tops, catapults, fifes, cradles, blasts and whistles.

I saw Stephen King making a ball. Four pint-bottle corks are tied together by a piece of cloth. Then woollen knitting thread is rolled around the corks and made into the shape of a ball. Then I sew a string through the thread to keep it together. I use them for hurling.

I have seen Bartley Murphy making rabbit snares. They are made by making a noose in a piece of thin copper wire about eighteen inches long, and tying the end of the wire to a peg. Then the peg is stuck in the ground at the mouth of the rabbit's burrow and the noose is set. When the rabbit gets caught in the noose he is choked.

I have seen Martin Connely making a hurley. First a piece of ash about one yard long, and with a turn at one end, is cut. Then it is pared with a pocketknife and a piece of broken glass, and the hurley is made.

**Hopscotch on Lower Merchant's Road.**

I saw Bartley Murphy making marbles. When I am in want of marbles, I get a piece of tar or candle grease and roll it between my palms and make it round. Then I leave it in a cold place to get hard.

I saw Pat Crowe making a buzzer. First two holes are put in the centre of the top of a boot polish tin. Then a string is passed through the holes and the ends are tied together. By stretching the string the buzzer spins around and makes the buzzer sound.

I saw Patrick Tully making a pipe. First a hole is put into a piece of wood about two inches long and an inch in diameter. Then another hole is bored with a knitting needle in another thin piece of wood about six inches long. This is called the stem and the other one is called the bowl. Then another hole is put in the side of the bowl and the stem is stuck into it.

I saw Bartley Murphy making a top. First a piece of wood is made into the shape of a top with a pen knife and then a nail is driven through the top of the top. They do not stay spinning long because they are a bit heavy.

I saw John Walsh making a catapult. I got a forked branch about nine inches long and two pieces of a motor tube, each about a foot long. I tied one piece of the rubber to one branch of the fork and the other piece to the other branch of the fork, and tied a piece of soft leather to the other end of the rubber. I used it for firing stones a great distance but could take no aim with it.

A cradle bird is made from sally rods. First I placed four rods in the shape of a square. I tied the corners with twine. Then I placed four more on top of these and tied them the same way. I continued on, making each square smaller than the one before it until it was finished. I held up one side of it by means of a *gabhlóg*. Then I attached another rod called the *slavín marbh* to this. If the bird alighted on this, the cradle bird would fall on him. I attached another rod shaped in a half circle to the cradle. If the bird touched this, the cradle would fall also. This is called the belly band. The four thick rods at the bottom of the cradle are the frame.

I made a fife from the barrel of a bicycle pump. I closed one end with a cork. I reddened a big nail in the fire. Then I bored six holes on one side, about one inch apart and all the same size. Then, near the top, and along the same side, I bored a bigger hole to blow into.

I made a blast by getting a cocoa tin and putting a little carbide and a little water into it. I put the lid on the box then. I put a hole in the bottom of the tin and I lit a match near the hole. The carbide exploded with a loud noise and blew the lid off.

*(S30: 9–13. Micheál Ó Griallais, Caisleán Gearr, Gaillimh.*
*Bhí an t-eolas seo ar fad agam féin.)*

# PASTIMES

### *Caitheamh Aimsire [Pastimes] (B)*

Súil ribe: Píosa sreanga agus súil a chur ar a cheann agus an ceann eile a chur amach ann agus é a chur ar an bpoll a mbeadh an coinín ag codladh ann agus nuair a bheadh sé ag dul isteach ann chuirfeadh sé a cheann isteach agus ní fhéadfadh sé a fhágáil ná go bhfaigheadh sé bás.

Gunna: Píosa de chrann troim a fháil agus píosa d'iarann a chur ins an tine agus nuair a bheas sé dearg, é a thógáil aníos agus é a shá isteach ins an mhaide agus beidh poll ins an mhaide ansin. Píosa maide eile a fháil nach mbeadh chomh mór leis an gceann eile agus é a shá isteach ins an bpoll agus bheadh an gunna déanta. Píosa luaidhe a fháil agus í a chur isteach ins an ngunna ins an taobh eile agus an maide a bhualadh le do lámh agus an luaidhe a bhrú amach.

Púicín: Píosa éadaigh a fháil agus é a chur ar do shúile. Rithfidh na gasúir agus an té a mbeirtear air, caithfidh sé a bheith ina phúicíneach.

An tlascaire: Bíonn fear amháin ina sheanfhear agus an chuid eile ina ndaoine a thagann isteach ins an ngarraí (aige). Fiafraíonn siad de an bhfuil cead acu a bheith ag spraoi ins an ngarraí. Deireann sé leo go bhfuil inniu ach nach mbeidh amárach agus tosaíonn siad ag rith isteach. An chéad duine a mbeirtear air caithfidh seisean bheith ina sheanfhear.

Trap a chur ins an áit a mbeadh an giorria ag dul agus nuair a sheas-fadh sé anuas ar an trap, choinneodh an trap greim ar a chois nó go gcaillfí é. Láighe agus píce agus bláthaí a fháil agus poll mór a dhéanamh ins an talamh agus na bláthaí a leagan anonn is anall air agus nuair a bheidh an coinín ag dul thar an bpoll titfidh sé síos ins an bpoll agus marófar é.

Rópa mór a fháil agus súil a chur ar cheann de agus cloch a chur ins an tsúil agus an rópa a chaitheamh leis an gcoinín agus marófar é.

Tobar uisce a fháil agus úll a chur síos ann agus an té a bheadh in ann an t-úll a thabhairt aníos lena bhéal, bheadh sé aige.

**TRANSLATION:**

Snare: Make a loop in the end of a piece of wire and place it on a hole where a rabbit would be sleeping. When the rabbit goes into the hole, he'll put his head into the snare and not be able to leave till he dies.

A gun: Get a piece of elder tree and put a piece of iron in the fire. When it's red hot, take it out and push it into the stick and make a hole. Get another stick then, not as big as the first, and put it into the hole and you'll have the gun made. Get a bit of lead and put it into the gun at the other side. Hit the stick with your hand and push out the lead.

Blind Man's Buff: Get a piece of cloth and cover your eyes. The children will run and the person who's caught will be 'on it' next time.

**St Brendan's boys.**

Fisherman: One child is the old man and the others come into his garden. They ask him if they can play in the garden. He says they can today but not tomorrow and they start running in. The first one to be caught must take the old man's role next time.

Put a trap in the hare's path. When he stands on the trap, it'll keep hold of his leg till he dies. Get a loy and a pitchfork and vegetation. Make a hole in the ground and lay the vegetation over and back on top of it. When the rabbit is going over the hole, he'll fall in and be killed.

Get a big rope and put a loop on one end of it and put a stone in the loop. Throw the rope at the rabbit and kill him.

Put an apple down into a well. The person who can lift the apple in his mouth can keep it.

*(S31: 235–7. Fuair mé an t-eolas seo ó m'athair a rugadh agus a tógadh ar an gCeathrú Rua. Pádraig Ó Bhailís, 3 Sráid an Teampaill, Gaillimh.)*

# 3

# BELIEFS AND CUSTOMS

Dreoilín, dreoilín, rí na n-éan,/ Lá Fhéile Stiofáin, gabhadh an t-éan./
Is mór é a mhuirín, is beag é féin,/ Éirigh suas a bhean an tí,/
Beir ar scian na coise buí,/ Agus gearr amach píosa don dreoilín.

*[Wren, wren, king of the birds,/ St Stephen's Day, the bird was caught./*
*His family is big though he is small,/ Get up woman of the house,/*
*Take the yellow handled knife,/ And cut a piece for the wren.]*

The traditions in this chapter, more than any other, take us right to the heart of the 1930s psyche, and point to essential differences between that time and our own. Then, almost every aspect of community life was governed by traditional observancess, and the beliefs and customs generated by them. Underpinning all their affairs was a strong understanding of the concept of 'luck'. This luck was a valuable commodity; it needed guarding and protecting at all times. It pertained to all areas of human existence: the house, the cow, making butter, going fishing and to areas of inter-personal relations such as meeting strangers or finding a marriage partner. There seemed to be an equilibrium in all things, which was to be maintained at all costs. The two ideas of luck and consequence walked hand in hand and care needed to be exercised. Actions could have consequences for good and ill. The traditional superstitious beliefs often overlapped with, or sat easily beside, what we might now call popular religion. Certain religious customs and emblems were credited with special, almost magical, powers. Some religious festivals were propitious times for ensuring the luck of an enterprise such as seed planting.

This corpus of traditions gives us a glimpse into the complex web of beliefs and customs that marked the daily, weekly and yearly round.

Belief in the fairies in their different guises was still alive to some extent in the 1930s. They were called the 'good' people, capable of intervening in human affairs in order to help, but also capable of causing great harm if annoyed. Actual belief in the fairies has always been very difficult to measure but the accounts here point at least to a residual belief and a knowledge of the actions required to protect people, stock and crops from their malign intent.

Weather, and particularly bad weather, is an important part of people's lives here in the west of Ireland. In the 1930s there was no Met Éireann, no smartphone app to call upon. But there was a huge body of local observation to draw on: you could look at the behaviour of birds or insects, the sea, the colours in your fire, whether there was a white ring around the moon. For fishing folk and farmers, this weather lore played a vital role in their daily affairs. They relied on it, pooling their resources of tried and tested signs and information to enable them to go about their daily tasks.

The whole calendar was punctuated by festival days, high days and holidays, each with its own customs and rituals. We can enumerate up to twenty festival days in chronological order, from St Brigid's Day on 1 February, through the year, to Epiphany on 6 January the next year, aside from local festivals such as patron or pattern days. Most of the festivals are religious and Christian in orientation and many function as 'marker' days, for planting and reaping, in the agricultural year. When a new task was being undertaken, people were observant of the day on which it was begun. Some days were auspicious, good for beginning work or getting married. And some were definitely to be avoided. 'Special days', such as Hallowe'en and May Day, had their roots in pagan antiquity. They were still observed, in a modified form, and keenly anticipated, particularly by the young people. They provided a break from the humdrum of daily life, an opportunity for dressing up, socialising and having fun. They were tied into the wider culture in a functional way, through the belief system and people's work activities. Christmas and New Year involved the making of a 'feast' – special food and drink and merry making to mark the end of one year and the beginning of the next.

For a whole range of everyday ailments and conditions, people were just as likely to avail of traditional medicine and cures as orthodox medicine, for themselves and their animals. There was a huge range of traditional

**Eyre Square, Galway, *c.* 1940s.**

cures available to them: verbal, manipulative, procedural and herbal. Some were the provenance of certain gifted individuals and others were common knowledge. For common conditions such as warts and sprains there was a plethora of remedies available, and availed of, it would seem. Even consumption, as tuberculosis was called, had its own range of folk remedies.

Marriage and death too were enveloped in traditional rites and understandings. The institution of marriage was beginning to change from an economic liaison between families to a romantic relationship between a man and a woman. But matchmaking and the arrangements associated with a dowry were still remembered, and still practised in certain cases. Up until thirty years before the time of the Schools' Collection, wake games had been played at night in the kitchen of the wake house in Castlegar parish. In a living link with a much different time, one pupil states his grandfather 'often played them'.

Many traditional understandings of life and its underpinning still held firm in the 1930s. Time, work and belief were integrated to a remarkable degree, while people lived on the land. Society would change and these understandings of how things worked would change along with it.

# WEATHER LORE

## *Seanchas i dTaobh na hAimsire [Weather Lore] (NB)*

Nuair a fheiceann tú an éanlaith ag eitilt go hard in san spéir, sin comhartha go bhfuil aimsir bhreá ag teacht. Ach nuair a fheictear iad ag eitilt go híseal, sin comhartha báistí.

Is minic a chíonn duine an fharraige ag éirí garbh. Bailigh ó sin go bhfuil stoirm ann. Ach is minic a thagann eagla ar mhairnéalaigh nuair a thagann calm go hobann. Deirtear go minic 'calm roimh an stoirm'.

Bailítear ó na feithidí eolas maith freisin. Feiceann tú an phéist ar an gcré roimh stoirm nó báisteach. Is maith go mór leis an t-uisce. Amuigh faoin dtuath, in sna tithe, bíonn na creagair ina dtost roimh thitim báistí. Bíonn siad ag 'chirpeáil' go mór roimh achar aimsir bhreá. Ní bhíonn na cuileoga go hard in san spéir ansin agus nuair a bhíonn an ghrian ag taitneamh feictear iad go hard ann.

Féach ar an dtine. Nuair atá sí go geal tá aimsir mhaith ag teacht, ach nuair atá sí go híseal tá drochaimsir ag teacht. Titeann an súiche freisin roimh bháisteach.

**TRANSLATION:**

When you see the birds flying high in the sky, that's a sign that good weather is coming. But when you see them flying low, that's a sign the rain is coming.

Often people notice the sea getting rough. That's a sign there's a storm coming. But sailors often get afraid when a sudden calm comes. They often say 'calm before the storm'.

The insects give good information too. You see the worm on the clay before a storm or rain. It likes the water. Out in the countryside, the crickets fall silent in the houses before rainfall. They chirp away before a period of good weather. The flies aren't usually high in the sky, but when the sun is shining they can be seen high up.

Look at the fire. When it is shining brightly good weather is on its way, but when the fire is low, bad weather is coming. The soot falls down too before heavy rain.

*(S31: 33. Pádraig Ó Dubhghaill. Fuair mé an seanchas ó Phádraig Ó Fáthaigh, Na Duganna, Gaillimh.)*

## Seanchas i dTaobh na hAimsire [Traditions About the Weather] (CGC)

Tá eolas ag na daoine thart anseo cén sórt aimsire atá le teacht ó na rudaí seo:

Ag éirí na gréine dá mbeadh an spéir go dearg, déarfadh siad go mbeadh báisteach ann.

Nuair a bios an ghaoth aneas bíonn báisteach air.

Nuair a bios fáinne bán ar an ngealach bíonn báisteach air.

Nuair a bhíonn an tuar ceatha le feiceáil go minic bíonn báisteach air.

Nuair a bios dath an tsionnaigh ar an spéir an-chomhartha báistí is ea é.

Dá mbeadh an spéir go dearg ag dul faoi don ghréin, déarfadh siad go bhfuil aimsir bhreá ann.

Nuair a bios ceo ann sin comhartha aimsir bhreá.

Nuair a thagann na gabhair abhaile deirtear go mbeidh aimsir gharbh againn.

Nuair a bios na cait ag scríobadh na ndoirse sin comhartha go bhfuil aimsir gharbh air.

Nuair a bhíonn go leor réalta san spéir bíonn aimsir bhreá air.

The Claddagh, *c.* 1925.

Nuair a bhíonn an madadh ag ithe féir ghlais in aice claí bíonn báisteach
   air.
Sí an ghaoth aneas is mó a thugann báisteach léi.
Dá dtiocfadh spideog in aice an tí bheadh sioc ann.

**TRANSLATION:**

The people around here know what kind of weather is coming from these
signs:
If the sky is red at sunrise, they would expect rain.
The south wind brings rain.
When there's a white ring around the moon there'll be rain.
A rainbow indicates rain.
When the sky is the colour of the fox, that's a great sign of rain.
If the sky is red at sunset they'd say there would be fine weather.
Fog is a sign of good weather.
When the goats come home, they say we'll have rough weather.
When the cats scrape the doors that's a sign of rough weather.
When there are lots of stars in the sky there'll be fine weather.
When the dog eats green grass beside the ditch it will rain.
The south wind is the main wind to bring rain.
If a robin came near the house there'll be frost.

*(S32: 58–61. Máirtín Mac Giollarnath, Cathair Gabhann; Peadar Ó Moráin;*
*Cathair Gabhann; Máirtín Ó Cuileanáin, Creig Buí, Baile Chláir na Gaillimhe.)*

# SEASONAL CUSTOMS

### *Lá Fhéile Stiofáin [St Stephen's Day] (P)*
Titeann Lá Fhéile Stiofáin ar an lá i ndiaidh Lá Nollag. Bíonn go leor buachaillí beaga ag dul thart leis an dreoilín. Bíonn an dreoilín thíos i mbosca
agus bíonn cuileann ar bharr an bhosca. Bíonn amhrán beag dá rá ag na
buachaillí beaga. Seo é an t-amhrán:

   Dreoilín, dreoilín, rí na n-éan,
   Lá Fhéile Stiofáin, gabhadh an t-éan.

**Presentation Secondary School, Galway, 1920.**

Is mór é a mhuirín, is beag é féin,
Éirigh suas a bhean an tí,
Beir ar scian na coise buí,
Agus gearr amach píosa don dreoilín.

Deir an duine a bhíonn ag éisteach leis go bhfuil sé sin go maith agus tugann sé pingin nó dhá phingin dóibh. Bíonn dhá bhuachaill agus bosca eatarthu. Nuair a bhíonn a sáith déanta acu, roinneann siad an t-airgead eatarthu. Ceannaíonn siad milseáin agus téann siad abhaile.

**TRANSLATION:**
St Stephen's Day falls on the day after Christmas Day. Lots of small boys go around with the wren. The wren is placed down in the bottom of a box with holly on top of it. The boys sing a little song. This is it:

Wren, wren, king of the birds,
St Stephen's day, the bird was caught.
His family is big though he is small,
Get up woman of the house,
Take the yellow handled knife,
And cut out a piece for the wren.

The person listening says that's great and gives them a penny or two. There are usually two boys and a box between them. When they have done enough, they divide the money between them. They buy sweets and go home.

*(S30: 456–7. Mairéad Ní Chomáin, 11, Cinn Uisce, Baile Cláir.*
*Fuaireas an scéal seo ó mo mháthair, Sorcha Uí Chomáin.)*

## *Nósanna a Bhí ag na Mná Óga Fadó ar Oíche Shamhna [Young Women's Customs at Halloween] (NC)*

Théadh na mná óga go dtí sruthán teorann agus thógaidís braon uisce as agus chuiridís blogam ina mbéal. Théidís ag éisteacht ag na doirse dúnta i dtrí theach den sloinneadh céanna agus dá gcloisfidís caint ar an ainm céanna fir ins na trí theach, bheadh súil acu gurbh é sin an t-ainm a bheadh ar an bhfear a phósfaidís. Muna gcloisfidís ainm fir ar bith dá lua, thitfeadh an drill ar an dráll acu, ag ceapadh nach bhfaigheadh siad fear ar bith agus go bhfanfaidís singil go deo.

D'fhaigheadh siad úll agus bhainidís an craiceann de gan é a bhriseadh óna chéile agus chaithidís siar thar a ngualainn é. Pé litir a dhéanfadh sé nuair a thitfeadh sé ar an urlár, sin é an chéad litir ar ainm an fhir a phósfaidís.

D'fhaigheadh siad úll agus bhainidís an craiceann de os comhair scátháin agus bhí sé ráite go bhfeicfeadh siad an fear céile a bheadh acu.

**TRANSLATION:**

The young women would go to a boundary stream and take a mouthful of water and keep it in their mouths. They'd go around listening at the closed doors of three houses of the same surname and if they heard the same man's name mentioned in the three houses, they'd hope that was the name of the man they were going to marry. If they didn't hear any man's name mentioned, they would be in despair, thinking that they would never get a husband and that they would always remain single.

They'd get an apple and peel it without breaking the skin and throw the peel over their shoulder. Whatever letter it made when it fell on the floor, that'd be the first letter in the name of the man they'd marry.

They'd take an apple and peel it in front of a mirror and it was said that they would see their future husband (in the mirror).

*(S31: 151–2. Bairbre Nic Dhonnachadha, 22 Tulach Naomh Doimnic, Gaillimh.)*

### Oíche Shamhna agus an Leipreachán [Halloween and the Leprechaun] (P)

Fadó, bhíodh go leor trácht ag na seandaoine ar an leipreachán agus ar na sióga oíche Shamhna.

Lá amháin, blianta ó shin, rug fear a bhí ag teacht abhaile ar leipreachán. Fuair sé é, fá scáth crainn, ag gréasaíocht bróg. Bhí pota mór óir aige. Rug an fear greim ar an leipreachán agus d'iarr sé air cá raibh an pota óir i bhfolach aige. Dúirt an leipreachán nach n-inseodh sé dó cá raibh sé. Nuair a d'fhéach an fear thart timpeall air féin arís bhí an leipreachán imithe.

Bíonn bosca snaoisín ag an leipreachán. Nuair a fheiceann sé na daoine ag faire air caitheann sé an snaoisín sna súile acu. An fhaid is a bhíonn siad ag sraoifeartaigh imíonn sé.

Oíche Shamhna, bíonn na sióga ag athrú áit chónaithe. Nuair a bhíonn siad ag athrú, caitheann siad seile ar na húlla agus ar na sméara. Deir siad nach ceart iad a ithe ón oíche sin amach.

Bíonn cleasanna ar siúl ag na daoine óga an oíche sin freisin. Bíonn siad ag faire go dtagaidh an oíche. Ag an suipéar, gearrann bean an tí cáca milis ina mbíonn fáinne. Bíonn siad ar fad ag faire ar an bhfáinne. Tá seanrá ann, an duine a gheibheann an fáinne gurb é an chéad duine a phósfaidh an bhliain sin.

Bíonn go leor spóirt ag na páistí beaga freisin. Bíonn siad ag tomadh i dtobán uisce agus ag déanamh go leor rudaí mar sin.

Is mór an trua nach dtagann an oíche sin níos mó ná uair amháin sa mbliain!

**TRANSLATION:**

Long ago, the old people used to talk about the leprechaun and the fairies at Halloween. One day, years ago, a man was coming home and found a leprechaun. He found him in under a tree, fixing shoes. The leprechaun had a pot of gold. The man grabbed him and asked him where he had the pot of gold hidden. The leprechaun said he wouldn't tell him where it was. When the man looked around again, the leprechaun was gone.

The leprechaun has a box of snuff. When he sees people looking at him, he throws the snuff in their eyes. While they are sneezing, he makes off.

On Halloween night, the fairies change abode. When they are changing, they spit on the apples and blackberries. People say they shouldn't be eaten after that.

Young people play tricks on that night too. They wait for night to come. At supper, the woman of the house cuts a sweet cake that contains a ring. Everyone wants the ring. There is an old saying that the person who gets the ring will be the first person to marry that year.

The small children have plenty of fun too. They go ducking (for apples) in a tub of water and that kind of things.

It's a great pity Halloween doesn't come more than once a year!

*(S30: 434–5. Cáit Ní Ioláin, 14, Baile Chláir, Rang 8.*
*Fuaireas an scéal seo ó Mhicheál Mac Cuimín, Cinn Uisce, Baile Chláir.)*

## May Day (P)

In some parts of the country it is the custom on May Day to decorate the house with green branches and to put up a May pole with flowers and eggshells.

*(S30: 448, Addie Molloy, Lower Salthill, Galway, 15 years.*
*I got this story from my mother who heard it from her mother.)*

## An Nollaig Trí Scór Bliain ó Shin [Christmas Sixty Years Ago] (C'b)

Sé an méid plúir a thagadh abhaile dhá chloch agus leathchloch 'Christmas Box'. Cheannaíodh siad ceithre phunt cuiríní agus punt rísíní, agus d'fhaigheadh siad leathphunt isteach leis. Cheannaíodh siad ceithre phunt de mhuiceoil Ameiriceá, agus cloigeann caorach, na scamhóga agus na haebhanna. Bhácáiltí cloch den phlúr le haghaidh Nollag Mhóir agus cloch eile le haghaidh Nollag Bhig agus bheadh leathchloch le haghaidh Lá Cinn. Bhruitheadh siad dhá phunt den bhfeoil le haghaidh Lá Nollag Mhóir agus dhá phunt le haghaidh Nollag Bhig. Bhíodh an cloigeann caorach, na haebhanna agus na scamhóga le haghaidh Lá Cinn.

Cheannaíodh siad pionta fuisce ar chúig phingin déag ins an teach ab fhearr i nGaillimh san am sin a dtugaidís tigh 'Katty Fiddle' (air). Chuireadh siad pionta uisce tríd an fuisce. D'óladh siad a leath oíche Nollag Mhóir agus an leath eile le haghaidh oíche Nollag Bhig agus dhéanadh siad punch de. Cheannaíodh siad péire coinnle agus d'fhaighidís coinneal bheag isteach (leo). Lasadh siad ceann de na coinnle oíche Nollag Mhóir agus an ceann eile le haghaidh oíche Nollag Bhig agus an choinneal bheag le haghaidh Lá Cinn. Bheadh an Nollaig thart ansin agus bheadh caitheamh mór ina diaidh acu. Chuireadh siad slán agus beannacht léi go ceann bliana mar ní bhfaigheadh siad píosa aráin nó braon te go dtiocfadh an Nollaig arís.

**TRANSLATION:**

They'd bring home two stone of flour and get half a stone for a 'Christmas Box'. They'd buy four pounds of currants and a pound of raisins, and they'd get half a pound in with it. They'd buy four pounds of American bacon, a sheep's head, lungs and liver. A stone of flour would be baked for Christmas Day and another stone for Little Christmas and there'd be a half stone for New Year's Day. They'd boil two pounds of the meat for Christmas and two pounds for Little Christmas. They'd have the sheep's head, the liver and lungs, for New Year's Day.

They'd buy a pint of whiskey in the best house in Galway, 'Katty Fiddle's'. They'd put a pint of water through the whiskey. They'd drink half of it on Christmas night and the other half on Little Christmas and they'd make punch with it. They'd buy a pair of candles and get a small candle in with them. They'd light one of the candles on Christmas night and the other on Little Christmas. They'd have the little candle for New Year's Day. Christmas would be over then and they'd miss it. They'd bid it farewell for another year, for they wouldn't get a bit of bread or a drop of whiskey till Christmas would come around again.

*(S30: 173–4. Seán Beaglach, 70, Coill Uachtair, Gort an Chalaidh, Gaillimh. Feilméara. 19 Eanáir 1938.)*

### Laethanta Áirithe [Special Days] (NB)

Dúirt mo mháthair liom go raibh pisreog ag baint le laethanta áirithe. Seo cuid de na laethanta sin: Lá Bealtaine, Lá Marú Chríost, Dé Luain.

THE SALMON FISHERIES, GALWAY.

The salmon fisheries, Galway, *c.* 1925.

Chuireadh an feilméara píosa éadaigh deirg ar na beithígh ar Lá Bealtaine agus ní thosaíodh sé ag treabhadh mar bhí pisreog ann. Cheap sé go mbeadh mí-ádh air muna ndéanfadh sé é sin.

Ní dhéanadh daoine tithe nua ar Lá Marú Chríost in onóir ár dTiarna Íosa Críost. Ba mhaith le daoine troscán a aistriú isteach i dteach nua Dé Luain agus Dé hAoine. Ceapann siad go mbeadh ádh mór orthu ar na laethe sin. Níor mhaith leo troscán a chur isteach Dé Domhnaigh.

Bhí eagla ar iascairí dul amach ar an fharraige mhór Dé hAoine freisin mar cheap siad go mbeadh an bás orthu dá ndéanfadh siad é sin.

Chuireadh na daoine coinnle ar lasadh sna fuinneoga oíche Nollag mar bhídís ag súil go dtiocfadh an Mhaighdean Mhuire isteach ina dteach.

Dúirt mo mháthair liom go raibh Lá Crosta na Bliana ar an 12ú lá de mhí Lúnasa. Tagann na bádaí iascaireachta le chéile ar an lá sin agus beannaítear iad. Bíonn tosnú ansin ar iascaireacht na scadán. Muna mbeadh an bheannacht speisialta sin ann, cheapfadh siad go mbeadh siad gan éisc ar bith.

**TRANSLATION:**

My mother told me there were superstitions associated with certain days: May Day, Good Friday, and Mondays.

The farmer put a piece of red cloth (flannel) on the animals on May Day. He wouldn't begin ploughing (on that day) because there was a superstition about it. He believed he would have bad luck if he did.

People didn't build new houses on Good Friday, in honour of Our Lord Jesus Christ. People would like to move furniture into a new house on Monday and Friday. They'd think they'd have great luck on those days. They wouldn't like to move in furniture on a Sunday.

Fishermen were afraid to go out to sea on Friday too, because they believed they might die if they did.

They used to put lighted candles in their windows on Christmas Eve because they hoped the Virgin Mary might come into their house.

My mother said that 12 August is 'the cross day of the year'. The fishing boats come together on that day and they are blessed. The herring fishing starts on that day. If they didn't get that blessing, they believe there wouldn't be any fish.

*(S31: 78–9. Pádraig Ó Dubhghaill. Fuair mé an t-eolas seo ó*
*Bhean Uí Dhubhghaill, 39, Na Duganna, Gaillimh.)*

## Laethanta Áirithe Eile [Special Days] (NB)

Dúirt mo mháthair liom nach gcuirfeadh feilméara síol prátaí i dtalamh thar Aoine an Chéasta agus cabáiste thar an 17ú lá de Mhárta. Saghas pisreoige a bhí ann, ach níl sé ann anois.

Chuala mé go minic ar Laethanta na Bó Riabhaigh. Tá ainm eile air ná 'Gearrtha Craicinn na Seanbhó'. Bíonn an t-am sin den bhliain ann i dtosach an Aibreáin. Deir na seandaoine go mbíonn deich lá eile ag Mí na Márta agus bíonn an aimsir chomh fuar sin agus nach mbíonn i gceart ag mí Aibreáin ach fiche lá. Deirtear gur ghearr an fuacht an craiceann den seanbhó.

Ansin, chuala mé trácht go minic ar Fhómhar na nGéanna. Sa séasúr seo, bíonn na géanna ag ithe an méid cruithneachta nó an conlach a bhíonn fágtha tar éis baint na cruithneachta. Amuigh faoin dtuath, maraítear géanna ar lá fhéile Mháirtín a bhíonn ann ar an séú lá de mhí na Samhna. Ansin, cuirtear cuid fola na ngéanna ar an ndoras in onóir Naomh Máirtín mar cailleadh é i muileann agus chuaigh a chuid fola ar an dtalamh.

Bíonn dhá lá dhéag na Nollag ann ó Lá Nollag go dtí an séú lá d'Eanáir. Nollaig Bheag a thugtar air sin nó Nollaig na mBan, mar chuaigh an Mhaighdean Mhuire isteach sna tithe fadó agus bheannaigh sí na mná i ngach teach a ndeachaigh sí isteach ann.

**TRANSLATION:**

My mother told me that no farmer would plant seed potatoes on Good Friday, or cabbage on 17 March. It was a kind of superstition, but it's not held any longer.

I often heard of the Days of the Brindled Cow. It's also called 'Skinning the Old Cow'. That's at the beginning of April. The old people say that March gets ten more days and the weather is so cold that April really only gets twenty days. They say the cold skinned the old cow.

I often heard of the Geese Harvest. In this season, the geese eat whatever wheat or stubble is left on the ground after the wheat has been harvested. Out in the countryside a goose is killed on St Martin's Day, on 6 November. Then the goose's blood is put on the door in honour of Saint Martin, because he was killed in a mill and his blood spilled on the ground.

The twelve days of Christmas are between Christmas Day and 6 January. This is called Little Christmas or Women's Christmas, because the Virgin Mary went into the houses long ago and she blessed the women in every house she entered.

*(S31: 81–2. Pádraig Ó Dubhghaill. Fuair mé an t-eolas seo ó Bhean Uí Dhubhghaill, 39, Na Duganna, Gaillimh.)*

### Unlucky Days (NB)

One of the unlucky days of the year is November day [Halloween]. On that night the people will not go outside the doors, because they think they will have bad luck for the year around.

**Claddagh girls.**

Another unlucky day in the year is the first day in May. The farmers will not go ploughing on that day because they think they will do everything wrong, and they might meet with an accident when they are ploughing.

The people in the Claddagh long ago, in the olden times, would never cut their hair on Monday, because they thought they would have misfortune and bad luck.

If you broke a cup, they thought you would break another thing in the house before the end of the week was out.

*(S31: 83. Martin Cox. I got this information from Mrs Cubbard, 57,*
*Lr Fairhill Rd, Galway.)*

### Laethanta Áirithe [Certain Days] (C'b)

Ní ceart gruaig dhuine a bhearradh Dé Luain: 'Lomadh Luain nó fuadach seachtaine.'

Deirtear nach ceart luatha a chaitheamh amach Dé Luain. Deirtear nach ceart airgead a chur amach as an teach Dé Luain.

Níor mhaith le daoine pósadh Dé hAoine nó breith linbh.

Ní ceart uisce salach a chaitheamh amach Dé Luain.

Ní ceart pósadh ar an Mháirt, mar sin é lá na sióg.

Ní ceart obair a dhéanamh an chéad lá den bhliain.

Ní ceart síol a chur Luan Cásca.

Dá gcuirfí síos síolta Aoine an Chéasta bheadh siad ádhúil, nó aon rud eile mar sin.

Ní ceart dusta an tí a chur amach ar an tsráid an chéad lá den bhliain.

**TRANSLATION:**

It isn't right to cut a person's hair on Monday: 'Monday's clipping, a week of plunder.'

They say it's not right to throw out ashes on Monday, or let money go out of the house on that day.

People wouldn't like a wedding or a child to be born on Friday.

Dirty water shouldn't be thrown out on Monday.

It's not right to marry on Tuesday because that's the day of the fairies.

It's not right to work on the first day of the year.

It's not right to plant seeds on Easter Monday.

If seeds were planted on Good Friday, they'd be lucky, or anything else like that.

It's not lucky to sweep the dust of the house out on to the street on the first day of the year.

*(S30: 184–5. Peaits Ó Fáthaigh, 65, Baile an Dubhlaoich, Feilméara. 28 Feabhra 1938.)*

### An Bhrídeog [The Brídeog] (C'b)

Bíonn Lá Fhéile Bríde ann ar an chéad lá de mhí na Feabhra. Tagann cailíní thart le brídeog an oíche sin. Sé an rud brídeog bábóg déanta as tuí. Déanann siad an bhrídeog as tuí agus cuireann siad éadach geal uirthi.

Cuireann siad dhá shúil uirthi agus béal le peann luaidhe. Téann siad thart chuig na tithe agus deireann siad rann ag gach doras. Faigheann siad pingin nó dhá phingin i ngach teach. Nuair a bíos siad réidh, comhaireann siad an t-airgead agus roinneann siad é idir an méid cailíní a bíos ann. Fágann siad i leataobh an bhrídeog go dtí an chéad bhliain eile. Nuair a thagann siad isteach i dteach, deireann na seandaoine 'Go raibh muid beo ins an am seo arís.'

**TRANSLATION:**

St Brigid's Day falls on 1 February. Girls come round with a *brídeog* on that night. The *brídeog* is a doll made from straw. They make the *brídeog* from straw and put a white cloth on it. They put two eyes and a mouth on her with a pencil. They go around the houses and say a rhyme at every door. They get a penny or two at every house. When they are finished, they count the money and divide it among all the girls. They leave the *brídeog* aside until the next year. When they come into a house, the old people say, 'May we be alive this time next year again.'

*(S30: 182. Cáit Nic an Chródha, Baile an Dubhlaoich, Gaillimh.)*

# SUPERSTITIOUS BELIEFS

### Cosaint an Pháiste [Protecting the Child] (CGB)

Bhí Naomh Seosamh agus an Mhaighdean Mhuire ag siúl thart lá amháin. D'fhág siad Íosa Críost istigh i gcliabhán. Nuair a tháinig siad abhaile bhí an tlú ina lámh aige agus bhí barr an tlú ina bhéal aige. Rinne siad an-ionadh de sin.

Mar gheall air sin, má bhíonn páiste ina chodladh san gcliabhán, deirtear gur ceart an tlú a chur trasna ar an gcliabhán má bhíonn muintir an tí ag dul amach, ionas nach n-éireoidh aon cheo don pháiste.

**TRANSLATION:**

St Joseph and the Virgin Mary were out walking one day. They left Jesus Christ in the cradle. When they came home he had the tongs in his hand and the tip of the tongs in his mouth. They were very surprised.

Because of that, if a child is asleep in the cradle, they say the tongs should be placed across the cradle if the people of the house are going out, so that nothing will happen to the child.

*(S32: 145. Nóra Bn. Uí Dhubhagáin, 62, Móinteach, a d'inis.)*

### Pisreoga Iascaireachta [Fishing Superstitions] (NC)

Bhí seanbhean thiar i gConamara fadó agus bhí triúr mac aici agus nuair a théidís amach ag iascach, d'éiríodh an tseanbhean agus thugadh sí sluasaid tine dhearg léi agus chaitheadh sí an bóithrín ina ndiaidh í agus deireadh sí thar a gceann agus thar a gcosa, gach drochrud, sin ag ceapadh nach rachadh na daoine maithe in aice leo.

An bhean chéanna freisin, rinne sí rud eile le han-phisreoga. Chuaigh an triúr mac amach ag iascach lá amháin. Bhí siad imithe dhá lá agus nuair nach bhfaca sí ag teacht iad, thosaigh sí ag ceapadh go raibh rud éicint suas. Fuair sí báisín uisce agus chuir sí trí chupán ins an mbáisín agus thug sí ainm do gach ceann acu. Thug sí Tomás ar cheann acu, Seán ar cheann eile agus Peadar ar an cheann deireanach. Nuair a d'fheiceadh sí ceann de na cupáin ag dul síos, deireadh sí, 'Á, tá Peadar bocht dá bháitheadh.' Le han-phisreoga a dhéanadh sí é seo. Nuair nach bhfeiceadh sí ag dul go han-domhain iad, deireadh sí, 'Níl siad imithe fós, buíochas le Dia.'

**TRANSLATION:**

There was an old woman back in Connemara long ago and she had three sons and when they'd go out fishing, the old woman used to get up and take a shovelful of red coals and throw it down the road after them, and she'd say all kinds of bad things after them, believing that the fairies wouldn't go near them.

This same woman too, she did something else very superstitious. One day the three sons went out fishing. They were gone two days and when she didn't see them returning, she started thinking that something was wrong. She got a basin of water and put three cups into the basin and gave a name to each one. She called the first one Tomás, the second Seán and the last Peadar. When she'd see one of the cups sinking, she'd say, 'Ah, poor Peadar

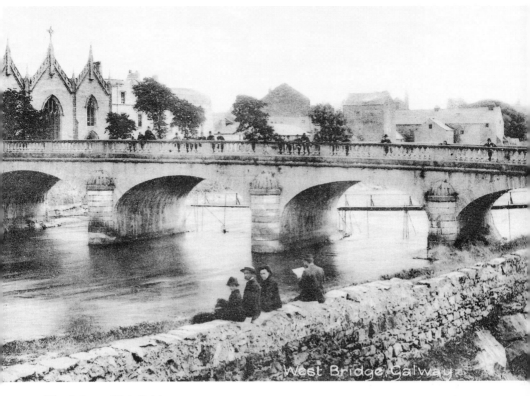

**The Salmon Weir Bridge,** *c.* **1925.**

is drowning.' Through great superstition she'd do that. When she wouldn't see the cups going down deeply, she'd say, 'They're not gone yet, thanks be to God.'

*(S30: 155–6. Cáit Ní Bhradha, Cnoc an Dioláin.)*

## *Pisreoga [Superstitions] (P)*

Nuair a bhíonn fear nó bean ag dul chuig an aonach, caitheann bean an tí seanbhróg ina ndiaidh, ag ceapadh go mbeadh an t-ádh leo ansin agus go ndíolfaidís pé rud a bheadh acu le díol ag an aonach.

Bíonn crú capaill crochta ar dhoras an scioból ag daoine, iad ag ceapadh go mbeadh an t-ádh ar an scioból agus ar gach a bheadh istigh ann. I gcorrtheach, d'fheicfeá crú capaill crochta thuas in aice leis an lampa agus páipéar ar dhath an airgid casta timpeall air. Bíonn an lampa ag scalladh air agus bíonn sé go han-deas.

Ceaptar nuair a fhaightear seamróg a mbíonn ceithre dhuilleog uirthi go mbeadh an t-ádh ar an duine a gheobhadh í.

Nuair a éiríonn bó tinn gearrtar píosa beag dá cluas agus caitear piobar isteach ann. Uaireanta, déantar scoilt i dteanga an bheithígh. Uaireanta, bíonn ribín dearg ar ruball na mbeithígh. Ceapann na daoine má bhíonn ribín dearg ar ruball na bó nach nglacfaidh na síóga seilbh uirthi.

**TRANSLATION:**

When a man or woman goes to the fair, the woman of the house throws an old shoe after them, so they will have luck and sell whatever they have to sell at the fair.

People have a horseshoe hung on the stable door, to bring luck to the stable and everything in it. In some houses you'd see a horseshoe hung up beside the lamp and silver paper round it. The lamp shines on it and it looks lovely.

They believe that anyone who finds a four-leafed clover will have luck.

When a cow gets sick, they cut a piece from her ear and shake pepper into the ear. Sometimes they cut a nick in an animal's tongue. Sometimes they put a red ribbon on the cattle's tails. They believe the red ribbon will prevent the fairies from taking a cow away.

*(S30: 466–8. Lil Ní Nuanáin, 13, Bóthar na hOllscoile, Gaillimh.*
*Tomás Ó Coincheannáin as an Spidéal a thug dom na nósanna seo.)*


## Pisreoga [Superstitons] (M)

Nuair a thagann duine isteach i dteach ba cheart dó dul amach an doras céanna a dtáinig sé isteach. Tugann sé an t-ádh amach leis. Ní ceart splanc tine a ligint amach as an teach Dé hAoine gan an barr a bhaint den splanc. Ní ceart beirt as an teach pósadh an bhliain chéanna. Deirtear nach ceart d'aon duine pósadh i mí na Bealtaine. Ní ceart duine a bhualadh le maide saileoige. Ní ceart uaigh a oscailt ar an Luan. Tá sé de nós ag na daoine fós píosa flainnín beannaithe a chur ar ruball na bó ar fhaitíos go ndéanfaí drochshúil uirthi. Ní ceart filleadh ar ais nuair a bheifeá ag dul ar thuras fada. Ní ceart salann a ligean amach as an teach Dé hAoine.

**TRANSLATION:**

When a person comes into a house, he should leave by the same door he entered or he'll take the luck with him. A lighted ember shouldn't be allowed out of the house on a Friday without removing the top. Two people from one house shouldn't marry in the same year. It is said that no one should marry in May. You should never strike anyone with a sally rod. A grave shouldn't be opened on a Monday. People still have the custom of putting a piece of blessed flannel on the cow's tail, for fear she'd be 'blinked'. You shouldn't turn back if you're going on a long journey. Salt shouldn't be allowed out of the house on a Friday.

*(S30: 108. Nóra Ní Mhaoldomhnaigh a scríobh.)*

## Pisreoga (C'g)

1. If you leave water in which you washed your feet in the house during the night, you will not be able to sleep.
2. If you were going out playing cards and someone stuck a darning needle in the back of your coat, unknown to you, you'll win at the cards.
3. Always put a little drop of water in milk which you are giving away.
4. If a *fiach dubh* [raven] flies over the house someone will die in the house before long.
5. If you went to the mearin wall between your own and a neighbour's field and put your reaping hook in a hole in the wall and repeated, 'Butter on my hook' for about an hour, you would have all your neighbour's butter and he'd have none.
6. Leave twelve potatoes on the hearth every night, lest the good people want them.
7. If a big knife fell on the floor, a tall man will come in.
8. Give no milk away and give out no fire on May Day.
9. A funeral takes the longest way to the chapel.
10. Begin spring sowing on Friday.
11. On New Year's Day, do not move a corpse.
12. After supper, leave five potatoes on a corner of the table for the dead.
13. If you bring in water at night, put a small coal into it or the fairies will bring it [away].

14. Put a grain of salt in your right shoe before going on a journey.
15. Don't leave for a fair until the cock crows.
16. On the day before getting married, each of the persons should get the loan of three things to wear.
17. When going into a new house, never bring the cat.
18. Never count potatoes.
19. Never wave a burning stick in the house.
20. If you jump on a person lying on the ground, he will grow no more.
21. If you let a spoon fall, a stranger will come to the house.
22. Never go out with the sign of the cake [of bread] on your hands. The cake will not be nice.
23. Never sleep out on May Day or the fairies will follow you.
24. Do not spill salt if you are eating dinner in the fields.
25. If the soles of your feet are itchy you will be walking in a strange place.
26. If your left hand is itchy it is a sign you are getting money.
27. If your left hand is itchy it is a sign you are going to shake hands.
28. It is right to put the sign of the cross on a cake.
29. If you hear the banshee someone will die in your house.
30. If you hear the clock striking two for nineteen nights you will die on the twentieth.
31. Whoever the cat first looks at after washing his face will be the first to die.
32. Make the sign of the cross on any place on which you fall.
33. Kick a hen if she cackles [like a rooster] or she will bring bad luck.
34. Do not break any old delph.
35. If, when cutting your nails beside the fire, a piece flies into the fire and is burned you will get a sore toe or finger.
36. Do not stir a heap of old shoes or the fairies will give you a disease.
37. Do not build an extension to a house southwards because it is unlucky.
38. If you fall in a graveyard you will soon die.
39. Milk the first of the cow's milk on to the ground for the fairies.
40. If a robin flies round in the chapel some one in the parish will soon die.
41. A lost frost-nail should be put in the purse. If you lose the purse you will find it again.
42. Do not sleep between two doors.
43. Do not light two candles on the same table.

44. Do not leave shoes on a table.
45. Do not bring out a can with a trace of milk in it.
46. After milking a cow put a little water in the milk.

*(S30: 70–5. Written by Micheál Ó Griallais, Caisleán Gearr, Gaillimh.)*

# THE FAIRIES

## Fairy Forts (NB)

My mother often told me about fairy forts. One day a man was ploughing his land and there was a fort in part of the field, and there was a tree growing on top of the fort. It was in the man's way and he dug it up. During all that night, he didn't rest or sleep. When he got up next morning, he told his people and when they heard the story, they advised him to plant the tree again. So he planted it again and he got rest and a good sleep after that.

*(S31: 90–1. Pádraig Ó Coisdealbha. I got these stories from Mrs Costello, 22 Beattystown, Galway.)*

## Na Sióga Ag Goid Bó [The Fairie Steal a Cow] (B)

Bhí fear ann fadó agus ní raibh aon cheird aige ach a bheith ag baint fraoich agus dá dhíol. An lá seo, chuaigh sé amach idir dhá loch agus ghearr sé leis gur shuigh sé síos ag ligean a scíth. Ní raibh sé i bhfad mar sin go bhfaca sé a bhó féin agus thosaigh sé ag dul abhaile léi. Is gearr go dtáinig sé go dtí páirc ina raibh na sióga ag bualadh báire. Bhí an-spóirt aige (leo) ach is gearr gur buaileadh an liathróid ins an tsúil air agus bhí sé dall. Nuair a fuair sé amharc a shúile ar ais bhí an bhó imithe. Chuaigh sé dá cuardach agus ní raibh aon tuairisc le fáil uirthi.

Ar maidin nuair a dhúisigh sé chuaigh sé amach agus chonaic sé caisleán mór. Nuair a bhí sé ag breathnú ar an gcaisleán, chonaic sé an bhó agus dhá fhear dá faire. Thairg siad dhá phunt is deich scilling (ar an mbó) dó ach ní raibh aon mhaith ann. Thairg siad trí phunt dó agus thóg sé é. Ach nuair a chuaigh sé abhaile ní raibh aige ach póca folamh.

**St Brendan's National School.**

**TRANSLATION:**

Long ago there was a man who had no trade but to cut heather and sell it. One day he went out between two loughs cutting heather. He sat down to take a rest. He wasn't long there until he saw his own cow and he set about taking her home. In a short while he came to a field where the fairies were playing hurling. He had lots of fun with them and it wasn't long until the ball hit him in the eye and he was blind. When he got his eyesight back, his cow was gone. He searched for her but she was nowhere to be found.

Next morning when he woke up he went out and saw a big castle. When he was looking at the castle he saw his cow and two men herding her. They offered him two pounds and ten shillings for the cow but that wasn't enough. They offered him three pounds and he took it. But when he went home all he had was an empty pocket.

*(S31: 186. Written down by the teacher, T. Mac Eochaidh.)*

## Na Daoine Maithe [The Fairies] (NC)

1. Bhí sé ina ghnás fadó dá mbeadh duine ag dul chuig tórramh, (go gcuirfeadh sé) gráinnín salainn ina bhéal, ag ceapadh nach rachadh na daoine maithe in aice leis.

2. Dá dtitfeadh duine amuigh ar an tsráid, sé a dhéanfaí nuair a thiocfadh sé isteach ná gráinnín salainn a chur ina bhéal ar eagla go dtabharfadh na daoine maithe (na sióga) leo é.

3. Nuair a bhíonn siad ag déanamh ime, cuireann siad splanc faoin gcuinneog ar eagla go dtabharfadh na sióga uathu é.

4. Fadó, an oíche roimh Lá Bealtaine, théadh na daoine amach agus d'fhaighidís píosa beag de chrann Bealtaine agus chuiridís ar na ba agus ar na caoirigh é ar eagla go dtabharfadh na daoine maithe leo an bainne ó na ba agus an olann ó na caoirigh.

**TRANSLATION:**

1. Long ago it was the custom for anyone going to a wake to put some salt in his mouth, believing the fairies wouldn't go near him.

2. If a person fell out on the street, when he'd come in they'd put some salt in his mouth, for fear the fairies would take him away.

3. When they make butter, they put a lighted ember under the churn, for fear the fairies would steal the butter.

4. Long ago, on the eve of May Day, people would go out and get a small piece of May tree and place it on the cows and sheep, for fear the fairies would take the milk from the cows and the wool from the sheep.

*(S31: 156–7. Bairbre Nic Dhonnchadha, 22, Tulach Naomh Doimnic, Gaillimh.)*

## Fairy Abduction (O'm B)

One night, there was a man and his wife and family sitting around the fire and a knock came to the door. The man was getting up to open it when someone struck him with a sod of turf on the back. A great number of fairies came in and they started beating the man and his wife and children. They brought the man away with them. After a few days, he came back to his wife and he said to her, 'You can save me tomorrow night. We will have a race and I will be on the third horse and when I will be passing you out,

**Stacking turf, Carrowbrowne 1930s.**

throw a sod of turf at me and I will be saved.' Next night when he was passing her out, she threw a sod of turf at him and he was saved. The reason
the fairies beat him was because he had no water in [the house] and he kept
enough water in the house after that.

*(S32: 359–60. Written down by Pádraic Mac an Ríogh, Uarán Mór,*
*as told by his grandmother.)*

### The Leipreachán (P)

In Ireland, the people used to say that there was such a man as the *leipreachán*
and that this man used to be dressed in a red hat and green shoes. It was
also said that he lived in a fort or in some lonely place and that he had a pot
of gold. Any person who found the *leipreachán*, he would give them the pot
of gold and he would make them so rich that they would not be in need of
money as long as they lived.

It is many a person this *leipreachán* played tricks on. When the *leipreachán* would be talking to the person who would be trying to get the pot of gold from him, he would say to the person, 'Look at the big dog – take care he does not bite you!' This was a trick that the *leipreachán* had, to make the person look back, for if the person looked back but once, the *leipreachán* was gone and then the person would be without the pot of gold. Needless to say, at the present day, you would not hear people say that there are any of them about.

*(S30: 444. Written by Bridie Connolly, 13, New Line, Galway.*
*I got this story from my aunt, who got it from her mother.)*

### Dia Luain, Dia Máirt (O'm B)

There was a man one time and he had a hump on his back. One night he was out late and on his way home he had to pass by a big fort. As he was passing by, he heard a voice singing, '*Dia Luain, Dia Máirt; Dia Luain, Dia Máirt; Dia Luain, Dia Máirt.*' '*Agus Dia Céadaoin!*' says the man with the hump. 'You put length in my song,' says the voice. Out came a little man in a red jacket. 'Follow me,' says the little man, 'and I will make you rich for life.' All of a sudden a door opened in the side of the fort and they went in. The first thing the little man did was to take the hump off the man and hang it up on the wall. He filled his pockets with gold and silver. Then he told the man to close his eyes and when he opened them, he was outside the fort and he went home. Everyone was asking him where did he leave the hump and he told them all about it.

There was another man in the place and he had the same kind of a hump and he said, 'I will go tonight and maybe they will take the hump off me too.' So he went that night and as he was passing the fort, he heard the voice saying, '*Dia Luain, Dia Máirt, Dia Céadaoin!*' '*Diardaoin, Dia hAoine, Dia Sathairn agus Dia Domhnaigh!*' says the man with the hump. 'You spoiled my song,' says the voice and out came the little man in the red jacket and he very vexed.

'Follow me,' says the little man and he brought the man with the hump into the fort and he put the other man's hump on top of his own and he was worse than ever then.

*(S32: 407–8. Written down by Máirtín Ó Mogháin, as told by his mother who heard it from her mother thirty years ago.)*

# THE EVIL EYE

### The Bad Eye (P)

About a hundred years ago the people of Tuam used to think that a person with a bad eye could take away the butter from your cows.

There lived in Marley a woman who had a few cows. When she churned her milk she could not get any butter. There was an old man passing at the time dressed in old clerical clothes. He went into the house and took the churn dash from the woman. She was very distressed and told him that she had been churning for a couple of hours and still had no butter. He began to churn and soon the churn was full of butter. He told her that he had her butter and from that time on the woman had no churning.

*(S30: 450. Written by Bea Mangan, Upper Salthill, Galway, 12 years. I got this story from my grandmother who got it from her father.)*

# DEATH TRADITIONS

### Wakes of this Parish (C'g)

Celia King of Ballygurrane described a wake in Carrabrowne. She said the corpse was laid out on a long low table raised up on six chairs beside one of the kitchen walls. Ropes were tied to the rafters over the corpse and from the ropes sheets were hung on three sides, to form curtains. There was also another sheet on top, which formed a ceiling. The corpse could only be seen on one side. Persons kneeling down could not see it either because it was raised up about five feet above the floor. This wake took place about seven years ago.

Up to about thirty years ago, games were played at wakes in this parish. They were generally played at the wakes of fairly old people. The young men present took part in them. They were played in the kitchen. They began at midnight and were continued until the wake was over in the morning.

Of all the games that were played at wakes in those days, Hurra-harra was the most popular. The young men sat round in a circle facing each other on the kitchen floor. One sat in the middle of the circle. Those in the circle had a *súgán* (straw rope) with a knot on the top. They passed this around quickly under their knees from one to another and each was looking for an opportunity to give a blow of it to the man in the centre. If, however, the man in the centre succeeded in catching the *súgán*, then the person who held the other end of it had to take his place in the centre of the circle.

Two men stood facing each other on the kitchen floor. Each held both the others' hands. Several other pairs of men did the same thing until there was a line of pairs a few feet apart. Then another man jumped over the hands of each pair until he reached the end of the row.

The following is another game which was played at wakes in this locality. To see who had the stronger hand, two men stood facing each other on the kitchen floor. They clasped each other's right hand and each tried to force the other's hand downwards. The left hand was not allowed to be used. They continued at this until they discovered who had the strongest right arm.

My father described these games to me. He himself never saw them played but his father, who often took part in them, often told him of them.

(S30: 3. Micheál Ó Griallais ó Hanraoi Ó Griallais, 45, Caisleán Gearr, Gaillimh.)

## MARRIAGE CUSTOMS

### Marriage (NB)

Long ago the people of Galway used to get married on Mondays, Wednesdays and sometimes Saturdays. If they got married on Tuesday, Thursday or Sunday, they would have no luck. The man always puts the woman in front of him when they are leaving the church.

Long ago, in the time of our great-grandfathers, or our great-grandmothers, the man used never see the woman, until on the morning when they were to get married. The people used never get married in the month of May. The mother of the girl that was to get married used to give some stock to the man, such as cattle and money. If the girl gets married in blue, she is sure to come through, and if she gets married in red, she wishes for dead. The man sometimes gives the priest three pieces of money, to get blessed. When the money is blessed, the priest hands it back again to the girl, for which she is to buy a pot and a piece of iron.

*(S31: 57. Martin Cox. I got this information from Paddy Doyle, New Docks, Galway.)*

## Póstaí [Marriages] (NB)

Dúirt na daoine a bhí ann fadó má bhí duine marbh sa séipéal agus má pósadh daoine ann, ní bheadh aon áthas ar na daoine sin. Dúirt siad freisin an chéad duine de na daoine a pósadh a rachadh amach as an séipéal i dtosach, sin an duine a gheobhadh bás i dtosach.

Fadó, fadó, pósadh daoine ina dteach féin. Bhí mo sheanmháthair i dteach uair amháin nuair a bhí pósadh ar siúl. Nuair a phósann duine, faigheann sé féiríní ó mhuintir na háite, agus má bhíonn a athair saibhir faigheann sé talamh agus beithíoch agus airgead. Sin nós a bhí ag na daoine fadó.

**TRANSLATION:**
Long ago the people said if there was a corpse in the church when people got married, they wouldn't have a happy marriage. They said too that the first married person to go out the door (of the church) would be the first to die.

Long, long ago, people married in their own house. My grandmother was once at a wedding in a house. When a person marries he gets small gifts from the local people, and if he has a rich father he gets land, an animal and money. That's a custom the people had long ago.

*(S31: 59. Uinseann de Búrca. Fuair mé é seo ó mo sheanathair, Uinsenn de Búrca, 79,*
*Plás Naomh Seán, Gaillimh.)*

# CURES

## *Leigheasanna [Cures] (NC)*

Sileadh Síadháin: Nuair a bhíonn do theanga bheag tite anuas ar do theanga eile tugtar sileadh síadháin air agus sé an chaoi chun sin a leigheas ná spúnóg a chur siar i mbéal an duine agus trí ribe áirithe i mullach a chinn (a tharraingt?) agus é seo a dhéanamh trí lá i ndiaidh a chéile.

Craosghalar: Sin sórt spota geal a bhíonn ar theanga duine agus sé an chaoi le é a leigheas ná duine ar bith nach bhfaca a athair ariamh a anáil a chur naoi n-uaire siar (i mbéal an duine atá tinn) gach aon lá go ceann trí lá.

Tine Dhia: Sé an chaoi le é seo a leigheas ná fáinne óir a chuimilt dó. Deirtear gur fearr fáinne pósta mar tá sé beannaithe. Ansin cuirtear comhartha na croise air agus beidh sé leigheasta.

Fiolún: Tá luibh ann ar a dtugtar Dréimire Mhuire agus tá bláth deas gorm air. Baintear é seo Lá Bealtaine roimh éirí na gréine agus duilleog de a bhruith ar bhainne gabhair agus an bainne a thabhairt don duine agus beidh sé leigheasta ansin.

**TRANSLATION:**

Dropped palatine uvula (*sine siain*): When the little tongue (at the back of the soft palate) has fallen down on your other tongue, that's called *sileadh síadháin* and the way to cure it is to place a spoon back into the person's mouth and [pull?] three hairs on top of his head. That has to be done three days in a row.

Thrush: That's a kind of white spot on a person's mouth. The way to cure it is a person who never saw his father breathe nine times into the mouth of the sick person, every day for three days.

Erysipelas: The way to cure this is to rub it with a gold ring. They say a wedding ring is best because it is blessed. Then the sign of the cross is made and it will be healed.

Felon: There's a plant called lady's ladder [the lesser centaury] and there's nice blue flowers on it. It is picked on May Day before sunrise and a leaf of it is boiled in goat's milk and the milk given to the person and he'll be cured.

*(S31: 158. Bairbre Nic Dhonnchadha, 22, Tulach Naomh Dominic, Gaillimh.)*

### *Old Remedies of this Parish (C'g)*

Sore foot: Wash it in the tide when the tide is going out.

A sore on our face: Rub a spit on it before you eat anything in the morning.

Hiccup: Hold in breath as long as you can.

Swollen hand: Rub the juice of boiled *flidheach* [chickweed] on it three times a day.

*Oigherach* [sores from cold or chafing]: Wash in potato water.

Freckles: Wash in buttermilk.

A scrape: Rub in soot three times a day.

Bronchitis: Put some worms in a small bag round your neck and when the worms have died the bronchitis will go.

Toothache: Wash your mouth in salt and water.

Scald: Shake flour on it.

Leg asleep: Lash your leg with nettles.

Cuts: Wash the cut in salt and water.

Nose bleed: Put a stone on the back of your neck.

Bruises: Keep bruised part in cold water and the pain will go.

Rash: Rub sulphur and unsalted butter on the rash.

Pain in stomach: Drink boiled onion in milk.

Weakness: Slap backs of person's hands.

Mumps: Heat cloves of garlic and put them on the mumps.

Pain in back: Rub on mustard and cover with flannel.

Measles: Drink milk left behind by a ferret.

Whittle (Whitlow): *Flidheach* [chickweed] and a dead snail mixed. Apply for two hours.

*Craosghalar* [thrush]: A person who has never seen his father has a cure.

Sore ear: Put a small piece of black wool in it.

Bunions: Wash feet three times a day for three days in bog water.

Stonebruise: Bruise your finger three times against the stone that caused it and it relieves the pain.

Nettle sting: Apply the *capóg shráide* [common dock] to the affected part.

Sore lip: Apply cream to it.

Worms in a child: Boil garlic root in milk for fifteen minutes. Strain it and drink the milk before going to bed every night for three nights.

Varicose veins: Fast from midnight. Next morning, while fasting, wet your finger on soap and rub on veins every day for four weeks.

Bleeding: To prevent a cut from bleeding, place a cobweb on it.

Baldness: Rub in the marrow of a hen's bones.

Skin rash: Rub the gravy of a roast rabbit on it.

Heartburn: Eat a piece of a raw turnip.

Lizard in stomach: Lizards jump into your mouth if you stoop too near water when at the well, or if you lie down in the bog. For a cure, mount a white horse and then eat a lot of salt. Go to a well, then stoop over it from the horse's back. The lizard will jump out of your mouth into the water.

Consumption: Eat watercress.

A cold: (i) Rub warm goose grease on your chest for three successive nights and cover with flannel.

(ii) Heat butter and mix with sugar and drink it every morning and evening.

(iii) Rub hot lard and pepper on your chest.

(iv) Drink hot cabbage broth.

Warts: (i) Wash in granite stone water.

(ii) Melt sugar and soap and apply as a poultice.

(iii) Count the number of warts you have. Get the same number of pebbles and wrap them in a paper and leave it on the road. The warts will grow on the first person who takes up the paper and at the same time they will leave you.

(iv) Rub a *greabhal* [dropwort?] on it and it will fall off.

Sprain: (i) Knock a crack out of the injured part and go to a waterfall or current and put it in the water.

(ii) Rub goose grease on it.

Sty: (i) Wash the sty in cold tea without milk or sugar.

(ii) Make the sign of the cross on it with your mother's marriage ring nine times a day for nine successive days.

Thrush: (i) Let a person who has never seen his father breathe three times into the patient's mouth.

(ii) If a pup died before it saw its mother, that mother would have the cure for thrush. All that is needed is to show the mother to the sick person.

Headache: (i) Drink strong black tea without sugar.

(ii) Keep your head over the steam of strong tea.

Burns: (i) Rub a cobweb on a few times a day.

(ii) Rub the juice of ivy leaves on the burn.

Chincough [Whooping cough]: (i) The seventh son in a house has a cure for it.

(ii) Bore an auger hole in the door. Put a frog in the hole and another in a jug. When the frogs die, the chincough will go.

(iii) A man who owns a white horse has the cure. Ask him and do whatever he says.

(iv) Let young children ride on a white horse.

(v) Boil roots of nettles and eat them at once.

(vi) Eat the leavings of a married couple named John and Julia.

Boils: (i) A poultice of linseed meal.

(ii) A poultice of bread and water.

(iii) A poultice of soap and sugar.

(iv) Drink lime water for a week.

Thorns: (i) Poultice with boiled potatoes.

(ii) A piece of the fox's tongue applied as a poultice will draw out a thorn that has sunk deeply into the flesh.

Pain in back: (i) Go through the window of a house that was enchanted long ago.

(ii) Boil a field mouse in milk and drink the milk.

Pain in knee: (i) Wash it in potato water.

(ii) Rub goose grease on it.

Corns: (i) Walk barefoot in soft places in the bog.

(ii) Go through rocks. Dip corns in first stone in which there is water.

(iii) Wash corns in paraffin.

*(S30: 42–5. Nóra Bhreathnach, Caisleán Gearr. Fuair mé an t-eolas seo ó a lán daoine.)*

### Leigheasanna [Cures] (NB)

Chuala mé pisreog. Nuair a bhíodh pianta ar bhuachaill nó ar chailín ina gcnámha, chuireadh na seandaoine fá dhris (nó faoi bholg asail) iad trí huaire agus d'imigh an galar uathu. Cuireadh iasc beo i mbéal duine agus ní bhíodh pian ina fhiacail uaidh sin amach.

**TRANSLATION:**

I heard this superstition. When a boy or girl had pains in their bones, the old people would pass them under a rooted briar or a donkey's belly three times and the disease would leave them. A live fish would be placed in a person's mouth and he'd have no pain in his tooth after that.

*(S: 31, 71–2. Pádraig Ó Dubhghaill. Fuair mé an t-eolas seo ó Bhean Uí Dhubhghaill, 39, Na Duganna, Gaillimh.)*

### St Augustin's Well (NB)

... The people used to go down to St Augustine's well on the last Sunday in the month of August. They wash their eyes in it. Although the salt water goes over the well, the water (in it) still remains fresh. Another cure was to swallow a live frog to cure malaria fever. The fever was caught in foreign countries.

*(S31: 74. Martin Browne. I got these from Mrs Raftery, Fair Hill, Galway. Her age is above 78 years. 7 February 1938.)*

# 4

# ORAL LITERATURE

Rinne siad bainis mhór ansin agus cruinniú mór dá réir. Bhí mé féin ag an
mbainis. Nuair a bhí an bhainis thart, fuair mé builín a chosain sé pingine agus
péire stocaí bainne ramhair agus bróga páipéir. Níor mhair na bróga páipéir i
bhfad agus níor mhair na stocaí bainne ramhair chomh fada sin féin. Nuair a
bhí siad caite, b'éigean dom na bonnacha a thabhairt don talamh ach bhí mé
ag baint plaic as an mbuilín go raibh mé sa mbaile.

*[They had a big marriage feast then and many guests came. I was at the marriage feast*
*myself. When it was over, I got a sixpenny loaf, a pair of buttermilk stockings and some*
*paper shoes. The paper shoes didn't last long and even the buttermilk stockings didn't*
*last that long either. When they were worn out, I had to go barefoot but I was eating the*
*sixpenny loaf till I got home.]*

Always and everywhere, people use language not just to exchange information, but creatively, to put a shape on their world, to amuse themselves,
to discuss and understand life better. The Schools' Collection gives us an
insight into the corpus of oral literature, stories and legends of every kind,
which was in currency before much of it was displaced by commercial and
electronic media and before the Irish language gave way to English in many
of the survey areas here.

There are stories about every aspect of life in this particular place. Stories
make sense of people's lived experience and process it for the generations
to come. They allow people to dream, to engage in fantasy and escapism,
to ponder certain questions. Each story's texture comes from the particular way it is fashioned, from the moulding of language, the use of idiom,
regional and personal dialect. Storytellers use body language and eye con-
tact and vary their tone for emphasis and atmosphere. Silence and laughter
are part of the experience too, though they do not appear in the recorded
tale on the printed page.

There are folktales here, the oral counterpart of contemporary light, popular literature or the film on DVD. The listeners suspend their disbelief and

**William Street, Galway, c. 1940s.**

enter into the conventions of a magical world, where all kinds of exciting events can take place. Usually, an unpromising hero or heroine makes good by using their guile to outwit the powers that be. Many of these folktales are local variants of international types that have crossed linguistic and cultural borders easily, because of their timeless and placeless quality. The commercial traffic at Galway harbour brought in more than wine and rum. There was a cultural cargo too, which was just as eagerly awaited. The traditional ending from one of the Galway stories (which is placed at the beginning of this chapter) gives an indication of the fictional almost 'other-world' quality of many of the narratives; tales to thrill and delight for a while, before teller and listener must return to a much more mundane reality.

Supernatural and religious stories are the verbal counterpart of the beliefs and customs in the last chapter. They recount people's encounters with the fairies, the *Cailleach Bhéara*, ghosts and other creatures from the spirit world, as well as the community's local understandings of biblical figures.

141

These encounters with the supernatural are often firmly located in the local landscape: a mermaid at Pier Head, the banshee crying in a trench in a bog, a fabulous eel in Lough Corrib or the wonderful water horses in Lough Reagh. In many cases, the religious stories present a moral tale in the form of a homespun parable or an aetiological legend to explain the characteristics of something like the robin's red breast and crooked beak. Many religious stories resemble a folk version of stories in the New Testament.

Humorous stories were, and still are, particularly popular. They present an audience with their own human foibles and the humorous situations that arise as a result. More than any other genre of oral literature, short pithy humorous stories have survived the transition to a modern technological culture. We still need to laugh, it seems.

In the hard times of the 1930s, people used stories to educate themselves, to remember the important events and people, to entertain themselves and sometimes to escape from reality for a while. It was a vital part of their existence.

## TALES OF WONDER AND ENCHANTMENT

### The Glass Door (O'm B)

Once upon a time, there was a little boy and he was an only son. One day his father and mother went to the town nearby. There was a field outside the house and they called it the hill. They put the cow out on the hill and they put the little boy to mind the cow. In the grass he saw a little glass door. He opened it and down he went.

There was a big house below and a king and lots of young people along with him. The king asked the little boy whether he would like to go to Philadelphia and they were there in less than five minutes. The king asked him what would he like to bring home and he said he would like to bring an ounce of tobacco for his father at home in Derryhesk in Ireland. 'It isn't an ounce but a fifty pound roll of tobacco [you will take home],' said the king. 'Go back to that merchant and get a fifty pound roll of tobacco.' Then the king took a gold clew [ball of thread] from his back and gave it to the boy saying, 'If the merchant does not give you the tobacco, drop the end of this clew on the floor and he will see what he will see.'

The boy did as he was directed. He went to the merchant and asked for a fifty pound roll of tobacco. 'That will be £10,' says the merchant. 'I haven't a penny in my pocket, not to mind £10,' says the boy. 'Get out,' said the merchant and the boy dropped the clew on the floor and he was hardly outside the door when the house was in a blaze.

The king told the boy to go back and ask the merchant for the tobacco and he would save his house. The merchant gave him the tobacco and the boy took the clew from the floor and the house was saved.

Then the king asked the boy what he would like to bring home. 'A yard of silk,' said the boy. 'It isn't a yard but fifty yards you will take home,' said the king. Then he told the boy to do the same thing as before. The boy took the clew and went over to the silk merchant and asked for fifty yards of silk. 'That will be £10,' said the merchant. 'And where would I get £10?' said the boy. 'I have not a penny in my pocket.' 'Get out, get out!' said the merchant and the boy dropped the clew on the floor and the house was on fire. Then the king told the little boy to go back and ask the merchant could he give him the silk and he would save his house. [And he did.]

Then the king asked the boy what other place he would like to go and he said he would like to go to Spain to see the king's house. And they were there in less than five minutes. They went in and they saw ten thousand dinners and they ate and they drank enough. And when they were ready, the boy fell asleep. After a while the king (of Spain) came in and his men came in and there was nothing left on the table. They found the boy and his head on the table and the king shook him up and he handcuffed him and ordered him to be hanged.

They put him up on the table and the king asked him had he any request to ask and the boy said he had. He asked him what was it, and the boy said he'd had a little cap when he fell asleep in the hill. And they gave it to him and the boy said when he had the cap on him, 'I wish and I wish I was home in Derryhesk in Ireland,' and off he flew.

*(S32: 397–9. This story was taken down by Máirtín Ó Mogáin, Uarán Mór, from Pat Costello, Gleann na Sgáil. The latter has spent all his life in the district.)*

### Jackeen na Spúnóg [Jackeen of the Spoons] (F)

Bhí buachaill ann aon uair amháin agus Jack na Spúnóg an t-ainm a bhí air. An fáth a raibh an t-ainm air, bhíodh sé ag goid spúnóg ó dhuine uasal a raibh sé ag obair leis. Fuair an duine uasal amach go mbíodh sé ag goid agus dúirt muna ndéanfadh sé dhá rud go gcuirfí chun báis é.

An chéad rud a bhí air a dhéanamh an capall a raibh an fear uasal ag marcaíocht air de ló agus d'oíche a ghoid.

Nuair a d'inis an buachaill é sin dá athair, dúirt seisean, 'Ní bheidh tú in ann é sin a dhéanamh go deo.' 'Ná bíodh faitíos ar bith ort,' a dúirt Jackeen. D'imigh sé ansin agus fuair sé dhá bhuidéal poitín.

Nuair a tháinig sé chomh fada leis an gcró ina raibh an capall, chaith sé é féin ar an talamh agus thosaigh sé ag osnaíl. Lig sé air féin go raibh sé ar meisce. Nuair a chuala na fir a bhí taobh istigh é, tharraing siad isteach é agus chuir siad in aice na tine é. Thosaigh Jackeen ag cur suas an bhuidéil as a phóca sa chaoi is go bhfeicfeadh na fir é. Nuair a chonaic siad an buidéal, thóg siad as a phóca go réidh é.

Bhí siad ag dul ar meisce ansin agus chuir Jackeen suas an buidéal eile. Nuair a fuair siad an buidéal eile, thit an triúr acu ar an talamh, bhí siad chomh hólta sin. Fuair Jackeen an capall agus thug sé chuig an duine uasal é.

An dara rud a bhí air a dhéanamh, an braillín a bhí istigh faoin duine uasal agus a bhean a ghoid. An oíche seo ar chuma ar bith, fuair duine as an mbaile céanna bás. D'imigh Jackeen agus thóg sé an corp as an gcónra agus chuaigh sé suas ar bharr tí an duine uasail seo. Cheangail sé rópa ar an bhfear caillte seo. Bhí an duine uasal ag faire agus nuair a chonaic sé an corp in aice na fuinneoige, thóg sé a ghunna agus chaith sé leis. Dúirt sé lena bhean, 'Tá Jackeen marbh agam agus caithfidh mé imeacht anois agus é a chur.'

D'imigh an duine uasal seo leis an gcorp agus nuair a fuair Jackeen imithe é, chuaigh sé isteach agus dúirt sé le bean an duine uasail, 'Brúigh isteach, tá mé caillte leis an bhfuacht.' Nuair a bhí an bhean ina codladh, tharraing Jackeen amach an braillín agus d'imigh leis. Bhí fearg an domhain ar an duine uasal ansin ach dúirt sé le Jackeen muna n-inseodh sé faoin gcleas a d'imir sé air, go dtabharfadh sé céad go leith punt dó.

Dúirt Jackeen nach labhródh sé faoi agus fuair sé an t-airgead.

**TRANSLATION:**

Once upon a time there was a boy whose name was Jack of the Spoons. He was called that because he used to steal spoons from the gentleman he was working for. His boss found out he was stealing and said he'd put him to death unless he'd complete two tasks.

The first thing he had to do was to steal the horse his master used to ride day and night. When Jack told his father what he had to do, the father said, 'You'll never be able to do that.' 'Never fear,' said Jack. Off he went and got two bottles of poteen.

When he came up to the shed where the horses were, he threw himself down on the ground and started sighing. He pretended to be drunk. When the men inside heard him, they pulled him in and put him beside the fire. Jack pulled up the bottle he had in his pocket so the men would see it. When they saw it, they took it out of his pocket quickly.

Then they were getting drunk and Jack pulled up the other bottle. When they got the second bottle, the three of them got so drunk they fell on the ground. Jack got the horse and brought it to his master.

The second thing he had to do was to steal the sheet the master and his wife were sleeping on. That night a local man died. Jack went and took the body from the coffin. He climbed up on top of his master's house. He tied a rope around the dead man. The gentleman was keeping watch and when he saw the body beside the window, he picked up his gun and shot at it. He said to his wife, 'I've killed Jackeen and now I must go and bury him.'

Off he went with the body and when Jack got him away, in he went and said to the man's wife, 'Push in, I'm frozen with the cold.' When the woman was asleep, Jack pulled out the sheet and headed off. The gentleman was furious, but he told Jack if he didn't tell anyone about the trick he'd played on him, he'd give him £150.

Jack said he wouldn't speak about it and then he got the money.

*(S30: 289–91. Fuair mé an scéal seo ó Dhoiminic Ó Faodhagáin, 44,*
*Freeport, Bearna. 4 Márta 1938.)*

### Truth and Lies (O'm B)

Once a man was walking the road and he had a long journey to go. He was going along and he met a tramp. They were walking along and they were talking about everything. The tramp asked the other man, 'Which is the best, a lie or the truth?' The man said the truth was the best. 'No,' said the tramp. 'I got more out of the lie.' 'No,' said the man, 'the truth is the best.' 'Well,' said the tramp, 'we won't argue any more, but the first person we meet on the road we will ask him and whatever he says will be law and whoever wins will pluck the two eyes out of the other fellow. Will you agree to this?' said the tramp. 'I will,' said the man. 'I will agree.'

They went on till they met a man and they told him their story. 'Well,' said the man, 'I would say the lie is the best. I got more out of the lie than the truth.' 'Good,' said the tramp, 'I won.' 'Come on,' said he to the man, 'till I pick out your eyes.'

They went inside the wall and the tramp left the man stone blind. The man was moving around and he was near a graveyard. He went into a tomb to sleep. At twelve o'clock he heard three cats coming in and they sat around the coffins and began to talk. One cat said to the others that he knew a girl who was blind. 'And now,' said he, 'there is a bottle under that stone and if she rubbed it on her eyes three times she would have her sight as good as ever.'

The man was afraid to draw his breath and at three o'clock they left. The man moved around till he got the bottle. He rubbed it three times on his eyes and he had his sight as good as ever. He put the bottle in his pocket and went out the road. The first man he met was the tramp and he said, 'Is this you?' ''Tis,' said the man. 'I thought I plucked the eyes out of your head!' said the tramp. 'You did,' said the man, 'and I slept in the graveyard. I got a bottle and it cured me. Now,' said the man, 'which is the best, the lie or the truth? I will pull the two eyes out of you.' 'But leave me in the graveyard first that I may get the bottle,' said the tramp. 'All right,' said the man.

The tramp went into the graveyard and the man picked out his eyes. He slept in the same tomb and the cats came in again and one of the cats said, 'There was someone listening to us last night, the bottle is gone. Come on till we search!'

So they got the tramp and tore him to pieces.

*(S32: 355–7, Written down by Seán de Búrca, Gleann na Sgál, Uarán Mór.*
*Told by Pat Costello, Gleann na Sgál.)*

### Triúr Iníon [Three Daughters] (F)

Bhí bean ann fadó agus bhí triúr iníon aici. Lá amháin dúirt an cailín ba shine, 'Rachaidh mise ar lorg oibre amárach.' Dúirt an mháthair léi sular imigh sí, 'Cé acu is fearr leat (píosa den) bhuilín aráin seo agus mo bheannacht, nó an builín ar fad gan mo bheannacht?'

'Ó,' a dúirt an cailín, 'tabhair dom an builín ar fad agus is cuma faoin bheannacht.'

Ansin, d'imigh sí agus bhí sí ag siúl i rith an lae go dtáinig sí chomh fada le teachín beag a bhí ar leataobh an bhóthair.

Bhuail sí an doras agus labhair guth éicint ón taobh istigh. 'Tar isteach,' a dúirt an tseanbhean a bhí ina suí cois na tine. 'Is tú atá ag teastáil uaim. Anois cíor mo ghruaig dom ach ar t'anam ná breathnaigh suas an simléar.'

Thosaigh an cailín ansin ag cíoradh a gruaige agus nuair a fuair sí an deis d'fhéach sí suas agus chonaic sí mála mór óir thuas ann. Dúirt sí léi féin, 'Beidh sin agamsa nuair a gheobhas sí seo bás.'

Tar éis tamaill, dúirt an tseanbhean léi, 'Faigh an seáláil sin agus imigh go dtí an tobar agus líon é le huisce. Agus ná tar anseo muna bhfuil sí líonta agat, nó beidh an cloigeann bainte díot.'

D'imigh an cailín ach níor fhéad sí é a dhéanamh.

Ansin tháinig sí abhaile agus ní dhearna an tseanbhean tada léi ach an cloigeann a sciobadh di.

Ansin dúirt an dara cailín go rachadh sí féin amach ag lorg oibre. Nuair a bhí sí ag imeacht, d'fhiafraigh an mháthair di an rud céanna, agus dúirt sí, 'Cén mhaith do bheannacht? Tabhair dom an builín.' Fuair sí an builín agus d'imigh sí agus tharla an rud céanna di.

Ansin dúirt an tríú cailín, 'Rachaidh mise amach ar lorg oibre freisin.' Nuair a bhí sí ag imeacht, d'fhiafraigh an mháthair an rud céanna di.

'Tabhair dom leath an bhuilín agus do bheannacht,' a deir sí.

D'imigh sí go dtáinig sí chomh fada leis an teachín céanna. Chuaigh sí isteach agus dúirt an tseanbhean léi, 'Cíor mo ghruaig ach ar t'anam ná breathnaigh suas an simléar.'

Nuair a bhí an ghruaig cíortha aici, bhreathnaigh an cailín suas an simléar agus chonaic sí an mála mór. Ansin dúirt an tseanbhean, 'Faigh an seáláil agus imigh go dtí an tobar. Líon le huisce é agus ná tar anseo muna mbeidh sé líonta agat.'

D'imigh an cailín go dtáinig sí chomh fada leis an tobar agus chuala sí éan beag ag rá léi, 'Líon an seáláil le caonach agus cré agus coinneoidh sé an t-uisce ar feadh an lae.'

D'imigh sí abhaile agus bhí an tseanbhean lánsásta.

Tar éis tamaill, thit an tseanbhean ina codladh agus chuir an cailín a lámh suas an simléar agus sciob sí an mála léi. Ní raibh sí ach ag rith amach an doras nuair a dhúisigh an tseanbhean. Rith an cailín isteach sa muileann agus rith an tseanbhean isteach ina diaidh. Nuair a chuir an tseanbhean a cloigeann isteach ins an rotha, chuir an muilleoir an rotha thart agus bhain sé an ceann di. Ansin d'imigh an cailín abhaile go sona sásta.

**TRANSLATION:**

Long ago there was a woman and she had three daughters. One day the eldest daughter said, 'I'll go and look for work tomorrow.' Before she left, her mother asked, 'Which would you prefer a piece of this loaf and my blessing, or the whole loaf and no blessing?'

'Oh,' replied the girl, 'give me the whole loaf and it doesn't matter about the blessing.'

She set off and walked all day until she came to a small little house beside the road.

She knocked on the door and a voice answered from inside. 'Come in,' said an old woman, who was sitting beside the fire. 'You're just the person I need. Now, comb my hair for me, and whatever you do, don't look up the chimney.'

The girl began combing her hair and when she got a chance she looked up and saw a bag of gold. She said to herself, 'I'll have that when this one dies.'

After a while, the old woman said to her, 'Take that shawl and go to the well and fill it with water. And don't come back here unless it's filled or you'll lose your head.'

Off went the girl but she couldn't do the task.

When she came home the old woman just cut off her head.

Then, the second girl said she would go out to look for work. When she was leaving, her mother asked her the same question, and she said, 'What good is your blessing? Give me the loaf.' She got the loaf and set off and the same thing happened to her.

Then the third girl said, 'I'll go out and look for work too.' When she was leaving, her mother asked her the same question.

'Give me half the loaf and your blessing,' she replied.

She went off till she came as far as the same small little house. In she went and the old woman said to her, 'Comb my hair, but for goodness sake don't look up the chimney.'

When she had combed the hair, the girl looked up the chimney and saw the bag of gold. Then the old woman said, 'Take the shawl and go to the well. Fill it up with water and don't come back here if it's not full up.'

Off the girl went to the well where she heard a small bird saying, 'Fill the shawl with moss and clay and it will hold water all day.'

She went back home and the old woman was delighted.

After a while, the old woman fell asleep. The girl put her hand up the chimney and snatched the bag. She was just running out the door when the old woman woke up. The girl ran into a mill and the old woman after her. When the old woman put her head on the wheel, the miller turned it and it took off her head. The girl went off home as happy as could be.

*(S30: 256–9. Bailíodh an scéal seo ó Dhoiminic Ó Faodhagáin, Freeport, Bearna, Gaillimh. 44 bliain, feilméara. Chuala sé an scéal ag Seán Ó Faodhagáin, 22–25 bliain ó shin. 25 Samhain 1937.)*

## Triúr Iníon [Three Daughters] (C'b)

Bhí fear ann fadó agus bhí triúr iníon aige. Bhí fear an-saibhir sa mbaile in aice leofa agus bhí pósadh geallta aige don iníon ba shine. Bhí sochraid sa mbaile ansin agus chuaigh an fear saibhir chuig an tsochraid. Bhí maide ina láimh aige; maide daor a bhí ann. Nuair a chuaigh sé isteach sa reilig, leag sé an maide suas le doras thuamba agus nuair a bhí an corp curtha, níor smaoinigh sé ar a mhaide a thabhairt leis nó go raibh sé sa mbaile. Bhí sé ag éirí deireanach.

Ansin sa tráthnóna, chuaigh sé go dtí an bhean óg a raibh an pósadh geallta aige dithe agus d'fhiafraigh sé di an dtiocfadh sí chuig an reilig i gcoinne a mhaide. Dúirt sí leis nach dtiocfadh. 'Má théann tusa,' a deir sé leis an darna iníon, 'is tú a phósfas mé.' 'Ní rachainn ann,' a deir sí, 'dá mbeinn gan pósadh go deo.' 'An dtiocfása liom ann?' a deir sé leis an tríú iníon. 'Agus is tú a phósfas mé má théann tú ann.' 'Rachaidh mise ann duit,' a deir sí. D'imigh sí ansin agus chuaigh sí go dtí an reilig agus bhí sé deireanach san oíche nuair a bhí sí ann. Chuaigh sí go dtí an tuamba san áit a raibh an maide leagtha. Nuair a bhí sí ag dul ag breith ar an maide, dúirt fear a bhí curtha san tuamba an maide a fhágáil ansin.

'Oscail an doras atá ar an tuamba seo agus lig amach mé,' a deir sé. 'Cén chaoi a bhféadfadh mé an doras a oscailt agus glas air?' a deir sí leis. 'Cuir isteach do mhéar bheag i bpoll an ghlais agus osclóidh sé dhuit,' a deir sé. Chuir agus d'oscail sé. 'Bain an clab den chónra agus tóg aniar anois mé,' a deir sé, 'mar tá mé lag. Tá mé anseo le céad bliain gan aon ghreim a ithe.' Rug sí air agus thóg sí aniar é. 'Gabh faoi m'ascaill anois,' a deir sé, 'agus tabhair leat mé chuig teach go bhfaighe mé ruainne le n-ithe.'

Thug sí léi ansin é nó gur casadh teach leofa. 'Rachaimid isteach anseo anois,' a deir sí. 'Tá an t-uisce coiscrithe sa teach sin,' a deir sé. 'Ní fhéadfadh muid a dhul isteach ann.' Shiúladar leofa gur casadh teach eile leofa. 'Rachaimid isteach anseo,' a deir sé, 'mar níl uisce glan nó uisce salach ann.' Chuaigh siad isteach ansin agus d'oscail an doras dóibh. 'Féach an bhfuil gráinne mine a dhéanfadh cáca', a deir sé léi. Chuartaigh sí thart agus fuair sí an mhin. 'Tá an mhin agam anois,' a deir sí leis, 'ach níl uisce nó bainne agam a dhéanfadh é.' 'Féach an bhfaighfeá scian mhaith dhomsa,' a deir sé léi. Fuair sí an scian dó.

Fuair sé bowl (babhla) agus chuaigh sé siar sa seomra chuig leaba a raibh an dá bhuachaill óg ina gcodladh inti. Ní raibh ag fear an tí ach iad. Ghearr sé píobáin an dá bhuachaill óg; líon sé an bowl lena gcuid fola agus níor lig sé deoir de i bhfásta. 'Déan an cáca leis an bhfuil agus cuir chuile dheoir de ann,' a deir sé. Rinne sí an cáca leis an bhfuil agus bhruith sí é. Níor airigh aon duine iad. Thug sé píosa den cháca dithe féin agus dúirt sé léi é a ithe. Dúirt sí leis go gcaithfeadh sí a dhul amach ar an tsráid. Chuaigh sí amach agus sháigh sí an píosa cáca suas i mbunsop an tí. Tháinig sí isteach agus bhí an cáca ite aige roimpi. D'fhiafraigh sé di ar ith sí an píosa a thug sé di. Dúirt sí gur ith. 'Tabhair leat anois mé,' a deir sé, 'agus fág san áit chéanna aríst mé.' Rug sí ar a ascaill ansin agus thug sí léi amach é.

Níor airigh aon duine sa teach iad ag teacht nó ag imeacht. Nuair a bhí scaithimh den bhóthar siúlta acu, dúirt sé léi fanacht ina seasamh. 'An bhfeiceann tú an talamh sin istigh?' a deir sé léi, 'Sin an talamh a bhí ag mo mhuintir sa seansaol agus chuir an chuid eile den dream sin a raibh muid istigh anois acu amach mo mhuintirse agus chuir siad draíocht ormsa agus ní aithneoidh aon duine mé ach bhí cuimhne agam féin go raibh mé beo. D'iarr mé impí gan mé bás a fháil go mbainfinn sásamh díobhtha, mar sin iad an dream a chuir isteach ins an gcónra mé agus a chuir mé ins an tuamba. Ní raibh i ndán dom aon bhás a fháil go dtiocfadh duine go dtí mé a mbeadh misneach aige agus a dhéanfadh liom mar a rinne tusa. An bhfeiceann tú na trí leacht cloiche atá i ndiaidh,' a deir sé,' a chéile taobh istigh den chlaí? Tá trí phota óir fúthu sin; gheobhaidh tú iad lá ar bith is maith leat a theacht dá gcoinne.' D'imigh siad leofa ansin go dtí an tuamba.

'Cuir isteach ins an tuamba mé agus cuir an clab air, agus dún an tuamba orm.' Rinne sí é. 'Téirigh abhaile anois,' a deir sé. 'Agus tá mise ag dul a fháil bháis,' a deir sé. D'imigh sí ansin agus thug léi an maide agus chuaigh sí abhaile. Chuaigh sí a chodladh agus í trom tuirseach tar éis na hoíche. Nuair a d'éirigh sí i gceann scaithimh, chuala sí caoineadh mór ar fud an bhaile. D'fhiafraigh sí cén fáth an caoineadh. Dúradh léi go raibh beirt mhac lena leithéid seo d'fhear marbh de bharr na hoíche agus gan fios cé a rinne é.

Chuaigh sí chuig an teach agus fuair sí an t-athair agus an mháthair ag caoineadh agus ag béiceadh agus an teach lán le daoine. Dúirt sí leis an athair na daoine a chur amach agus go ndéanfadh sí féin maith dóibh dá bhféadfadh sí. Dúirt sí leofa a dhul amach go ceann tamaill. Chuaigh siad amach. Chuaigh sí féin amach agus thug sí léi an píosa cáca a bhí sáite aice sa bhunsop agus thug sí isteach é. Chuir sí síos i mbáisín uisce te é agus d'fháisc sí an fhuil as amach. Thug sí braon de le hól do na buachaillí a bhí marbh. D'éirigh siad suas chomh maith agus a bhí siad ariamh. Bhí ionadh mór faoi chéard a bhí déanta. Scaip na daoine agus chuaigh siad abhaile.

'Céard a d'fhéadfadh mé a dhéanamh leat ar son an mhaith atá déanta agat dúinn?' a d'fhiafraigh an t-athair. 'Fear acu a thabhairt dom le pósadh,' a deir sí. 'Tabharfaidh mé duit duine ar bith acu,' a deir sé. 'Tógfaidh mé an fear is sine,' a deir sí. 'Sé is córa dom.'

Pósadh iad ansin. Nuair a bhí an pósadh thart, chuir sí fios ar a dearth-áir féin. Ansin, shiúil sí féin agus a deartháir agus an fear pósta amach. Chuaigh siad go dtí an áit a raibh na trí phota óir. Thóg siad iad. Choinnigh sí dhá cheann dóibh féin agus ceann don deartháir. Bhí a sáith ansin acu an fhaid is a mhair siad.

Rinne siad bainis mhór ansin agus cruinniú mór dá réir. Bhí mé féin ag an mbainis. Nuair a bhí an bhainis thart, fuair mé builín a chosain sé pingine agus péire stocaí bainne ramhair agus bróga páipéir. Níor mhair na bróga páipéir i bhfad agus níor mhair na stocaí bainne ramhair chomh fada sin féin. Nuair a bhí siad caite, b'éigean dom na bonnacha a thabhairt don talamh ach bhí mé ag baint plaic as an mbuilín go raibh mé sa bhaile.

**TRANSLATION:**

Long ago there was a man who had three daughters. A very rich man lived beside them and he had promised to marry the eldest daughter. There was a funeral and the rich man went to the funeral. He had a walking stick in his hand, a costly walking stick. When he went into the graveyard, he leant the stick up against the door of a tomb. When the body was buried, he forgot about the stick until he was back home. It was getting late.

Then in the evening he went to the young woman whom he had promised to marry and asked her if she'd go to the graveyard for the stick. She said she wouldn't. 'If you go,' he said to the second daughter, 'I'll marry you.' 'I wouldn't go,' she replied, 'if I were never to marry anyone.' 'Would you come with me?' he asked the third daughter. 'And if you do, it's you I'll marry.' 'I'll go for you,' she replied. Off she went and it was late at night when she reached the graveyard. She went to the tomb where the stick was. When she was about to take hold of it, a man who was buried in the tomb told her to leave the stick alone.

'Open the door of this tomb and let me out,' he said. 'How can I open the door and it locked?' she asked. 'Put your little finger in the keyhole and it'll open for you,' he said. She did that and it opened. 'Take the lid off the coffin and lift me up,' he said, 'for I am weak. I'm in here for a hundred years without a bite to eat.' She took hold of him and lifted him up. 'Support me now,' he said, 'and take me to a house till I get a bite to eat.'

She took him with her till they came to a house. 'I'll go in here now,' she said. 'There's holy water in that house,' he said. 'We can't go in there.' They walked on until they came to another house. 'We'll go in here,' he said, 'for there's neither clean nor dirty water in it.' In they went and the door opened for them. 'See if you can find a bit of meal to make a cake,' he said to her. She searched around and found the meal.

'I have the meal now,' she said, 'but I have no water or milk to make it.' 'See if you can find me a good knife,' he said. She got him the knife. He got a bowl and went into a room where there was a bed with two boys sleeping in it. They were the only sons of the house. He cut the two young boys' throats, filled the bowl with their blood and didn't let one drop of it go to waste. 'Make the cake with the blood and put every single drop in,' he said. She made the cake with the blood and cooked it. No one heard them.

He gave her a piece of the cake and told her to eat it. She said she needed to go out on the street. Out she went and shoved the cake up under the eaves of the house. When she came in, he had eaten the cake. He asked her if she had eaten the piece he gave her. She said she had. 'Take me now,' he said, 'and leave me in the same place again.' She took his arm then and brought him out. No one in the house heard them coming or going.

When they had walked a little way along the road, he told her to stand still. 'Do you see that ground in there?' he asked her. 'That's the land my people had in olden times and they were put out of it by the same people whose house we've just been in. They put a spell on me so no one would recognise me, but I still remembered I was alive. I pleaded not to die till I had revenged myself on them, for that's the crowd who put me in the coffin in the tomb. I wasn't destined to die till someone courageous like you would come and do what you did for me. Do you see the three gravestones standing beside each other inside the ditch? There's three pots of gold under them; you'll get them any day you wish to come here for them.'

They continued on to the tomb. 'Put me into the tomb now,' he said, 'and put the lid on it and close it up.' She did as he asked. 'Go home,' he said. 'I'm going to die now.'

She took up the stick and made for home. She went to sleep, exhausted after the night. When she got up later, she heard a terrible keening throughout the whole place. She asked what was going on. She was told that the two sons of a certain man had been killed the night before and no one knew who had done it.

She went to the house and found the father and mother weeping and wailing and the house full of people. She asked the father to send the people away, that she'd help them if she could. She asked the parents to go outside for a while. Out they went. She went outside and got the piece of cake she had pushed in under the eaves and brought it in. She placed it in a basin of hot water and squeezed the blood out of it. She gave a drop of the blood to the dead boys to drink. They got up, as well as they had ever been. Everyone was astonished at this. The people scattered and went home.

'How can I repay you for the help you have given us?' asked the father. 'Give me one of these boys to marry,' she replied. 'I'll give you either one of them,' said the father. 'I'll take the eldest,' said she, 'he's the best for me.'

They had a big marriage feast then and many guests came. I was at the marriage feast myself. When it was over, I got a sixpenny loaf, a pair of buttermilk stockings and some paper shoes. The paper shoes didn't last long and even the buttermilk stockings didn't last that long. When they were worn out, I had to go barefoot but I was eating the sixpenny loaf till I got home.

*(S30: 232–6. Seán Ó Beaglach, Coill Uachtair, Gort an Chalaidh, Gaillimh. Feilméara, 80 bliain. 25 Iúil 1938.)*

### An Buachaill Glic [The Cute Boy] (F)

Bhí bean ann aon uair amháin agus bhí triúr mac aici. Lá amháin dúirt an mac ba shine go rachadh sé ag iarraidh a fhortúin. Dúirt an mháthair leis fanacht go maidin. Nuair a tháinig an mhaidin rinne sí dhá cháca. Dúirt sí leis an mhac cé acu a thógfadh sé, an cáca beag agus a beannacht nó an cáca mór agus a mallacht. (Ghlac sé an cáca mór.) D'imigh sé agus sheas an mháthair amach san doras ag cur a mallacht ina dhiaidh go raibh sé imithe as amharc. Bhí sé ag imeacht go dtáinig sé chomh fada le teach feilméara.

Thosaíodar ag caint ansin agus d'iarr an feilméara den mhac an mbeadh sé sásta dá bhfaigheadh aon cheann acu locht ar an gceann eile go mbainfí an dá chluas de. An chéad lá eile, dúirt an fear leis an mbuachaill aimsire a mháthair a thógáil amach ag siúl agus ní bhfuair sé bricfeasta ar bith. Nuair a tháinig an buachaill ar ais, d'iarr sé a bhricfeasta. Sé an rud a dúirt an fear leis, 'Tá mo bhricfeasta féin ite agam, is cuma liom fútsa.'

Tharla an rud céanna an chéad lá eile ach an tríú lá, nuair a tháinig an buachaill ar ais, d'iarr sé a bhricfeasta agus dúirt an fear, 'Tá sé ite agam féin agus is cuma liom fútsa. An ndóigh ní fhaigheann tú locht air sin?' 'Muise, faighim agus is fada mé ag fáil locht ort,' a deir an buachaill. 'Déanfaidh sin,' a deir an fear. 'Tiompaigh thart anseo go mbainfidh mé an dá chluas díot.' Bhain sé an dá chluas de agus chuaigh sé abhaile maol.

Tharla an rud céanna don dara mac.

Ach an tríú mac, nuair a bhí seisean ag imeacht d'fhiafraigh a mháthair de cé acu a thógadh sé, an cáca beag agus a beannacht nó an cáca mór agus a mallacht. Dúirt sé go dtógfadh sé an cáca beag agus a beannacht. D'imigh sé ansin agus sheas an mháthair amach san doras ag cur a beannachta ina dhiaidh. Bhí sé ag imeacht ansin go dtáinig sé chomh fada le feilméara a bhí amuigh san bpáirc. D'iarr an buachaill obair air. Dúirt sé go dtabharfadh sé obair dó ach an mbeadh sé sásta leis seo, dá bhfaigheadh ceann acu locht ar an gceann eile go mbainfí an dá chluas de agus nach bhféadfadh sé dul abhaile go nglaofadh an chuach, agus ní ghlaodh an chuach ansin ar chor ar bith.

An chéad lá eile, ba é an obair a bhí le déanamh aige an tseanbhean a thógáil amach ag siúl. Nuair a chuaigh siad amach, d'iarr an tseanbhean air cén t-ainm a bhí air. An freagra a thug an buachaill di, 'Dhóigh mé féin! Dhóigh mé féin!' Nuair a tháinigeadar chomh fada le tom neantóga, chaith sé an tseanbhean isteach ann. Tháinig siad abhaile agus í ag screadaíl 'Dhóigh mé féin! Dhóigh mé féin!' 'Cén neart atá agamsa ort,' a deir an fear, 'nuair a dhóigh tú tú féin?' Dúirt an tseanbhean ansin go gcaithfí an buachaill sin a dhíbirt as an áit.

Ins an tráthnóna, chuaigh an fear síos go dtí an SeanDall Glic le plean a fháil leis an mbuachaill a chur as an teach. Dúirt an SeanDall Glic an méid seanbhróga a bhí thart a bhailiú agus a rá leis an mbuachaill muna mbeadh na bróga gréasaithe aige ar maidin go gcaithfeadh sé imeacht. I lár na hoíche, chuaigh an buachaill amach agus mharaigh sé an tarbh a bhí amuigh ins an gcró agus bhain sé an gréas as. Chuir sé ar na bróga é. Chuaigh sé a chodladh ansin agus bhí sé ina shuí roimh an fhear eile. D'iarr an fear cá bhfuair sé an gréas. 'Mharaigh mé an tarbh a bhí amuigh ins an gcró,' a deir sé. 'Ar ndóigh, ní fhaigheann tú locht air?' 'Ní fhaighim,' a deir an fear eile.

An chéad lá eile, chuaigh an fear síos go dtí an SeanDall Glic agus dúirt sé gur mharaigh an buachaill an tarbh air. Dúirt an SeanDall Glic a rá leis an mbuachaill dhá shúil déag agus súil chorr a chur ar phláta ar an mbord agus iad a bheith réidh aige ar maidin.

I lár na hoíche, chuaigh an buachaill amach agus mharaigh sé an capall rása a bhí amuigh ins an gcró agus bhain sé na súile as. Ansin mharaigh sé sé chaora agus bhain sé na súile astu. Ansin, d'fhág sé ar an mbord iad. Nuair a d'éirigh an fear ar maidin, d'iarr sé cá bhfuair an buachaill na súile. Dúirt seisean gur mharaigh sé na caoirigh agus an capall rása. 'Ar ndóigh, ní locht a fhaigheann tú air sin,' a deir sé. 'Ní fhaighim,' a deir an fear eile.

An tráthnóna céanna, chuaigh an fear síos go dtí an SeanDall Glic agus dúirt sé leis gur mharaigh an buachaill na caoirigh agus an capall rása. Dúirt sé leis go gcaithfidís plean eile a fháil.

Dúirt an SeanDall Glic ansin an tseanbhean a chur amach sa sceach amuigh sa gcoill agus nuair a rachadh an fear thairsti, déarfadh sí 'Cuckoo! Cuckoo!' Ar maidin, d'fhiafraigh an fear den bhuachaill aimsire ar mhaith leis dul amach ag siúl. Dúirt an buachaill go mba mhaith leis. Bhíodar ag imeacht agus ag imeacht go dtáinig siad chomh fada leis an áit a raibh an tseanbhean. Nuair a chuadar thart léi, dúirt an tseanbhean, 'Cuckoo!' Nuair a chualadar an tseanbhean á rá, dúirt an fear leis an mbuachaill, 'Tá an t-am agat dul abhaile.' 'Fan ort,' a deir an buachaill agus fuair sé spalla agus rois leis go dtí an crann. Leis sin, dúirt an tseanbhean arís, 'Cuckoo!' Chaith an buachaill an spalla agus thit an tseanbhean anuas as an gcrann.

'Anois, cén sórt cuaiche atá ann?' a deir an buachaill.

Ins an tráthnóna, chuaigh an fear síos go dtí an SeanDall Glic agus dúirt sé gur mharaigh an buachaill an tseanbhean agus nach ndéanfadh an plean sin. Bhí fathach mór ina chónaí ar oileán ins an am agus ba chóir an buachaill a chur amach chuige (a dúirt an SeanDall Glic). An chéad mhaidin eile thug an fear litir agus trí mhuca don mbuachaill. Ní raibh a fhios ag an mbuachaill céard a bhí istigh san litir ach séard a bhí inti (teach-taireacht) gan an buachaill a ligean slán as an oileán. Bhí an buachaill ag imeacht go dtáinig sé chomh fada le háit bhog. Ansin tharraing sé na cluasa agus na rubaill de na muca.

Bhí sé gar dá bhaile féin agus thug sé na muca abhaile chuig a mháthair. Ansin tháinig sé go dtí an áit a raibh na cluasa agus na rubaill agus sháigh sé síos san talamh iad.

Ansin chuaigh sé ar ais go dtí an fear agus dúirt sé go raibh na muca báite air. Chuaigh an fear in éineacht leis agus dúirt an buachaill leis greim a fháil ar an ruball agus rug sé féin greim ar na cluasa. Ansin dúirt an bua-chaill leis, 'Tarraing!' Tharraing an fear agus tháinig an ruball leis agus thit sé siar isteach san bpuiteach. 'Tá sé sin slogtha,' a deir an buachaill. Rinne sé an rud céanna leis an bpéire eile.

Nuair a bhí sé sin déanta, d'iarr sé den bhfear an bhfuair sé locht air. 'Maise faighim, agus is fada mé ag fáil locht ort!' a deir an fear. 'Déanfaidh sin,' a deir an buachaill. 'Tiompaigh thart anseo go mbainfidh mé an dá chluas díot.'

Ansin, chuaigh an buachaill go dtí an áit a raibh an fathach. Nuair a tháinig sé chomh fada leis an tigh, chuaigh sé suas ar bharr crainn mhóir. Tháinig an fathach amach agus dúirt sé, 'Faighim boladh an Éireannaigh bhradaigh!' Leis sin, rug sé ar chloch agus rinne sé gaineamh di.

Chaith an fathach suas cloch chuig an mbuachaill. Tar éis tamaill, tháinig an buachaill anuas agus thug an fathach isteach chuig an tae é. Bhí bó le hithe ag gach duine acu agus dúirt an fathach go gcaithfeadh sé oiread a ithe leis féin. Chuaigh an buachaill amach agus fuair sé craiceann caorach. Chuir sé thart air féin é. Ansin, tháinig sé isteach agus thosaigh sé ag ithe. Ach chuile sheans a gheobhadh sé, chaitheadh sé píosa mór den bhó síos idir é féin agus an craiceann caorach.

Nuair a bhí sin ite acu, d'iarr an fathach air a theacht amach ag rith. Thosaíodar ag rith agus bhí an fathach ag dul amach thar an mbuachaill. Tar éis tamaill, dúirt an buachaill, 'Tabhair dom scian go ligfidh mé cuid de seo amach.' Thug an fathach an scian dó agus ghearr sé suas an craiceann caorach agus tháinig an fheoil amach. Rith sé ansin agus bhí sé ag dul amach thar an bhfathach. Dúirt an fathach, 'Tabhair dom do scian go ligfidh mé cuid de seo amach.' Thug an buachaill an scian dó agus ghearr sé suas a bholg agus thit sé marbh ar an dtalamh.

Rith an buachaill go dtí an bhean (tí) agus dúirt sé léi go raibh an fathach marbh. Rith an bhean amach agus nuair a fuair an buachaill an bhean imithe, chuaigh sé siar sa seomra agus fuair sé mála óir thiar ann.

Amach leis agus an mála óir ar a dhroim aige. Ansin chuaigh sé abhaile chuig a mháthair.

**TRANSLATION:**

Once upon a time there was a woman who had three sons. One day the eldest son said he would go off and seek his fortune. His mother asked him to wait till morning. When morning came she made two cakes of bread. She asked her son which would he choose, the small cake and her blessing or the large cake and her curse. [He took the big cake.] Off he went and the mother stood in the doorway sending curses after him till he was out of sight. He kept going till he reached a farmer's house.

He and the farmer began talking and the farmer asked him to agree that if either of them ever found fault with the other, he'd forfeit his two ears. Next day, he told the servant boy to take his mother out for a walk. He hadn't got any breakfast. When he came back, the boy asked for his breakfast. The man said, 'I've eaten my own breakfast and I don't care about you.'

The same thing happened next day. But on the third morning, when the boy came back, he asked for his breakfast and the man said, 'I got my own and I don't care about you. Of course, you're not finding any fault with that?' 'Well indeed and I am and 'tis a long time now I'm finding fault with you,' answered the boy. 'That'll do,' said the man. 'Turn around now till I cut off your ears.' He cut off his two ears and the boy went home without them.

The same thing happened to the second son.

But when the third son was setting off, his mother asked him which would he choose, the small cake and her blessing or the large cake and her curse. He said he'd take the small cake. Off he went and his mother stood in the doorway blessing him. He walked on till he came to a farmer who was out in the field. The boy asked him for work. The farmer said he'd give him work if he would accept this: if either of them found fault with the other they'd have their ears cut off, and he couldn't go home until the cuckoo would call, and no cuckoo ever called in that place.

Next day, the boy's work was to take the old woman out for a walk. When they went out the old woman asked him what was his name. He gave her this answer, 'I burned myself! I burned myself!'

When they reached a bunch of nettles, he threw the old woman into it. They came home and she screaming, 'I burned myself! I burned myself!' 'What can I do about it if you burned yourself?' said the man. The old woman said then they'd have to get rid of the boy.

That evening, the man went down to the SeanDall Glic [the Clever Old Blind Man] to find a plan to get rid of the boy. SeanDall Glic told him to collect up all the old shoes that were around and tell the boy if he didn't have them all greased by morning, he'd have to leave. In the middle of the night, the boy went out and killed the bull that was in the shed and took the grease from it. He greased the shoes. He went to sleep then and was up and awake before the other man. The man asked him where did he get the grease. 'I killed the bull that was out in the shed,' he said. 'Of course you don't find fault with that?' 'No, no,' said the man.

Next day, the man went down to SeanDall Glic and said that the boy had killed his bull. SeanDall Glic said to tell the boy to put six pairs of eyes the same, and one odd pair, on a plate on the table and to have them ready by morning.

In the middle of the night, the boy went out and killed the racehorse which was out in the shed, and took out its eyes. Then he killed six sheep and took out their eyes. He left the eyes on the table. When the man got up next day, he asked where did the boy get the eyes. He said he killed the sheep and the racehorse. 'Of course you don't find any fault with me for that?' he said. 'No! No!' said the man.

That same evening, the man went down to SeanDall Glic and told him the boy had killed the sheep and the racehorse. He said they'd have to find another plan.

SeanDall Glic said then to put the old woman out in a bush out in the wood and when the boy would pass, she'd say, 'Cuckoo! Cuckoo!' Next morning the man asked the servant boy if he'd like to go for a walk. He said he would. They were walking and walking till they came to the place where the old woman was. When they passed her, the old woman said, 'Cuckoo! Cuckoo!' When they heard it, the man told the boy, 'It's time for you to go home.' 'Wait a minute,' said the boy. He picked up a pebble and threw it at the tree. With that, the old woman called again, 'Cuckoo! Cuckoo!' The boy threw another pebble and she fell out of the tree.

'Now, what kind of a cuckoo is that?' said the boy.

That evening, the man went down to SeanDall Glic and told him the boy had killed the old woman and that plan wouldn't work either. At that time, there was a giant living on an island in that place and the boy should be sent out to him [said SeanDall Glic]. Next morning, the man gave the boy a letter and three pigs. The boy didn't know what was in the letter but it was a message not to let him get away from the island. The boy kept going until he reached a soft place. Then he pulled the ears and tails off the pigs.

He was near his own home and he took the pigs home to his mother. He went back to the ears and tails and shoved them into the ground.

He went back to the man and told him that his pigs were drowned. The man returned to the place with him and the boy told him to take hold of a tail. He took hold of the ears himself. Then the boy said, 'Pull!' When the man pulled, the tail came away with him and he fell back into the mud. 'It's swallowed up,' said the boy. He did the same with the other two sets of ears.

Then he asked the man did he find any fault with him. 'Indeed and I do, and I have done this very long time!' answered the man. 'That'll do,' said the boy. 'Turn around here till I cut off your two ears.'

Then the boy went to where the giant was. When he came to the house, he went up to the top of a big tree. The giant came out and said, 'I smell the blood of a thieving Irishman!' He grabbed a stone and ground it into sand.

The giant threw a stone up at the boy. After a while, the boy came down and the giant took him in for tea. Each of them had to eat a full cow and the giant said the boy had to eat as much as himself. The boy went out and got a sheepskin and put it around his body. He came back in and started to eat. Every chance he got, he'd throw bits of food down between himself and the sheepskin.

When they had eaten everything, the giant asked him to come out for a run. They started running and the giant was passing out the boy. After a while the boy said, 'Give me a knife till I get rid of some of this.' The giant gave him a knife and he cut the sheepskin and the food came out. He ran then and was able to pass out the giant. 'Give me the knife till I get rid of some of this,' said the giant. The boy gave him the knife and he cut up his stomach and fell dead on the ground. The boy ran to the housekeeper and told her the giant was dead. She ran out and when the boy got her out, he went to the room and found a bag of gold there.

Off he went with the bag of gold on his back, home to his mother.

*(S30: 295–300. Fuarthas an scéal seo ó Mháire Ní Íarnáin, 45, Foramoile. Feilméara. 26 Aibreán 1938.)*

## Teileascóp, Fáinne, Gunna agus Snáthaid [Telescope, Ring, Gun and Needle] (P)

Bhí fear ann fadó agus bhí ceathrar mac aige. Bhí na mic tuirseach sa mbaile agus chuaigh an ceathrar acu amach ar thóir oibre. Nuair a tháinig siad chuig an chrosbhóthar chuaigh an ceathrar acu slí amháin. Casadh fear ar an mac is sine agus d'iarr sé air cá raibh sé ag dul. Dúirt sé go raibh sé ag tóraíocht oibre agus dúirt an fear go raibh sé ar thóir buachaill aimsire. Dúirt an fear nach raibh aon rud sa domhan aige ach teileascóp agus go bhfeicfeá gach rud sa domhan tríd. Casadh an fear ar an dara mac. D'fhiafraigh sé de an raibh a fhios aige cá bhfaigheadh sé buachaill aimsire agus go dtabharfadh sé fáinne dó a ghoidfeadh gach rud sa domhan. Casadh an fear ar an tríú mac agus dúirt sé an rud céanna leis. Dúirt sé go dtabharfadh sé gunna dó a mharódh gach rud a shocródh sé air. Casadh an fear ar an mac is óige. Dúirt sé an rud céanna leis. Dúirt sé go dtabharfadh sé snáthaid dó a d'fhuafadh rud ar bith. Rud ar bith.

Lá agus bliain, tháinig na deartháireacha le chéile ar ais ag an gcrosbhóthar. Dúirt an mac is sine leis an darna mac, 'Táimid ar ais arís chomh bocht leis an lá ar fhágamar an baile. Is beag fáilte ag ár n-athair romhainn.' 'Ta mé mar thú,' ar an darna mac. 'Tá mise chomh dona leat,' ar an tríú mac. Dúirt an mac is óige an rud céanna.

Chonaic an t-athair iad ag teacht agus chuir sé fáilte rompu. Chuir sé síos tae agus chuir sé arán ar an mbord agus thug sé beatha dóibh. D'fhiafraigh an t-athair den mac is sine cén chaoi ar dhein sé. 'Fuair mé teileascóp agus nuair a bhreathnaíonn tú tríd, feiceann tú gach rud sa domhan.' 'Maith go leor,' arsa an t-athair. Dúirt sé an rud céanna leis an darna mac. 'Fuair mise fáinne a ghoidfeas gach rud sa domhan.' 'Maith go leor,' arsa an t-athair. D'iarr sé ar an tríú mac. 'Fuair mise gunna a mharódh rud ar bith a shocraím air.' 'Maith go leor,' arsa an t-athair. D'iarr sé ar an mac is óige. 'Fuair mise snáthaid a d'fhuafadh gach rud,' arsa an mac is óige.

'Maith go leor,' arsa an t-athair. 'Breathnaigh san gcrann sin thall,' a deir sé leis an mac is sine, 'agus féach an bhfuil aon nead ann.' 'Tá,' ar seisean, 'agus lon dubh ina luí inti agus cúig ubh fúithi.' 'Éirigh,' a deir sé leis an fhear a fuair an fáinne, 'agus goid iad sin agus ná corraigh an t-éan.' Ghoid sé iad. Thug sé chuig an athair iad. 'Socraigh ar cheithre choirnéal an bhoird iad,' (a dúirt sé.) 'Éirigh,' a deir sé leis an tríú mac, 'agus déan dhá leath dóibh.' Rinne sé sin. 'Éirigh,' a deir sé leis an mac is óige. 'Fuaigh iad sin mar a bhí siad cheana.' (Rinne sé sin.) 'Imigh,' a deir sé leis an dara mac, 'agus fág san áit chéanna arís iad agus ná corraigh an t-éan.' Rinne sé sin.

'By Deaid,' ar seisean, 'tá an cheird agaibh.' D'fhan siad go dtí maidin lá arna mhárach. Chuaigh an t-athair amach agus chonaic sé an rí ag teacht agus bhí coach aige agus dhá chapall fúithi. 'Tá rud éigin suas,' ar seisean. Chuir sé suas a lámh agus stad sé an rí. 'An bhfuil trioblóid ar bith ort?' ar seisean. 'Tá,' arsa an rí, 'ach is beag an mhaith dom thusa.' 'Ní bheadh a fhios agat,' ar an fear. 'Tá ceathrar mac agam atá in ann rud ar bith a dhéanamh.' 'Tá go maith,' arsa an rí. 'Ghoid fathach m'iníon aréir agus níl a fhios agam cá bhfuil sí.'

'Gabh amach,' arsa an t-athair leis an mac is sine, 'agus breathnaigh tríd an teileascóp agus féach cá bhfuil sí.' Bhreathnaigh sé agus bhí sí féin agus an fathach sa Domhan Thoir.

Chuaigh an ceathrar mac amach i mbád agus dúirt an rí go dtabharfadh sé an iníon le pósadh don fhear is fearr. D'imigh leo agus ghoid fear an fháinne í. Nuair a dhúisigh an fathach bhí an bhean imithe agus chuaigh sé ina diaidh. Agus bhí siad ag dul isteach insan mbád nuair a chonaic siad an fathach ag teacht. Chaith fear an ghunna leis agus fuair an fathach bás. Bhí an oiread teannaidh leis an fhathach gur thit sé sa mbád agus rinne sé dhá leath de. 'Táimid réidh anois,' ar siadsan. D'éirigh fear na snáthaide agus d'fhuaigh sé an bád sa chaoi chéanna a raibh sé. Tháinig siad abhaile slán sábháilte go dtí an rí. Bhí áthas an domhain air. 'Cé agaibh an fear is fearr chun an bhean a thabhairt dó?' ar seisean. 'Mise a chonaic í,' arsa an fear is sine. 'Mise a ghoid í,' arsa an darna fear. 'Bhí sibh marbh ar fad,' arsa an tríú fear, 'murach mise.' ('Mise a chóirigh an bád,' arsa an fear is óige.)

'Níl a fhios agam céard is fearr dom a dhéanamh,' arsa an rí. 'Ach tabharfaidh mé fortún (daoibh uilig) a mbainfidh sibh maireachtáil as,' ar seisean. Chuaigh siad abhaile agus bhí siad saibhir as sin amach.

**TRANSLATION:**

Long ago, there was a man and he had four sons. The sons were fed up at home and they set off to look for work. When they came to the crossroads, the four of them went the same way. The oldest son met a man who asked him where he was going. He said he was looking for work and the man said he was looking for a servant boy. The man said he had nothing in the world [to give him] but a telescope that you could see everything in the world through. The man met the second son. He asked him did he know where he'd get a servant boy. And he'd give him a ring that'd steal everything in the world. The man met the third son and said the same to him. He said he'd give him a gun that would kill anything he wanted. He met the youngest son and said the same thing. He said he'd give him a needle that'd sew up anything, anything at all.

In a year and a day, the brothers came together again at the crossroads. The oldest son said to the second, 'We're back here again as poor as we were the day we left home. Our father won't have a great welcome for us.' 'I'm the same as yourself,' said the second son. 'And I'm as bad,' said the third. The youngest said the same.

The father saw them coming and welcomed them. He made tea and put bread on the table and gave them food. He asked the eldest son how did he get on. 'I got a telescope and when you look through it, you can see every-thing in the world,' said he. 'Good enough,' said the father. He asked the second the same thing. 'I got a ring that'll steal everything in the world,' said he. 'Good enough,' said the father. He asked the third son. 'I got a gun that'll kill anything I choose,' said he. 'Good enough,' said the father. He asked the youngest son. 'I got a needle that'll sew up everything,' said the youngest.

'Well and good,' said the father. 'Look in that tree over there,' says he to the eldest, 'and see is there a nest in it.' 'There is,' said he. 'A blackbird is in it, sitting on five eggs.' 'Get up,' says he to the lad who got the ring, 'and steal those eggs and don't disturb the bird.' He stole them and gave them to the father. 'Now, place them on the four corners of the table,'(said he.) 'Get up,' says he to the third son, 'and make two halves of them.' He did. 'Get up,' says he to the youngest son. 'Sew those up, just as they were before.' He did that. 'Go now,' says he to the second son, 'and leave them back in the same place and don't disturb the bird.' He did that.

'By Dad,' says the father, 'ye have the craft all right.' They stayed till next morning. The father went out and saw the king coming in a coach drawn by two horses. 'Something's wrong,' said the father. He raised his hand and stopped the king. 'Is there anything wrong?' he asked. 'Oh yes!' answered the king, ' but you're not much use to me.' 'You wouldn't know about that,' said the man. 'I have four sons who can do anything at all.' 'Good enough,' said the king. 'A giant stole my daughter last night and I have no idea where she is.' 'Come out,' said the father to his eldest son. 'Look through the telescope and find out where she is.' He looked. She and the giant were in the Eastern World.

The four sons went out in a boat and the king said he'd give his daughter in marriage to the best man of them. Off they went and the man with the ring stole her. When the giant woke up she was gone and he set off after her. They were just getting into the boat when they saw the giant coming. The man with the gun shot him and the giant died. He was so big that when he fell on the boat he made two halves of it. 'That's the end of us now,' said they. But the man with the needle got up and repaired the boat as good as ever it was. They came home safe and sound to the king. He was thrilled. 'Who is the best man of you, till I give him this woman in marriage?' he asked. 'It was I that saw her,' said the oldest. 'It was I that stole her,' said the second. 'You were all dead,' said the third, 'if it weren't for me.' ('It was I who fixed the boat,' said the fourth.)

'I don't know what to do,' said the king. 'I'll give each of you a fortune to grant you a living for the rest of your lives.' They went home and they were rich from that time on.

*(S30: 445–7. Nóra Ní Dhroighneáin, 12, An Caisleán Nua, Gaillimh. Rang 7. Fuaireas an scéal seo ó mo mháthair. Fuair sise é ó na seandaoine san áit ar rugadh í, An Spidéal.)*

# SUPERNATURAL LEGENDS

### *A Ghost (O'm B)*

Long ago, there was a man in Oranmore who made chairs. His name was Andy Malone. One day a man came in to him and he gave him an order to make four chairs. This man was from Island Eddy and his name was Thomas Keane. Andy Malone told him that he would make him the chairs if he would promise to call for them on that day week. 'I am very poor and I want the money,' he said. 'Dead or alive, I will come,' said Thomas.

That day week, Andy was waiting all day for him to call and in the evening he came in and he was all wet. He left his hand on the four chairs and then he disappeared. Andy was wondering what had happened and next day he heard that when Thomas Keane was coming out to the quay of Clarenbridge a sudden squall came and upset the boat and drowned him.

*(S32: 361. Written by Páraic Mac an Ríogh. Told to him by his grandmother.)*

## Bean na Luibhe [The Herb Woman] (NC)

Bhí beirt fhear ag dul amach ag iascaireacht ar Dhug na Gaillimh maidin le héirí na gréine tuairim dhá bhliain ó shin agus chonaic siad bean ag baint luibhe ag an mBalla Fada agus nuair a chonaic fear acu í, chrom sé síos sa mbád agus dúirt sé leis an bhfear eile cromadh, go raibh an bhean ag baint luibhe agus go bhfaigheadh an chéad duine a d'fheicfeadh sí bás. 'Sin seafóid,' a deir an fear eile agus níor thug sé aon aird air. Bhí an bád ag seoladh amach nuair a sheas an bhean suas agus chonaic sí duine de na fir ina sheasamh sa mbád. Cúpla nóiméad ina dhiaidh sin, tháinig stoirm mhór agus sciobadh amach as an mbád an fear agus báthadh é. Deirtear gur tógadh é in éiric an fhir a bhí leigheasta ag an luibh.

**TRANSLATION:**

Two men were going out fishing from Galway Dock at sunrise one morning about two years ago and they saw a woman gathering herbs at the Long Wall. When one man saw her, he told the other to bend down, that the woman was gathering herbs and the first person she'd see would die. 'That's nonsense,' said the other fellow and he paid no heed to it. The boat was sailing out when the woman stood up and she saw one of the men standing up. A few minutes later, a great storm rose and the man was swept out of the boat and drowned. They say that he was taken in place of the man who was cured by the herb.

*(S31: 154. Cáit Ní Bhradha, Cnoc an Dualam, Gaillimh.)*

## Seán Ó hAnlaí [Seán Hanley] (B'p)

Tuairim is céad bliain ó shin, bhí fear barrúil gurbh ainm dó Seán Ó hAnlaí ina chónaí in aice le Sruthair, áit atá in oirthear na Gaillimhe. Ar nós riar mór feilméaraí eile ní raibh mórán de mhaoin an tsaoil aige. Lá amháin, d'imigh sé lena chapall agus a chairt le hualach cruithneachta ar an margadh go Tuaim, mar cruithneacht a bhí sé de sheift acu san am sin leis an gcíos a íoc agus bhí riar mór cíosa glaoite ar Sheán. Dhíol sé an chruithneacht agus fuair sé airgead go leor air. Is cosúil go raibh dúil mhór san ól aige mar d'ól sé a sháith. D'éirigh siléig éigin dó agus bhí sé deireanach san oíche sular fhág sé Tuaim. Bhí sé ag triall leis abhaile nó go raibh sé trí mhíle amach as Tuaim, an áit a dtugtar Cnoc Meá air. Bhí teach ansin ar leataobh an bhóthair agus bhí na soilse ba bhreátha dá bhfaca sé riamh ag scartadh amach tríd na fuinneoga agus bhí an doras ar oscailt. Bhí ceol agus damhsa sa teach agus is cosúil go raibh dúil i ngal tobac aige mar chuaigh sé isteach ag deargadh a phíopa. Nuair a chuaigh sé isteach, chroith fear an tí lámh leis agus ar seisean, 'Céad míle fáilte romhat a Sheáin Uí Anlaí.' Agus chuir gach duine sa teach idir fhear agus bhean an fháilte chéanna roimhe.

'Tháinig mé isteach,' arsa Seán, 'le mo phíopa a dheargadh.'

'Tá fáilte romhat sin a dhéanamh,' arsa fear an tí. 'Cén fáth nach bhfanfá go maidin ag éisteacht leis an gceol is an damhsa?'

'Tá capall scáfar foilsceach fé mo chúram agus caithfidh mé dul abhaile léi,' arsa Seán.

'Má fhanann tú,' arsa'n fear, 'cuirfidh mise fear abhaile léi atá in ann í a cheansú chomh maith leat féin.'

'Bhuel,' a deir Seán, 'ba mhaith liom é a fheiceáil sula ligim mo chapall abhaile leis.'

'Siúd é thíos sa gclúid é,' arsa an fear.

'Ara, an é an séicleach údan thíos atá chomh sean leis an gceo?' arsa Seán.

'Éirigh i do shuí a ghaiscígh agus taispeáin do Sheán Ó hAnlaí céard atá tú in ann a dhéanamh,' arsa fear an tí.

D'éirigh an séicleach de léim agus is beag nár phlúch sé a raibh sa teach lenar thit de luaith buí as a sheanbhalcaisí. Bhí matal trasna an tí agus chuaigh sé de léim anonn thairis agus de léim eile anall.

'Dar fia,' arsa Seán, 'ba cheart go mbeadh sé seo in ann í a thabhairt abhaile.'

Leis sin, amach leis an scológ agus siúd abhaile leis an gcapall. D'fhan Seán ag éisteacht leis an spóirt nó go raibh sé thart. Ansin, chuir bean an tí leaba bhreá chlúimh faoi réir do Sheán agus dúirt leis dul ar a shuaimhneas go maidin.

Chuaigh an scológ abhaile leis an gcapall agus chuir sa stábla í. Bhí bean Sheáin is na páistí ina gcodladh agus chuaigh an scológ a chodladh freisin. Ar maidin, nuair a dhúisigh an bhean, bhí Seán básaithe lena taobh sa leaba ach ar ndóigh ní hé Seán a bhí ann ach síóg.

166

Frítheadh gléas tórraimh faoi réir do Sheán is bhí sochraid air lá arna mhárach agus cuireadh é agus éagmais mhór a bhí ina dhiaidh. Ach ní raibh gá leis, ní raibh Seán básaithe in aon chor. Is cosúil gur, in ionad bheith oíche amháin leis na síóga, is amhlaidh bhí sé dhá oíche is lá leo. Ach nuair a dhúisigh Seán ní i leaba chlúimh a bhí sé ach i dtulán fraoigh ar thaobh Chnoc Mheá. Ghluais leis chomh trén agus a d'fhéad, ag triall abhaile. Bhí sé ina mheán oíche nuair a shroich sé an teach. Bhí an bhean is na páistí ina gcodladh. Bhuail sé ar an doras. D'fhiafraigh an bhean de cé a bhí ann.

'Mise Seán,' ar seisean.

'As ucht Dé agus béal na húlaíochta ort a Sheáin Uí Anlaí,' ar sise, 'agus fan uaim, mar tá mo dhóthain trioblóide agam le dhá lá is gan tú teacht arís.'

Leis sin, chuimhnigh Seán go raibh rud éigin suas agus dúirt leis féin go rachadh sé a chodladh sa gcoca tuí go mbeadh solas an lae aige. Ach is gearr a bhí sé sa tuí nuair a tháinig beirt bhuachaill leis an sagart i gcoinnibh na muice a bhí ag an mnaoi ag cleithiúnas ocht bpunt d'airgead iasachta a bhí tugtha ag an sagart do Sheán. Bhí siad ag tiomáint na muice amach an bóithrín nuair a d'airigh Seán iad. Siúd amach leis ina ndiaidh.

'Cáil sibh ag tabhairt muc mo mhná?' ar seisean leo.

Siúd leo abhaile agus bun a n-anama amuigh. D'fhiafraigh an sagart dóibh cá raibh an mhuc. Dúirt leis go dtáinig Seán ina ndiaidh nuair a bhíodar dá tiomáint amach. Dúirt an sagart leo go gcaithfidís dul ar ais ach dúirt siadsan nach rachadh mura dtiocfadh sé féin leo.

'Déanfaidh sin,' ar seisean.

Siúd leo chun bealaigh go dtáinig siad chuig an teach. D'fhan na buachaillí amuigh ar an mbóithrín agus chuaigh an sagart isteach. Nuair a bhí sé ag tabhairt amach na muice, labhair Seán.

'Cáil tú ag tabhairt mo mhuc?' ar seisean.

'As ucht Dé agus béal na húlaíochta ort a Sheáin Uí Anlaí agus fan uaim,' ar seisean. 'Maithim do do bhean na fiacha agus achainí ar bith eile a iarrfaidh tú orm gheobhaidh tú é.'

'Bhuel,' arsa Seán, 'íocfaidh tú an bille a bhí glaoite orm ina leithéid seo de shiopa in Áth Chinn agus coinneoidh tú plúr agus gach rud a bheas ag teastáil uainn i rith na bliana linn agus caithfidh tú é sin a shíniú ar pháipéar faoi láimh domsa.'

'Déanfaidh mise sin duit agus fáilte,' arsa an sagart agus na cosa ag sciorradh uaidh agus é ag rith ón taibhse más taibhse a bhí ann. Ag teacht ar ais do Sheán ó theach an tsagairt, cé chasfaí dó ach buachaill an tiarna agus capall Sheáin aige in ómós an chíosa a bhí glaoite ar Sheán. Ar ndóigh, ba ghearr le mo dhuine a chosa a thabhairt leis nuair a chonaic sé an taibhse go ndeachaigh sé abhaile don tiarna. D'fhiafraigh an tiarna de cá raibh an capall agus dúirt sé leis gur chas Seán Ó hAnlaí air agus gur bhain sé de í. Ar ndóigh, níor chreid an tiarna é. Dúirt an buachaill leis munar chreid sé é dul agus é a bhaint de é féin. D'imigh an tiarna agus deifir mhór air. Bhí an srian aige ar an gcapall agus é ag imeacht léi nuair a labhair Seán sa choca tuí.

'Cáil tú ag tabhairt mo chapaill?' ar seisean.

'As ucht Dé agus béal na húlaíochta ort a Sheáin Uí Anlaí,' arsa an tiarna, 'agus fan uaim, agus maithim duit an méid cíosa atá glaoite agam ort.'

'Ní dhéanfaidh sin,' arsa Seán. ' Caithfidh tú é a shíniú domsa ar pháipéar faoi do láimh, agus é a shíniú saor ó chíos fhaid is bheas uisce ag rith agus féar ag fás agus é a bheith déanta sula n-éireoidh an ghrian inniu.'

'Déanfaidh mise sin agus fáilte,' arsa an tiarna.

Agus deir an scéal go mba áthasach an fear é Seán ar maidin, a chuid fiacha íoctha, a theach is a thalamh saor ó chíos go brách, agus an méid ceoil is spóirt a bhí aige leis na sióga.

**TRANSLATION:**

About a hundred years ago, a funny man called Seán Hanley lived beside Shrule, in east Galway. Like a lot of other farmers, Seán wasn't very well off. One day, he headed off with his horse and cart and a load of wheat to the market in Tuam. It was wheat they used to sell to make the rent money and Seán owed a lot of rent. He sold the wheat and got plenty of money for it. It seems he was very fond of a drink because he drank his fill then. He got delayed and it was late at night before he left Tuam. He was making his way home until he was three miles outside Tuam, a place which is called Knockma. There was a house there beside the road and the brightest lights he had ever seen shining out from the windows. The door was open. There was music and dancing in the house and it seems he liked a bit of a smoke because he went in to light his pipe. When he went in, the man of the house shook his hand and said, 'A hundred thousand welcomes, Seán Hanley.' And everyone in the house, women and men, welcomed him the same way.

'I came in,' he said, 'to light my pipe.'

'You're welcome to do that,' said the man of the house. 'Why don't you stay till morning for the music and the dancing?'

'I've a very frisky horse and I must go home,' said Seán.

'If you wait,' said the man, 'I'll send a man home with her, a man who can control her as well as yourself.'

'Well,' said Seán, 'I'd like to see that man before I let my horse home with him.'

'There he is over in the corner,' said the man.

'What! That old codger down in the corner who's as old as the hills?' exclaimed Seán.

'Get up my fine fellow and show Seán Hanley what you're fit for,' said the man of the house.

Up jumped the old man, almost suffocating everyone in the house with all the red ashes that fell out of his clothes. There was a mantle across the house and he jumped over it one way and back again the other.

'Gosh,' said Seán, 'this fellow should be able to take her home.'

With that, the fellow came out and headed home with the horse. Seán stayed listening to all the fun until it was over. Then, the woman of the house made ready a lovely soft feather bed for him and told him to rest till morning.

The servant went home with the horse and put it in the stable. Seán's wife and children were asleep and the servant went to sleep too. In the morning, when Seán's wife woke up, Seán was dead beside her in the bed, but of course it wasn't Seán but a fairy.

A wake was prepared for Seán and, next day, a funeral. He was buried and there was much grief after him. But there was no need for it as Seán wasn't dead at all. It seems that, instead of spending one night with the fairies, he had actually spent two nights and a day with them. But when Seán woke up, it wasn't in a feather bed he was but in a clump of heather on the side of Knockma. He set off home as quickly as he could. It was midnight when he reached the house and his wife and children were asleep. He knocked on the door. The woman asked who was there.

'It's Seán,' he said.

'For the love of God, Seán Hanley,' said she, 'keep away from me, for I've had enough trouble this last three days and you not to come back again.'

With that, Seán realised that something was wrong and he said to himself he'd sleep in the haystack till daylight. But he wasn't long there till two boys who worked for the priest came to take the pig which his wife owed, for the eight pounds the priest had loaned Seán. They were just driving the pig out the boreen when Seán heard them. He jumped out after them.

'Where are you taking my wife's pig?' he asked.

The two raced home with their hearts in their mouths. The priest asked where was the pig. They told him that Seán had come after them as they were driving it back. The priest said they'd have to go back, but they said they wouldn't unless he'd come with them.

'I'll do that,' he said.

They went back to the house. The boys stayed outside on the boreen and the priest went in. When he was taking out the pig, Seán spoke.

'Where are you taking my pig?' he asked.

'For the love of God, Seán Hanley, keep away from me,' said the priest. 'I forgive your wife her debts and you'll get any request you ask.'

'Well,' said Seán, 'you'll pay the bill I owe in such a shop in Headford and you'll keep us in flour and anything else we need for the next year. And you'll have to sign that promise on a piece of paper for me.'

'I'll do that and welcome,' said the priest, his feet skidding under him as he ran away from the supposed ghost. When Seán came back from the priest's house, who should he meet but the landlord's servant taking away his horse in repayment for the rent Seán owed. Of course, it didn't take the servant long to run off when he saw the ghost, tearing home to the landlord. The landlord asked him where was the horse and he said he'd met Seán Hanley and that he'd taken it back. Naturally, the landlord didn't believe him. The boy said if he didn't believe him to go and take it from Seán himself. Off went the landlord in a great hurry. He had just put the rein on the horse, ready to leave, when Seán spoke out of the haystack.

'Where are you taking my horse?' he said.

'For the love of God, Seán Hanley,' said the landlord, 'keep away from me, and I forgive you any rent you owe me.'

'That won't do,' said Seán. 'You'll have to sign a promise for me on paper, to have the land free from rent as long as water flows and grass grows, and get that done before sunrise.'

And the story goes that Seán was a happy man next morning, his debts paid, his house and land free from rent forever, and all the fun he'd had with the fairies as well.

*(S30: 412–6. Máire Ní Nuadháin, Pollach, a scríobh síos óna hathair Éamonn Ó Nuadháin (feilméara), Pollach, Maigh Cuilinn. Márta, 1938.)*

## An tÓl [Drink] (M)

Tuairim is leathchéad bliain ó shin, bhí fear ag obair i nGaillimh. Maidin amháin, chonaic sé fear in aice le teach ósta agus ghlaoigh an fear isteach air. Thug sé pionta uisce beatha dó agus d'ól sé é. An mhaidin ina dhiaidh sin, tharla an rud céanna, agus gach maidin eile. Aon oíche amháin, nuair a bhí an fear ag dul abhaile ghlac sé an pledge. Ar maidin, thug an fear isteach aríst é. Bhí an ghloine ina láimh aige nuair a chonaic sé gur cosa bó a bhí ar an bhfear eile. Chaith sé an t-uisce beatha leis an bhfear agus ní fhaca sé uaidh sin amach é. Bhí sé ag ceapadh gurbh é an diabhal a bhí ann.

**TRANSLATION:**

About fifty years ago, there was a man working in Galway. One morning he saw a man beside a hotel and the man called him in. He gave him a pint of whiskey, which he drank. Next morning, the same thing happened and every other morning too. One night, when the man was going home, he took the pledge. Next morning, the man took him in again. He had the glass in his hand when he saw that the other man had hooves (instead of feet). He threw the whiskey at the fellow and never saw him again. He was thinking it was the devil was in it.

*(S30: 80. Bríd Ní Phroinseas a scríobh síos. 5 Deireadh Fómhair 1938.)*

An Chéad Chomaoineach, Mionloch, 1935.

## An Chailleach Bhéarach [The Hag of Beare] (P)

Bhí bean ann fadó agus an Chailleach Bhéarach an t-ainm a bhí uirthi. Bhí sí ina cónaí i nGort a' Chalaidh agus bhí draíocht aici.

Gach bliain, bhíodh sí ag marú fear. D'iarr sí fear a' bhaint féir gach bliain agus mharaíodh sí gach ceann acu. D'iarr sí fear uair agus bhí faitíos mór air go maródh sí é. Bhí an fear seo pósta agus d'inis sé an scéal dá mhnaoi.

Sé an sórt mná a bhí ina bean, cailín as Maigh Eo a tháinig a' lorg oibre. Nuair a tháinig sí go dtí an teach seo choinnigh sé féin agus a athair í mar chailín aimsire. Tar éis tamaill, phós an fear óg í agus mhair an triúr go sona sásta.

Nuair a d'inis an fear di go raibh an Chailleach Bhéarach dhá iarraidh, dúirt sise nach mbeadh an Chailleach in ann é a mharú dá ndéanfadh sé an rud a déarfadh sí féin leis.

Dúirt sí leis ansin a dhul go Maigh Eo agus bhí gabha ann a raibh an-cháil air. Dúirt sí leis a rá leis an ghabha seo speal a dhéanamh dó agus faobhar a chur ann le hallas a mhalaí agus deich mbior iarainn a dhéanamh dó.

Bhí go maith. D'imigh leis go dtí an gabha agus nuair a tháinig sé chuige, d'fhiafraigh an gabha de cé a chuir chuige é. Dúirt seisean gur chuir a bhean ann é. D'fhiafraigh an gabha de ansin cén fhaid a raibh an bhean aige, agus dúirt sé go raibh sí aige seacht mbliana agus lá, agus gur ag iarraidh obair a bhí sí ar dtús.

'Sin í m'iníon-sa,' arsa'n gabha. 'Tá sí imithe uaim le seacht mbliana agus lá agus ní fhaca mé ó shin í.'

Ansin, rinne an gabha an speal agus bhí áthas air gur chuala sé faoina iníon. Nuair a bhí an chéad speal déanta aige agus an faobhar curtha ann aige, thriail sé é agus dúirt sé nach raibh aon mhaith leis an speal sin mar bhris sé é. Rinne sé ceann eile agus bhí an t-allas ag titim dá bhaithis mar uisce. Chuir sé faobhar ar an speal leis an allas sin. Chuir sé an oiread air gur léim an t-ámharsóir (áibhirseoir?) amach tríd an bhfuinneog nuair a thriail sé é. Rinne sé na bioráin agus thug sé dó iad agus d'fhágadar slán ag a chéile agus d'imigh an fear abhaile.

Nuair a tháinig sé go dtí a bhean d'inis sé a chuid eachtraí di. Dúirt sí leis a dhul a bhaint an fhéir ag an gCailleach.

D'imigh sé a' bhaint an fhéir ansin agus chuir an Chailleach amach roimpi féin é. Gach seans a gheobhadh sé, sháigheadh sé bior síos sa bhféar agus bhíodh ar an gCailleach faobhar a chur ar a speal féin go minic agus ar sise, 'Faobhar, faobhar a bhainfeadh féar,' agus arsa'n fear , 'Ní hea, ach fear breá láidir is speal breá géar.'

Bhí sé ag cur na mbiorán sa mhóinfhéar mar sin go raibh siad ar fad curtha ann aige. Faoin am sin, bhí an buachaill chomh mear sin ag imeacht go dtáinig sé suas léi agus bhain sé na cosa di, mar sin é an chaoi a mbíodh sí féin ag baint na gcos de na fir a mharaigh sí (féin).

**TRANSLATION:**

Long ago, there was a woman and she was called the Hag of Beare. She lived in Gortachalla and she had enchantment.

Every year, she used to kill men. Every year, she asked for a man to cut her hay, and she used to kill every one of them. Once she asked a man to come to her and he was very afraid she'd kill him. This man was married and he told the story to his wife.

His wife was a Mayo woman who had come to that place looking for work. When she came to their house, he and his father kept her as a servant girl. After a while, the young man married her and the three of them lived happily together.

When the man told her that the Hag of Beare was looking for him, she said that the Hag wouldn't be able to kill him if he'd do what she'd tell him to do.

She told him to go to Mayo where there was a blacksmith who was very famous. She told him to ask this blacksmith to make a scythe for him and to put an edge on the blade of the scythe with the sweat of his brow, and to make him ten iron pins as well.

Well and good. Off he went to the smith and when he got there, the smith asked him who had sent him. He said his wife had sent him. The smith asked how long his wife was with him and he said she was there seven years and a day, that she had come looking for work at the beginning.

'That's my daughter,' said the smith. 'She's away from me for seven years and a day and I haven't seen her since!'

**Making a haycock, 1936.**

Then the smith made the scythe and he was very happy to have heard news of his daughter. When he had finished the first scythe and put a sharp edge on it, he tested it and said it was no good because it broke. He made another one and the sweat was falling from his brow like water. He sharpened the blade with the sweat. He put such an edge on it that the devil jumped out through the window when the smith tested the scythe. He made the pins and gave them to the man. They said farewell and the man went home.

When he came home to his wife, he told her the whole story. She told him to go and cut the hay for the Hag of Beare.

Off he went to cut the hay and the Hag sent him out in front of herself. Every chance he got, he'd stick a pin down into the grass, so that the Hag would often have to sharpen her own scythe. 'Blade, blade that'd cut hay!' she said. 'No,' said the man, 'but a fine strong man and a good scythe.'

He was putting the pins in the meadow like that until he had them all used up. By that time, he was moving so fast he caught up with the Hag and cut off her legs, because that's what she'd do with the men she used to kill before that.

*(S30: 17–9. An tSr. M. Colmán. Stiofán Ó Briain, 62, Ceathrú an Bhrúnaigh, do thug an t-eolas seo uaidh.)*

## Cloch Fhada [A Long Stone] (O'm C)

Tá cloch mhór ard in aice le mo theachsa. Tá sí suite i bpáirc. Seo scéal aisteach fúithi.

Nuair a bhí na daoine ag cur suas an chaisleáin i Ros Cam, tháinig an Chailleach Bhéarach thart agus thosaigh sí ag caint leis na fearaibh a bhí ag obair.

'Ní fada go mbeidh sibh suas chomh fada leis an spéir,' ar sise. Chuir sí draíocht orthu agus níorbh fhéidir leo cloch a chur suas tar éis sin. Tháinig fearg mhór orthu agus bhí slat ag duine acu. Rith sé i ndiaidh na caillighe agus tháinig sé suas léi ag an gcloch seo. Mharaigh sé ansin í. Cuireadh í faoin gcloch agus tá a lán seanscríbhneoireachta ar a barr.

Tá scéalta eile faoi freisin. Deirtear go bhfuil Rí na hÉireann curtha ann ach ní chreideann aoinne é. Deirtear freisin go raibh airgead agus ór i bhfolach ansin ag na seandaoine fadó.

**TRANSLATION:**

There's a big tall stone near my house, in a field. Here's a story about it.

When the people were building the castle in Roscam, the Hag of Beare came around and began to talk to the workmen.

'You'll soon be up as far as the sky,' she said. Then she put a spell on them and they couldn't build another stone after that. They got very angry. One of them had a stick and he ran after the Hag and caught up with her at this stone. He killed her there and she was buried under the stone and there's a lot of writing on top of it.

There's other stories about it too. It's said that the King of Ireland is buried under it but no one believes that. They also say that the old folk long ago had silver and gold hidden under it.

*(S32: 509–10. No name given.)*


## Tobar na Caillighe [The Hag's Well] (O'm C)

Tá Tobar na Caillighe suite in aice stáisiún Uaráin Mhóir. Deirtear gur lig an Chailleach Bhéara a scíth ansin nuair a bhí sí ag dul go dtí Ó Súilleabháin Béara.

Tá scéal eile faoi freisin. Nuair a bhí an Chailleach Bhéarra marbh, tháinig gach seanbhean ón áit chun a cuid éadaí agus a cuid gruaige a ní (sa tobar). Bhí táilliúir ina chónaí in Uarán Mór. Gach oíche ar a dó dhéag a chlog, théadh sé go dtí an tobar. Oíche amháin, in áit buicéad uisce fuair sé buicéad fíona. Gach seacht mbliain ina dhiaidh sin bhíodh fíon le fáil ann.

**TRANSLATION:**

The Hag's Well is situated beside Oranmore Station. They say the Hag of Beare rested there when she was going to join O'Sullivan Beare.

There's another story too. When the Hag of Beare died, every old woman in the place came and washed their clothes and hair in the well. A tailor lived in Oranmore. Every night at twelve o'clock, he used to go to the well. One night, instead of a bucket of water, he got a bucket of wine. Every seven years after that, there'd be wine in the well.

*(S32: 524. No name.)*

### An Eascann a Bhí i Loch Coiribe [The Eel in Lough Corrib] (F)

Bhí reilig in aice le Cunga ar bhruach Loch Coiribe. Bhí eascann mhór i Loch Coiribe agus chuile oíche thagadh an eascann seo isteach sa reilig agus chartaíodh sí an talamh. Bhaineadh sí na coirp as an talamh agus d'itheadh sí iad. An lá seo, cailleadh máthair an fhir seo agus dúirt an fear nach n-íosfadh an eascann a mháthairse. Fuair sé claíomh trom agus thosaigh sé ag faire uirthi. Bhí poll ins an doras agus chuir sí a cloigeann isteach ins an bpoll. Tharraing an fear óg buille uirthi agus bhain sé an cloigeann di. Thit braon fola ar a laidhricín agus d'fhág sé an laidhricín ar chloch agus ghearr sé de féin é, mar bhí fuil na heascainne nimhneach.

**TRANSLATION:**

There was a graveyard beside Cong on the banks of Lough Corrib. There was an eel in Lough Corrib and every night the eel would come into the graveyard and dig up the ground. She'd take up the bodies and eat them.

**Barna village in former times.**

One day, a man's mother died and he said he wouldn't let the eel get her. He got a heavy sword and kept watch. There was a hole in the door and the eel put her head through the hole. The young man struck her a blow and cut off her head. A drop of blood fell on to his little toe. He placed his toe on a stone and cut it off, because the eel's blood was venomous.

*(S30: 301. Fuarthas an scéal seo ó Pheadar Ó Conghaile, 63,*
*An Ceapach. Feilméara. 17 Bealtaine 1938.)*

### Each Uisce i Loch Riabhach [A Water Horse in Lough Reagh] (B'p)

Bhí fear saibhir ina chónaí ar bhruach Loch Riabhach tráth. Tiarna talún ab ea é agus bhí talamh Loch Riabhach ar fad faoi chíos aige ach bhí tionóntaí aige ar chuid de agus d'íocadh na tionóntaí seo cíos leis. Ruairí Ó Mórdha ab ainm dó. Aon bhliain amháin chuir sé píosa mór den talamh faoi arbhar.

San bhfómhar, nuair a bhí an t-arbhar aibí, chuaigh an tiarna amach ag breathnú air. Chonaic sé go raibh a lán díobhála déanta don arbhar. D'fhág sé garda saighdiúirí ag tabhairt aire dó an oíche sin. I lár na hoíche, tháinig ionadh mór ar na saighdiúirí nuair a chonaiceadar scata d'eachanna uisce ag teacht amach as an loch agus isteach san bpáirc leo. Thosaíodar ag ithe an arbhair chomh tréan agus d'fhéadadar agus nuair a bhí a sáith ite acu d'imíodar leo.

Lá arna mhárach, d'inis na saighdiúirí don tiarna fán rud a tharla agus d'ordaigh an tiarna dóibh breith ar cheann de na heachanna. Nuair a thit dorchadas na hoíche, chuadar amach ag faire ar na heachanna. Tharla an rud céanna a tharla an oíche roimh ré. Nuair a tháinig na heachanna isteach san bpáirc rith na saighdiúirí ina ndiaidh agus rugadar ar cheann acu. Tugadh abhaile chuig an tiarna é. Chuir an tiarna isteach i scioból é agus d'fhág sé ansin é go raibh sé roinnt ramhar. Nuair a bhí sé roinnt ramhar, bhí sé ina each chomh breá is a bhí in Éirinn. Ansin, chuir sé amach san rása é agus ní raibh capall ar bith in ann é a shárú.

Lá amháin, thug Ruairí féin an capall amach san rása. Bhuaigh an capall an rása. Ansin tháinig Ruairí abhaile agus gliondar chroí air, ach a mhuirnín mo chroí thú, céard a dhéanfadh an capall nuair a bhí sé ag dul thar Loch Riabhach ach léim mhór amháin a thabhairt agus dul isteach san loch. Tásc ná tuairisc ní bhfuair Ruairí ar an each uisce uaidh sin amach.

**TRANSLATION:**

Once upon a time a rich man lived on the banks of Lough Reagh. He was a landlord and he had all the land around Lough Reagh rented out. He had tenants on some of the land and they paid him rent. Rory O'Moore was his name. One year he planted oats on a large portion of the land.

In autumn, when the oats were ripe, the landlord went out to take a look at them. He saw that a lot of damage had been done. He left a guard of soldiers to look after the oats that night. In the middle of the night, the soldiers were amazed when a herd of water horses came out of the lough and into the field. They began eating the oats as fast as they could and when they had eaten their fill, off they went again.

Next day, the soldiers told the landlord what had happened and he orderd them to catch one of the horses. When darkness fell, they went out to wait for the horses. The same thing happened that night. When the horses came into the field, the soldiers ran after them and one was caught. It was brought home to the landlord. He put it into the stable and left it there until it was fattened up a bit. When it was fattened up, it was as fine a horse as was to be found in the whole of Ireland. Then he sent it out to race and no horse could beat it.

One day, Rory himself took the horse out to race. The horse won and Rory came home absolutely delighted. But oh my dear, what did the horse do when it was going past Lough Reagh but give one huge jump into the lough. Rory has had neither sight nor sound of the water horse since.

*(S30: 422–3. Máite Ní Chearra a scríobh síos óna seanuncail, Micheál Ó Flannacha, Barr na Crannaighe, Gaillimh. Bealtaine, 1938.)*

## *Returning Spirit (O'm B)*

Long ago, there was a ghost living out in the tide near Island Eddy. For several nights before severe weather the ghost would be shouting and screeching.

The older people then used to say that this ghost was a baker who lived in Kinvara, not far from Island Eddy. He used to sell loaves that were not a proper weight. When he died, he was sent out there to do penance for his sins.

*(S32: 456. Told by Mrs Trayers of Renville, Oranmore.)*

## Cloch an Ádha [The Lucky Stone] (O'm C)

Aon uair amháin, bhí spailpín ina chónaí i gConamara. Bhí a mhuintir an-bhocht agus ní raibh oiread is leithphingin rua acu.

Dúirt an spailpín lena mhuintir lá amháin go raibh sé ag dul go Gaillimh agus nuair a bhí sé ag teacht abhaile go déanach san oíche, shuigh sé síos ar thaobh an bhóthair agus cén áit ar shuigh sé ach ar Chloch an Ádha. Tá an chloch sin ar thaobh an bhóthair idir Conamara agus Gaillimh. Nuair a shuigh sé ar an gcloich, d'éirigh sí den talamh agus d'eitil sí agus an fear ina shuí uirthi.

Thuirling an chloch go talamh ag caisleán mór. Chuaigh an spailpín isteach sa gcaisleán agus bhí bord mór bia réidh. D'ith sé agus d'ól sé go raibh sé súgach sáthach. Chuaigh sé isteach sa seomra eile agus bhí leaba shócúlach chluthar ann agus luigh sé siar ar an leaba agus níorbh fhada gur thit an codladh air.

Nuair a d'éirigh sé ar maidin, bhí sé ina shuí ar an gcloich ar leataobh an bhóthair mar gur thug na sióga ar ais arís é nuair a bhí sé ina chodladh.

**TRANSLATION:**

Once upon a time, there was spalpeen living in Connemara. His family were so poor they didn't have as much as a red halfpenny.

One day, the spalpeen told his family he was going to Galway. When he was coming home late at night, he sat down on the roadside and where did he sit but on the lucky stone which is on the side of the road between Connemara and Galway. When he sat on the stone, it rose up from the ground and flew off with the man sitting on it.

The stone came down again at a big castle. The spalpeen went into the castle and saw a big table of food. He ate and drank till he was full to bursting. Then he went into another room where there was a lovely soft, comfortable bed. He lay down on the bed and it didn't take long for him to fall asleep.

Next morning when he woke up, he was sitting on the stone at the side of the road because the fairies had brought him back while he was asleep.

*(S32: 522–3. No name given.)*


## Three Witches (O'm C)

Once upon a time there lived three sisters who were very poor, yet they still had everything they wanted. Nobody seemed to know how they lived. They lived in the mountain, yet they had corn and potatoes.

A stranger bought a piece of land near them, and when he sowed anything in it, it never thrived. His cows had no milk and he did not know what to do with them. One night, he went out to give them a drink. While he was there a hare came into the field and sucked all the milk from one of the cows and then went away. The hare returned soon after and repeated this until he had the milk sucked from all the cows. The man went home and pondered over all he saw.

Next day, he got up early and went to see an old man. He told this man what he had seen. The man told him that hare was a witch. He told him also that there were three sisters living near him who had a charm. They could, for instance, take upon themselves any form they pleased. One of them took the form of a hare and drank all the cows' milk. Another, under the form of a horse, took turf, corn and hay. The other stayed at home. Sometimes she went under the form of a fly.

The old man told him not to go home that night but to go to a certain man and ask him for a greyhound. The man would not give the dog, but when he was told of the hare which was taking the milk from the cows, he consented to lend the dog. The dog was taken near the mountain. But the dog was too young and the hare left him far behind. The man did not send the dog home as he hoped the hare would come again. He got ready and set out on his horse and put the dog in front. They arrived at their journey's end and at dusk went to the field where the cows were. The hare came and drank the milk. They then let the dog after her. The dog could only take one bite of the hare. Then they went to the house of the sisters. They forced the door open and on doing so they saw a woman sitting in the corner in a pool of blood. She had to admit that it was she who had been drinking the milk of the cows.

*(S32: 525–6. No name given.)*

# AN BHEAN SÍ

### *A Banshee (O'm B)*

One day an old woman and her child came into a house where the woman of the house was churning. The old woman asked for milk for her child and she was refused. The woman of the house said that she would not give her as much as would dash out of the churn.

The old woman went away, but as she was going out she said, 'I will have the butter of the heir of this house tomorrow.' Next day, the son of the house was hunting and he fell off his horse and struck his head against the wall and was killed.

When he was killed, the banshee was heard to screech, so the people knew that the old woman who had called in for the milk was a banshee.

*(S32: 481. Written down by Donnchadh Ó Treabhair,*
*Rinn Mhíl, Uarán Mór. Told by his mother.)*

### *Bean Sí [Banshee] (P)*

Bhí fear amuigh faoin dtuath san aimsir fadó. Bhí sé ag baint mónadh in san bportach. Bhí sé deireanach nuair a d'fhág sé an portach tráthnóna agus bhí deifir air abhaile mar bhí tórramh sa mbaile.

Nuair a bhí sé in aice an trinse, chonaic sé bean agus í ag ní thíos in san trinse agus culaith gheal uirthi. Chuaigh sé chomh fada léi. Chuir sé 'Bail ó Dhia' uirthi. Tháinig fearg uirthi. Lean sí é agus dúirt sí go dtarrainge-odh sí an ghruaig dá chloigeann. Dúirt an fear léi fanacht amach uaidh ar mhaithe léi féin, nó bhuailfeadh sé leis an sleán í. Nuair a bhí sé ag dul go dtí an teach tórraimh, lean sí é go dtí an doras agus rug sí lán a crúib dá chuid gruaige léi.

182

**A day in the bog, Connemara.**

Bíonn an bhean sí i gcónaí ag gol agus ag caoineadh in aice le tobar nó le claiseanna uisce. Deir na seandaoine go mbíonn sí ag caoineadh i ndiaidh daoine nuair a bhíonn siad ag fáil bháis, agus go mbíonn sí ag caoineadh in aice an tí. Ní bhíonn sí ag caoineadh ach i ndiaidh cuid de na daoine.

**TRANSLATION:**
Long ago, there was a man who lived out in the country and he was cutting turf in the bog. It was late when he left the bog in the evening and he was in a hurry to get home as there was a wake going on.

When he was beside the trench, he saw a woman washing down in the trench and she was wearing a white garment. The man went up to her and saluted her in the name of God. She got angry. She followed him and said she'd pull the hair out of his head. The man told her to stay back from him, for her own sake, or he'd strike her with the turf spade. When he was going to the wake house, she followed him to the door and pulled a handful of hair from his head.

The banshee is always weeping and crying beside a well or a water channel. The old people say she keens people who are dying and she keens beside the house. She only keens some people.

*(S30: 436–7. Cáit Ní Ioláin, 14, Baile Chláir, Rang 8. Fuaireas an scéal seo ó*
*Mhicheál Mac Cuimín, Cinn Uisce, Baile Cláir.)*

# THE MERMAID

### *Mermaids on the Galway Coast (NB)*

A mermaid is a very queer kind of a creature. It is half a woman and half a fish. It is very rarely seen on the Galway coast.

A mermaid appeared three times out near the lighthouse. A party of young men that were out on a pleasure trip saw a mermaid. A few men were out fishing when a mermaid appeared. The men got a terrible fright. They beat it on the head a couple of times. It let three great roars and then it went.

*(S31: 139. Martin Browne, Fair Hill, Galway. I got this from Mrs Raftery whose age is 78 years.)*

### *The Mermaid at Pier Head (P)*

Once upon a time, there used to be a mermaid coming ashore at the Pier Head in the Claddagh village. As the tide went out the mermaid used to

Claddagh girls.

come in on the shore, and she used to sit down on the rocks and comb her hair. When the tide came in again she would swim into the sea. She was a half-person and a half-fish. She used to remain away during the winter months, out in the deep sea. She would return in the summer and then come to the shallows.

She had a lovely head of hair and was always seen combing it. It is said that boys once followed her but she disappeared suddenly and was never seen after that.

*(S30: 443. Written by Margaret Coyne, 14 years, Fair Hill House, Fair Hill, Galway. I got this story from a Claddagh man named Patrick Melia.)*

### Merman in Galway Bay (NB)

There is an interesting story about a merman which is to be seen in Galway Bay. In Galway Bay, there is a cave near the sea and a merman is supposed to live in it. One evening, two men in a boat were amazed to see a creature, a merman, coming towards them in the water. He tried to capsize the boat, but one of the men hit him with an oar. This creature swam off, and rumours still hold that he abounds in Galway Bay.

*(S31: 138–9. Patrick Doyle, from Mrs Doyle, 39, New Docks, Galway. 29 April 1938.)*

## RELIGIOUS STORIES

### An Dearg Daol [The Black Beetle] (NB)

Nuair a bhí Muire Máthair agus Naomh Seosamh ag teitheadh chun na hÉigipte le hÍosa, thug fir oibre a bhí ag cur síl bia agus cabhair dóibh. D'fhás an síol láithreach agus d'aibigh. Thosaigh na fir oibre ag baint an lá arna mhárach. Tháinig saighdiúirí Herod chucu ag cuardach an triúir.

Dúirt na fir oibre go fírinneach gur ghabh a leithéid de thriúr an tslí an lá a bhí an barr á chur acu. Cheap na saighdiúirí gur ráithe roimhe sin é agus nárbh iad an triúr ceart iad. Bhíodar ar tí iompú abhaile arís nuair a

185

labhair an dearg daol ón bhféar de ghlór lag. 'Inné, inné!' arsa sé. Thuig na saighdiúirí céard a tharla agus leanadar orthu sa tóir. Ní maith le héinne an dearg daol ó shin amach.

**TRANSLATION:**

When the Virgin Mary and Saint Joseph were fleeing to Egypt with Jesus, some working men who were sowing seed gave them food and alms. The seed grew immediately and ripened. The men began to harvest it the next day when Herod's soldiers came along looking for the family.

The men said truthfully that three people of that kind had gone past the day they were sowing the crop. The soldiers thought it was three months before and so it wasn't the right three people. They were just going to turn back home when the black beetle down on the grass spoke in a low voice. 'Yesterday, yesterday!' said he. The soldiers understood what had happened

**Saving the harvest, Carrowbrowne, 1930s.**

and they continued the search. That's why no one likes the black beetle from that time till this.

(S31: 123. Pádraig Ó Dubhghaill. 8 Márta 1938.)

## An Cros-Ghob [The Crooked-Beak] (NB)

Chéas na Giúdaigh Íosa Críost ar Aoine an Chéasta. Nuair a bhí ár Slánaitheoir tairnithe ar an gcroich, d'imigh siad abhaile agus d'fhág siad an chroich ina seasamh ansin agus Íosa céasta uirthi. Tháinig an t-éan agus dúirt sé leis, 'Saorfaidh mé thú, a Íosa.' Bhí trua mór aige dó.

D'fhéach sé chun na tairní a tharraingt amach ó chorp Íosa, ach bhíodar rómhór agus róláidir ar a ghob. Chinn air mar ní raibh a ghob sách láidir chun é a dhéanamh.

Ar an gcaoi sin, cham sé a ghob agus mar gheall air sin tugtar an 'cros-ghob' mar ainm air. Ainm eile a thugtar air ná 'spideog brollaigh dheirg', mar gur thit fuil dhearg Íosa air an t-am a bhí an fhuil ag titim go talamh.

**TRANSLATION:**

The Jews crucified Jesus Christ on Good Friday. When our Saviour was nailed on the cross, they went off home and left the cross standing there and Jesus crucified on it. A bird came and said, 'I'll free you Jesus.' He had great pity for him.

He tried to pull the nails out of Jesus' body, but they were too big and too strong for his beak. He failed because his beak wasn't strong enough to do it.

As a result, he bent his beak and now he's called 'crooked-beak.' He's also called 'robin redbreast', because Jesus' red blood fell on him as it was falling to the ground.

(S31: 123–4. Pádraig Ó Dubhghaill. 8 Márta 1938.)

## Íosa Críost agus an Dá Chrann [Jesus Christ and the Two Trees] (C'b)

Nuair a bhí Íosa Críost ag rith ó na Giúdaigh, tháinig sé chomh fada le háit a raibh crann troim. Chuaigh sé faoin chrann troim agus scar an crann amach ar fad agus níor shábháil an crann troim é ar chor ar bith. Nuair a tháinig na Giúdaigh, chonaic siad Íosa faoin chrann troim ach d'imigh sé orthu.

Ansin chuaigh Íosa faoi chrann cuilinn a bhí ag fás in aice na páirce. Ansin, scar an crann amach mar theach agus shábháil an crann cuilinn é. Ní fhaca na Giúdaigh Íosa faoin chrann cuilinn. Agus sin é an fáth gurb é an crann troim an crann deireanach a chuirfeas amach bileoga agus an chéad chrann a thiteas na bileoga de. Agus an crann cuilinn, bíonn sméara dearga ag fás air chuile bhliain agus ní chailleann sé ach corrbhileog agus bíonn sé glas chuile lá den bhliain.

**TRANSLATION:**
When Jesus was fleeing from the Jews, he came to a place where an elder tree was growing. He went in under the elder tree and it spread out but it didn't save him at all. When the Jews came, they saw Jesus under the elder but he got away from them.

Then he went in under a holly tree, which was growing beside the field. The tree spread out like a house and saved him. The Jews didn't see Jesus under the holly tree. And that's why the elder is the last tree to put out its leaves and the first to lose them. As for the holly tree, it has red berries every year and it only loses an odd leaf and it's green every day of the year.

*(S30: 216–7. Máirtín Ó Ruaidhín, 63, Coill Uachtair,*
*Gaillimh. Feilméara. 21.6.1938.)*

## Scéal Cráifeach [A Religious Story] (C'b)

Aon lá amháin, bhí an Mhaighdean Mhuire ag tobar i gcoinne uisce. Tháinig aingeal chuici agus dúirt sé go mbeadh sí ina máthair ag Dia. Bhí a hathair tinn agus nuair a tháinig sí abhaile, dúirt sí go mbeadh sí ina máthair ag Dia. Dúirt a hathair léi cromadh síos agus póg a thabhairt dó agus thug. Ansin, pósadh an Mhaighdean Mhuire agus Naomh Iósaef.

Aon lá amháin, bhí siad amuigh ag siúl agus tháinig siad go dtí gort oráistí. Chuir an Mhaighdean Mhuire dúil iontu. Dúirt sí le Naomh Iósaef

iad a bhaint, ach ní bhainfeadh sé aon cheann. Tháinig gaoth mhór agus
lúb an crann anuas agus bhain sí cuid.

Aon oíche amháin, bhí brionglóid ag an Mhaighdean Mhuire faoi Íosa.
Seo é a an rud a dúirt sé,

'Labhair liom a mháthair, cén fáth t'aisling?'

'Go mbeidh tusa do do chrochadh ar chrann na Páise. Go mbeidh do
chuid fola fíor uasal dá doirteadh go láidir.'

'Is fíor sin a mháthair. Aon duine a deireann t'aisling trí huaire ag dul
chun báis, rachaidh sé go dtí na Flaithis agus Áiméan a Chríost.'

Aon uair amháin sa tseanaimsir, nuair a bhí Íosa ag rith ó na Giúdaigh,
tháinig sé chomh fada le páirc ina raibh gabhair agus caoirigh. Ansin,
chuaigh sé faoin ghabhar le dul i bhfolach ó na Giúdaigh. Thosaigh an
gabhar ag léimint agus ag screadach. Ansin, chuaigh sé faoin gcaora agus
shábháil an chaora é agus ní fhaca na Giúdaigh Íosa faoin gcaora. Agus
sin é an fáth go bhfuil brat maith olla ar an gcaora agus níl ach fionnadh
ag fás ar an ngabhar agus bíonn sé fuar chuile lá sa mbliain.

**TRANSLATION:**

One day the Blessed Virgin was at the well for water. An angel came to her
and told her she would be the mother of God. Her father was sick and when
she came home, she told him she was to be the mother of God. Her father
told her to stoop down and kiss him and she did. Then the Virgin Mary and
St Joseph got married.

One day they were out walking and they came to a field of oranges. The
Virgin Mary wanted some. She asked St Joseph to pick them but he wouldn't
pick any. A great wind came and the tree bent down and she picked a few.

One night the Virgin Mary had a dream about Jesus. This is what he said,
'Tell me mother, what do you see in your vision?'

'That you will be hanged on the Passion tree. That your noble blood will
be spilled profusely.'

'That is true mother. Anyone who recites your vision three times before
death, he'll go to Heaven and Amen Oh Christ.'

Once upon a time, long ago, when Jesus was fleeing from the Jews, he
came to a field where there were goats and sheep. Then he went in under
a goat to hide from the Jews. The goat began jumping and shouting. Then
he went under a sheep and the sheep saved him because the Jews didn't see

him in there. And that's why the sheep has a good coat of wool. The goat has only fur and it feels the cold every day of the year.

*(S30: 221–2. Máire Bean Uí Ógáin, 80, Baile Dubhlaoich, Gaillimh. Bean fheilméara. 12 Iúil 1938.)*

### Ár dTiarna agus Naomh Peadar [Our Lord and St Peter] (F)

Bhí ár dTiarna agus Naomh Peadar amuigh ag siúl an lá seo agus tháinig siad suas le fear bocht. Dúirt Naomh Peadar go mba cheart dóibh rud éicint a thabhairt dó.

'Ná bac leis,' a dúirt ár dTiarna.

Bhí siad ag imeacht leo agus tháinig siad suas chomh fada le fear eile. Bhí sé ag breathnú go maith agus bhí éadach cineál maith air. Thug ár dTiarna scilling dó agus dúirt Naomh Peadar, 'Cén fáth nár thug tú an scilling sin don bhfear bocht eile; bhí sé níos boichte ná é sin!'

'Tá go maith,' a dúirt ár dTiarna.

Bhí siad ag imeacht leo agus chuaigh Naomh Peadar isteach go dtí an siopa seo agus cé bhí istigh roimhe ann ach an fear ar thug ár dTiarna an scilling dó.

'Tóg deoch,' a dúirt sé le Naomh Peadar. 'Ní ólfadh,' a dúirt Naomh Peadar, 'nach bhfuil sé sin ag teastáil uait féin?'

'Dia a thugas agus Dia a bhéarfas,' a dúirt an fear.

D'imigh Naomh Peadar amach agus d'inis sé an rud a dúirt an fear bocht d'Íosa. D'imigh siad leo agus fuair siad an fear bocht eile caillte ar an mbóthar.

'Á,' a dúirt Naomh Peadar, 'breathnaigh ansin anois, caillte leis an ocras atá sé sin.'

'Cuir do lámh ina phóca go bhfeice tú an bhfuil sé bocht,' a dúirt ár dTiarna.

Nuair a chuir Peadar a lámh i bpóca an fhir, bhí chuile phóca acu lán d'ór.

'Caith chuile phíosa acu sin amach sa bhfarraige,' a dúirt ár dTiarna.

Ach chuir Naomh Peadar píosa den ór ina phóca féin.

'Anois,' a dúirt ár dTiarna, nuair a bhí a fhios aige gur choinnigh Naomh Peadar cuid den airgead, 'fágaim an tsaint ag na sagartaibh.'

**TRANSLATION:**

Our Lord and St Peter were out walking one day and they met a poor man. St Peter said they should give him some alms.

'Don't bother,' said Our Lord.

Off they went and they came up to another man. He was looking well and he was fairly well dressed. Our Lord gave him a shilling and St Peter said, 'Why didn't you give a shilling to the other poor man? He was poorer than this one!'

'That's alright,' said Our Lord.

They were going on and St Peter went into a shop and who was in there but the man Our Lord gave the shilling to.

'Take a drink,' said he to St Peter. 'I won't,' said St Peter. 'Won't you need that money yourself?'

'God gave and God will give,' said the man.

St Peter went out and told Jesus what the poor man had said. On they went and found the other poor man dead on the road.

'Ah,' said St Peter, 'Look at that now, that poor man is dead with the hunger.'

'Put your hand in his pocket and see if he is poor,' said Our Lord.

Then Peter put his hand in the man's pockets. Every pocket was full of gold.

'Throw every piece of that out into the sea,' said Our Lord.

But St Peter put a piece of the gold in his own pocket.

'Now,' said Our Lord when he knew that Peter kept some gold for himself, 'I ordain that the priests will be forever greedy!'

*(S30: 293–4. Fuarthas an scéal seo ó Doiminic ÓFaodhagáin, 58, Freeport. Feilméara. 26 Aibreán 1938.)*

# ANIMAL STORIES

## *The Goat and the Wolf (O'm B)*

Once upon a time there was a goat and she had four kids. They lived happily in a little cabin away in the middle of the wood. One day the mother goat went to the town, bidding the four kids to stay until she came back and if anyone came not to let him in. She was long gone when a wolf came to the door of the cabin, rattling with his paws to let him in. The little kids asked, 'Who's there?' 'Your mother,' replied the wolf. The kids rushed to the door in excitement to welcome their mother. But when they opened the door, in jumps the wolf and killed three of the kids and swallowed them up. The fourth little kid hid under a big box and the wolf didn't kill him. Then the wolf sneaked away and he wasn't long until he got very tired and lay down to sleep at the edge of a well.

When the mother came home, the little kid told her the whole story. The mother was very upset and she took a knife and went in search of the wolf. She was going along and she came to the well and finding the wolf there fast asleep, opened him up with the knife and found her three kids inside. She got big heavy stones and packed them into the wolf and sewed him up again. Then they went home and they were watchful of wolves from that out.

After a time the wolf got up, having slept enough. He felt very heavy and he was very sorry for eating those kids at all. He got very thirsty and went into the well to get a drink. When he was going down he fell into the well and got drowned. And that was the end of this cruel wolf.

*(S32: 395–6. Written down by Micheál Ó Seachnasaigh. Story told by Mrs Shaughnessy, Glenascaul, Oranmore. She heard the story from her mother.)*

### Scéal an Mhadaidh Rua [The Story of the Fox] (C'b)

Bhí trí mhadadh ar bhruach an locha lá. Bhí siad deallruithe leis an ocras. Siad na trí mhadadh a bhí ann ná an madadh allaidh, an madadh uisce agus an madadh rua. Bhí siad ina suí ansin go ceann tamaill ag faire go mbeadh iasc ar fáil acu. Níor fhéad siad aon iasc a fháil. Ansin bhuail plean ar an madadh rua agus dúirt sé na trí dhrioball a chur san uisce agus chuir siad na trí dhrioball san uisce. I gceann tamaill, thóg an madadh rua a dhrioball as an uisce agus chroith sé é. Ansin chuir sé síos arís é agus dúirt sé leis na madaidh eile gan a ndrioball a chorraí go mbaineadh an t-iasc greim astu. Ansin thóg sé aníos arís a dhrioball féin agus dúirt sé an rud céanna arís leo. Ansin chuir sé síos arís ann é. I gceann tamaill, thóg sé aníos arís as é agus shuigh sé ar bhruach an locha. D'fhan an dá mhadadh san uisce. Tháinig an mhaidin agus bhí leac oighir ar an uisce. Bhí an dá dhrioball greamaithe don leac oighir. Bhí siad ag tarraingt agus ag tarraingt gur fhágadar leath a ndriobaill san uisce agus sin é an fáth go bhfuil drioball fada ar an madadh rua agus dhá dhrioball gearra ar an dá mhadadh eile.

**TRANSLATION:**

One day, there were three dogs on the bank of a lough. They were starving with hunger. These are the three dogs that were there: the wild dog, the water dog (otter) and the red dog (fox). They sat there for a while to see if they might get a fish, but they couldn't. Then the fox hit on a plan and he said they should lower their tails into the water. After a while, the fox lifted his tail out and shook it. Then he lowered it in again and told the others not to move their tails until they'd feel a fish biting. He lifted his tail again and said the same thing to the others. He put his tail back in. After a while, he lifted it out again and sat on the side of the lough. The other two stayed in the water. When morning came, there was as sheet of ice on the lough. The two tails were stuck fast in the ice. The two were pulling and pulling until they left half their tails in the water. And that's why the fox has a long tail and the others have short tails.

*(S30: 166–7. Máirtín Ó Ruaidhín, 63, Coill Uachtair, Gaillimh. Feilméara.*
*Fuair sé an scéal seo óna athair 30 bliain ó shin. 7 Nollaig 1938.)*

## *An Easóg agus An Luch Mhór [The Stoat and the Rat] (C'b)*

Bhí easóg agus luch mhór ag troid lá amháin. Bhí siad ag troid ansin go dtáinig fear ag breathnú orthu agus chonaic sé go raibh an luch mhór ag gnóthachtáil. Shíl sé cuidiú leis an easóg. Chuaigh sé taobh thiar den luch agus shíl sé cic a thabhairt dó ach rug an luch ar a mhéar agus ghortaigh sé é. Ansin stop an troid agus chuaigh an fear abhaile. Bliain ina dhiaidh sin, d'éirigh an mhéar an-tinn. Bhí an fear ag dul chuig dochtúirí ach níor fhéad siad aon mhaith a dhéanamh dó. Bhí sé ina shuí lá amháin ar an teallach agus a chos sínte amach uaidh. Tháinig an easóg isteach agus bileog ina béal aici. D'fhág sí an bhileog ar an méar thinn agus tháinig biseach uirthi.

**TRANSLATION:**

One day a stoat and a rat were fighting. They were fighting away until a man came along to look at them and saw the rat was winning. He thought to help the stoat. He went behind the rat and tried to give it a kick, but the rat caught his toe and hurt it. The fight stopped then and the man went home. A year later, the toe got very sore. The man went to many doctors but they couldn't do anything for him. One day, he was sitting by the fire with his foot stretched out in front of him. In came the stoat with a leaf in her mouth. She placed the leaf on the sore toe and it got better.

*(S30: 175. Micheál Ó Catháin, 55, Ceathrú an Bhrúnaigh. Feilméara. 26 Eanáir 1938.)*

# HUMOROUS STORIES

## *A Foolish Wife (O'm B)*

There was a man one time and he got married. One day he said to his wife there was a stocking of gold under the bed and he was keeping it for the grey sweep of spring. 'All right,' said Mary, his wife. The man went off to work in the morning. During the day, an old man came in looking for charity. He had a long grey beard and he sat down in the chair. Mary said, 'Are you the grey sweep of spring?' and the poor man didn't know what to say. And Mary said to him again, 'Are you the grey sweep of spring, because if you are my husband has something good for you?' 'That's what they call me, whatever,' said the man. And she went over to the room and brought out the stocking of gold and gave it to the man. And he went off and he wouldn't look behind him because he was in such a hurry.

When the man of the house came home, Mary said to him, 'Musha, do you know who was here today?' 'I don't,' says he. 'The grey sweep of spring, and faith,' said she, 'I gave him the stocking of gold.' 'You did!' says the man. 'I did,' said Mary. 'Musha, God help us,' said he. 'I have nothing now, but a grain of wholemeal ground the other day.'

The man went to work next day and when he was gone, Mary brought out the caiscein [*caiscín* – kiln-dried grain] to winnow it. She brought out the sheet and according as she was winnowing, it was going with the wind. And she came in to eat her dinner. When she came out, it was all gone. When the man came home at night, she said to him, 'I brought out the caiscein today to winnow it and I came in to eat my dinner. I wasn't ten minutes with all the clocks in the world and when I came out, it was all gone with the wind.' 'Musha, God help us,' said he, 'I have nothing now but a pig and I must kill it to grease the bit of cabbage that's in the garden.'

He killed the pig and salted it and when he was going to work next day, Mary went and got the meat and she left a bit on every head of cabbage that was in the garden. When the man came home at night, he ate his supper and went to bed. After a while, they heard the dogs barking and shouting. 'What brought the dogs around?' says he. 'Maybe 'tis eating the meat they are,' says Mary. 'What meat?' says he.' 'The meat,' says she, 'that was there in the tub and I brought it out to grease the cabbage.' 'Musha, God help us,' says the man and he said he would not stay there anymore.

So he went out and Mary went after him. He was so vexed he told her to pull the door after her. They were going along and she was pulling the door after her. At last, they came to a wood and Mary said to him that she saw a tree and that she would climb it, and Mary brought the door after her. After a while, a crowd of robbers came and they were after robbing a big castle. They came and seated themselves under the tree and they began counting the money.

Mary said to her husband, 'Will I let down the door on top of them?' 'Take care would you,' says he, and she said she would. So she let down the door and the robbers thought the sky had fallen on top of them. They ran for their lives and Mary and her husband came down off the tree. They gathered up the money and they went home and lived happily ever after.

*(S32: 456–8. Taken down by Páraic Ó Mogháin from his mother.)*


### Leaba Chluimhrí [A Feather Bed] (F)

Aon uair amháin casadh beirt fhear le chéile. Fear beathach agus fear tanaí a bhí iontu. Bhíodar ag siúl go dtáinigeadar go Bóthar na Sceiche. D'fhiafraigh an fear tanaí den bhfear eile cén sórt leaba a gcodlaíonn sé air. Dúirt seisean 'ar leaba chluimhrí'. Chuaigh an fear beathach abhaile agus d'fhan an fear eile ag siúl thart agus chonaic sé cleite. Thóg sé suas an cleite agus chuir sé ina phóca é. Nuair a chuaigh sé abhaile, chuir sé an cleite i dtaisce go dtí am codlata. Thóg sé síos an cleite agus leag ar an talamh é agus luigh sé siar air. Shíl sé go gcodlódh sé go sámh go maidin.

D'éirigh sé ar a sé a chlog agus ní raibh cnámh ann nach raibh pian ann. Dúirt sé, 'Go bhfóire Dia ar an bhfear a bhfuil na céadta faoi!'

**TRANSLATION:**

Once upon a time two men met. One was a fat man and the other was thin. They were walking until they came to Bush Road. The thin man asked the other what sort of bed he slept on. He said, 'on a feather bed.' The fat man went home and the other walked on and he found a feather. He picked it up and put it in his pocket. When he went home, he put the feather away safely till bed time. Then he took it down and laid it on the ground. He thought he would sleep soundly till morning.

He got up at six o'clock and he hadn't one bone in his body that wasn't sore. He said, 'May God help the man who has hundreds of those feathers under him!'

*(S30: 265–6. Fuarthas an scéal seo ó Mhicheál Ó Cruadhlaoich, 48, Foramoile. Feilméara. 14 Nollaig 1937.)*

### An Mac Críonna [The Wise Son] (F)

Bhí fear ann aon uair amháin agus rinne sé a chroí díchill ar a mhac éirí go luath ar maidin. Theip air sin a dhéanamh. Ní raibh an mac sásta bheith ina shuí roimh an mheán lae lá ar bith.

D'inis an t-athair scéal dá mhac agus shíl sé go ndéanfadh sin cúis.

'Fear áirithe,' a deir sé, 'a d'éirigh go moch lá amháin, chuaigh sé amach agus fuair sé sparán a raibh a lán airgid ann.'

D'fhreagair an mac é agus dúirt, 'An fear a fuair an sparán sin, ní raibh sé ina shuí chomh luath leis an té a chaill é!'

**TRANSLATION:**

Once upon a time there was a man and he did his very best to get his son to get up early in the morning. He failed completely. The son wouldn't get up any day before midday.

The father told his son a story that he thought would change him.

'There was a man,' he said, 'who got up early one day and he found a purse with a lot of money in it.'

The son answered, 'The man who found that purse wasn't up as early as the person who lost it!'

*(S30: 255–6. Fuarthas an scéal seo ó Doiminic Ó Faodhagán, 44, Freeport, Bearna, Gaillimh. Feilméara. 25 Samhain 1937.)*

## Ag Léamh [Reading] (F)

Bhí beirt fhear i dtraein lá amháin. Bhí páipéar nuachta ag duine acu, agus bhí sé á léamh. Nuair a bhí sé réidh leis thug sé don fhear eile é. Tharla nach raibh aon fhoghlaim ag an bhfear bocht. Thiompaigh sé an páipéar bun os cionn agus thosaigh sé ag breathnú air.

Dúirt an fear leis, 'Dá dtiompófá an taobh eile é, bheifeá in ann é a léamh níos fearr.' 'Ó,' arsa mo dhuine. 'Nach mbeadh duine ar bith in ann é a léamh mar sin?'

**TRANSLATION:**

One day there were two men in a train. One of them had a newspaper and he was reading it. When he had finished with it, he gave it to the other man. The other poor man had no education. He turned the paper upside down and began to look at it.

The first man said to him, 'If you were to turn it up the other way, you'd be able to read it better.' 'Oh,' said the second, 'Wouldn't anyone be able to read it like that?'

*(S30: 259. Bailíodh an scéal seo ó Mháire Ní Íarnáin, 45, Foramoile, Bearna, Gaillimh.)*

## Madadh Dílis [A Loyal Dog] (F)

Bhí fear ann agus bhí sé ar a bhealach go Gaillimh. Thit an oíche air agus chuaigh sé isteach i dteach ósta le haghaidh lóistín na hoíche. Teach é seo a mbíodh go leor daoine ag fanacht ann nuair a bhíodh siad ar a mbealach go Gaillimh. Chuir sé an capall sa stábla. Bhí sé féin

197

ag fáil réidh le dul a chodladh. Bhí madadh aige sa mbaile agus d'imigh sé uaidh. Nuair a chuaigh sé isteach sa seomra bhí an madadh ansin roimhe. Nuair a bhí sé réidh le dul isteach sa leaba, léim an madadh isteach roimhe.

Sórt leapa é seo a bhí os cionn abhann agus nuair a théadh daoine isteach inti chasadh sí thart timpeall agus bháití iad san abhainn. Nuair a chuaigh an madadh isteach san leaba, chas sí thart agus thit an madadh isteach san abhainn ach léim sé aníos arís. Nuair a chonaic an fear seo, chuir sé air a chuid éadaí agus chuaigh sé síos go dtí an chistineach. Nuair a chuala fear an tí é, d'iarr sé air céard a bhí air. Dúirt an fear go raibh sé ag dul ag breathnú ar a chapall. Chuaigh sé abhaile agus d'inis sé an scéal do na daoine eile agus ní dheachaigh aoinne ann níos mó.

**TRANSLATION:**

One time a man was on his way to Galway. Night fell and he went into a hotel for a night's lodging. This was a house plenty of people used to stay in when they were on their way to Galway. He put his horse in the stable. Then he got ready for bed. He had a dog at home that had run away. When he went into the bedroom, the dog was there, waiting for him. Just as he was ready to get into bed, the dog jumped in before him.

This bed was fixed above a river and when someone would get in, it'd turn over and they'd be drowned in the river. When the dog got into the bed, it turned over and the dog fell into the river. It jumped out again and when the man saw this he put on his clothes and went down to the kitchen. When the man of the house heard him, he asked what was wrong. He said he had to go out to look at his horse. He went home and told the story to everyone else. No one ever went to that house again.

*(S30: 305. Fuarthas an scéal seo ó Mháirtín Ó Fáthartaigh, 60, Baile Móinín. Feilméara. 17 Bealtaine 1938.)*

### Turas Traenach [A Train Journey] (NB)

Aon lá amháin bhí an traein ag dul ón gClochán go Gaillimh. Bhí bean uasal ar an dtraein agus tháinig fear tuaithe isteach. Thosaigh an fear ag caitheamh toit agus ní raibh an bhean sásta.

Bhí madadh beag ag an mbean uasal. Cúpla nóiméad isteach sa turas, rug an bhean ar an bpíopa agus chaith sí amach ar an bhfuinneog é.

Rug an fear ar an madadh beag ansin agus chaith sé eisean amach ar an bhfuinneog freisin. Tháinig an traein go stáisiún na Gaillimhe. Bhí na daoine amuigh ar an ardán agus thosaigh siad ag gáire nuair a chonaic siad an madadh beag ar thosach na traenach agus an píopa ina bhéal aige!

**TRANSLATION:**

One day the train was going from Clifden to Galway. There was a rich lady on the train and a country man came on board. The man began smoking his pipe and the lady was cross.

The lady had a little dog. A couple of minutes into the journey, she grabbed the pipe and threw it out the window.

The man grabbed the dog and threw it out the window too. The train came in to Galway. The people waiting on the platform began to laugh when they saw the little dog on the front of the train and a pipe in his mouth!

*(S31: 28. Pádraig Ó Dochartaigh. Fuair mé an scéal seo ó*
*Phádraig Ó Briain, An Cladach, Gaillimh.)*

## An Tarbh agus an Bád [The Bull and the Boat] (NB)

Bhí fear ina chónaí i gConamara agus bhí bád aige. Lá amháin bhí sé ag dul amach ag iascaireacht agus nuair a tháinig sé ar ais leag sé an bád in aice na páirce. Bhí tarbh mór crosta ins an bpáirc agus bhí sé ag ithe féir. Bhí an bád ceangailte le rópa féir agus fuair an tarbh boladh an rópa féir.

Chuaigh an tarbh síos go dtí an bád agus d'ith sé an rópa féir. Ansin, chuaigh sé isteach in san mbád agus d'ith sé an méid a bhí istigh in san mbád freisin.

Chuaigh an bád amach leis an taoide. Tháinig na fir amach ansin agus chuaigh siad ag argóint. An fear a raibh an tarbh aige, dúirt sé gur ghoid an bád an tarbh. Dúirt an fear a raibh an bád aige gur ghoid an tarbh an bád. Chuaigh siad go teach na cúirte agus socraíodh an cás eatarthu ansin.

**TRANSLATION:**

There was a man living in Connemara and he had a boat. One day he was out fishing and when he came back home he left the boat beside a field. There was a big cross bull in the field and it was eating grass. The boat was tied up with a grass rope and the bull smelled the grass.

The bull went down to the boat and ate the grass rope. Then it went into the boat and ate everything that was in it.

The boat went out with the tide. When the men came out, they started to argue. The man who owned the bull said the boat had stolen the bull. The man who owned the boat said the bull had stolen the boat. They went to court and the case was settled between them.

*(S31: 29. Máirtín Mac Cóiligh. Fuair mé an scéal seo ó*
*Phádraig Ó Laoidh, An Cladach, Gaillimh.)*

# 5

# PRAYERS, POEMS, PROVERBS AND RIDDLES

Eggs and rashers/ For the Castlegar slashers,/
Hay and oats/ For the Cloonacauneen goats.

After they had ceased using it as the vernacular every day, it has been noted that people often retained the Irish language in intimate areas of life, such as prayers, and sometimes in shorter, more structured artistic expression, such as poetry, song, proverbs and riddles. This trend holds true here in the Galway material too. In the folk prayers, language performs an almost ritualistic role – it will not change as fast as in normal speech events. God continues to speak Irish, it seems, when others have had to change to English.

One of the pupils notes that the old people had a prayer for every occasion, whether rising in the morning, milking the cow or seeing the first star. Many of these prayers were not part of 'official' religious practice. They were transmitted orally and tied to specific contexts. Because of that oral transmission, they show slight textual variation, from person to person and from place to place. They take us right to the heart of people's faith and piety, expressing their sense of gratitude for every blessing they encountered.

In local folk poetry and song, we find a kind of metrical and musical chronicle of the important events and people in a particular place. So it is with the amusing rhymes here from Castlegar parish. I have not translated the Irish language piece entitled '*An Drár*' as it is written in very idiomatic

**Shop Street, Galway, *c.* 1940s.**

language whose rhythm and sense resist a literal rendering in English. It is a funny piece about a local man whose undergarments have been stolen and his attempts to retrieve them. I have included it so that it will not be lost and will instead be remembered as part of the canon of unofficial oral literature in this area.

Every day, people's ordinary speech interactions are peppered with short, structured, creative linguistic items such as proverbs, tongue-twisters, riddles and sayings. In the proverbs and sayings, we see people using language imaginatively to look at the common happenings and problems which affect them. In each proverb, linguistic playfulness is combined with moral training and a philosophical perspective on life. Proverbs reflect the received wisdom of the community on many issues, big and small. Riddles and tongue twisters were very popular, especially with children, allowing them to use language playfully to test and sharpen

202

their wits. All is not as it seems, the riddle teaches. Akin to poetry, riddles illustrate that there are many ways of perceiving the same thing. The Irish-language expression for solving a riddle is, '*Tomhas a fhuascailt*', literally 'To liberate a riddle'. The riddle in turn liberates language, meaning and imagination each time it is posed.

Everything in this chapter celebrates the gift of language, for spiritual, educational and creative purposes, in what was a largely oral culture.

# FOLK PRAYERS

## *Paidreacha [Prayers] (N's)*

Bhíodh paidreacha le haghaidh gach ócáide ag na seandaoine.

1. Tar éis dúiseacht dóibh deiridís, 'Mar a thug Tú slán ón oíche sinn, go dtuga Tú slán ón lá muid.'

2. Nuair a bhíodh siad ag coigilt na tine, deiridís, 'Coiglímse an tine seo mar a choiglíos Críost cách – Bríd ina bun, Muire ina barr, cumhdaigh an tigh agus daoine go lá.'

3. Ag dul thar reilig dóibh, deiridís, 'Beannacht Dé le hanamacha na marbh.'

4. Nuair a bhíodh duine ag baint a chuid éadaí de, deireadh sé,
'Mo Thiarna Íosa a nochtaíodh de do chuid éadaí d'fhonn Thú a sciúrsáil ó mo pheacaí go léir,
Mo chroí ar do lámha a Thiarna ós Tú is fearr a cheannaigh sinn,
Cuirim cime m'anama ort a Rí na Cathrach Naofa,
Luím ar mo leaba mar luím ar an uaigh,
Déanaim m'fhaoistin go crua leat a Dhia,
Cros Dé fúm,
Cros Dé os mo chionn,
Cros an Athar ar an leaba ar a luím,
Agus braon na ngrás ar lár mo chroí agam
a thógfas ceo agus smúid na bpeacaí díom.'

5. Nuair a bíos duine ag cóiriú leapa, deireadh sé,
'Cóirímid leaba bheag luachra anseo,
In ainm an Athar, in ainm na hoíche a rugadh É,
In ainm Síol Éabha agus Ádhaimh,

**Convent of Mercy.**

In ainm a bhfuil d'ainglí i bhFlaitheas na ngrás,
I t'ainm féin a mhuirnín.'

6. Nuair a fheiceann duine an chéad réalt sa tráthnóna, deireadh sé,
'Míle buíochas do Dhia le haghaidh an chéad réalt anocht.'

**TRANSLATION:**

The old people used to have prayers for every occasion.

1. After waking up, they'd say, 'As You brought us safely through the night, may You bring us safely through the day.'

2. When they were banking the fire, they'd say, 'I bank this fire as Christ preserves us all – Brigid at its foot, Mary at its top; preserve the house and all the inhabitants till morning.'

3. Going past a graveyard, they'd say, 'God's blessing on the souls of the dead.'

4. When a person is undressing, he says:
   'My Lord Jesus who was undressed to be scourged for all my sins,
   My heart in your hand Lord, since it's you who redeemed us,
   I imprison my soul in you, King of the holy city;
   I lie on my bed as I lie on the grave,
   I confess my sins most earnestly God,
   The cross of God under me,
   The cross of God over me,
   The Father's cross on the bed where I lie
   And the drop of grace in my heart
   To take the mist and cloud of sin from me.'

5. When a person is making up a bed, he'd say:
   'I fix up this little rushy bed tonight,
   In the name of the Father, in the name of the night He was born,
   In the name of all Adam and Eve's children,
   In the name of all the angels in Paradise,
   In your name my dear Lord.'

6. When a person sees the first star in the evening, he'd say:
   'A thousand thanks to God for the first star tonight.'

*(S31: 20–1. An tSr. M. Colmán. Stiofán Ó Briain, 62,*
*Ceathrú an Bhrúnaigh, do thug an t-eolas seo uaidh.)*


### Paidreacha [Prayers] (NB)

Tá paidreacha mar seo ag na seandaoine: nuair a thagann duine isteach i dteach, deireann sé, 'Bail ó Dhia oraibh go léir.' Nuair a imíonn duine, deirtear leis, 'Go ngearraí do bhóthar leat.'

Ar éirí ar maidin, deirtear, 'Go dtabhraí Dia saor sinn tríd an lá.' Nuair a chuireann duine isteach ar dhuine eile atá ag obair, deireann sé, 'Bail ó Dhia ar an obair.' Nuair a bhíonn duine ag sraothairt, deirtear, 'Dia linn.' Bíonn beannachtaí i mbéalaibh na ndaoine i gcónaí. Nuair a bhíonn duine ag dul abhaile tar éis bheith ag caint le duine eile, deireann sé, 'Slán leat,' agus freagraíonn an duine eile, 'Slán leat go deo.'

**TRANSLATION:**

The old people have these prayers. When a person comes into a house, he says, 'May God bless you all.' When he is leaving, they say to him, 'May your road be shortened for you.'

Getting up in the morning, 'May God take us safely through this day.' When someone meets another person who is working, he says, 'God bless the work.' When a person sneezes, they say, 'God be with us.' There are always blessings on the people's lips. When someone is going home after talking to another person, he says, 'May you go safely.' The other person answers, 'May you go safely always.'

*(S31: 142-4. Patrick Doyle. Seanchas ó Mr Ó Neachtáin,*
*Scoil na mBuachaillí, An Cladach. 12 Bealtaine 1938.)*


## Ofráil na Maidine [Morning Offering] (NB)

Moladh go deo leat a Mhic Dé,
Thugais saor ón oíche mé;
A Mhuire Mháthair iarr ar do mhac
Go mbeidh bealach mo leasa gan bac.

**TRANSLATION:**

Every praise to you, Son of God,
You brought me safely from night;
Mother Mary, implore your son
That the way be safe before me.

*(S31: 142-4. Patrick Doyle. Seanchas ó Mr Ó Neachtáin,*
*Scoil na mBuachaillí, An Cladach. 9 Bealtaine 1938.)*


## Seanphaidir [Old Prayer] (NB)

I kiss the wounds of Thy Sacred hands,
With sorrow deep and true;
May every move of my hands today,
Be a million acts of love to You.

I kiss the wounds of Thy Sacred Feet,
With sorrow deep and true;
May every step I walk today,
Be a million acts of love to you.

I kiss the wounds of Thy Sacred Head,
With sorrow deep and true;
May every thought of mine today,
Be a million acts of love to you.

I kiss the wounds of Thy Sacred Heart,
With sorrow deep and true;
May every beat of my heart today,
Be a million acts of love to you.

*(S31: 142-4. Patrick Doyle. Seanchas ó Mr Ó Neachtáin,*
*Scoil na mBuachaillí, An Cladach. 12 Bealtaine 1938.)*

# RHYMES

### *Rhymes of Castlegar Parish (C'g)*

Eggs and rashers
For the Castlegar slashers,
Hay and oats
For the Cloonacauneen goats.
The scrapings of the pan
For the Loughthavarna clann.

One fine day in the middle of June,
They brought me to town to christen me soon,
'What name will we call him?'
said Fr Mulloy,
'We'll call him brave Paddy,
the Castlegar boy.'

There was a man who sowed a garden full of seed;
When the seed began to grow
like a garden full of snow,
When the snow began to melt
Like a bucket and a belt,
When the belt began to break
Like a ship upon the lake,
When the ship began to fly
Like a needle in the sky,
When the sky began to fall,
Lord have mercy on us all.

If you're livin' in Ireland,
If you're livin' in France,
If you're livin' at all,
Come to the Ballindooly dance.
Celia Fahy plays the pipes,
Stephen Ward says, 'Phat's that?'
Norah Hogan says, 'A stack of rats!'

They went to Hull
To hurl John Bull,
To hurl him in his lawn;
'Don't fret my men,
They won't get in,'
said the men of Castlegar.

Davy Phair was very fair,
As fair as fair could be;
Davy Phair didn't act so fair,
At the last fair day
With me.

One fine day in the middle of the night,
Two dead men got up to fight,
Two blind men were looking on,

Two cripples went for the guards,
And two dumb men told them to hurry on.

Two Mile Ditch is all rich –
The boxes are locked,
The men are gone to the bog,
The hens are clocking,
And they cannot lay.

Tom Dan, the wise old man,
Stole a pig and away he ran,
The peelers caught him by the tail,
And sent him in to Galway jail.

One for a jockey,
Two for a pair,
God bless the jockey,
And off with the mare.

If you don't venture,
You won't win;
If you don't search,
You won't marry
And then you'll be sorry.

Master Mick is a very good man,
He tries to teach us all he can,
He teaches us how
To read and write
And do arithmetic.
But he never forgets
To give us the stick.

*(S30: 20–6. Nóra Bhreathnach, Caisleán Gearr.*
*Ó Sheán Ó hEidhín, 40, Caisleán Gearr, Gaillimh.)*

### An Drár (C'b)

An té a thug mo dhrár uaim,
Go gcrapuighe Dia a lámhaí,
Go gcaille sé a mheabhair agus a amharc,
Go dtaga rud eile air,
A chuirfeas chun báis é,
Is measa naoi n-uaire ná an colar.
Thug sé mo dhrár uaim,
Ag teacht dhom ón táilliúir,
Bhí fuaite go dúthrachtach daingean.
Caithfidh mé gluaiseacht anois ar a thóraíocht,
Agus ní rí-mhaith an t-eolas atá agam,
Go dté mé go Dubhros agus go híochtar an chondae,
Go Tobar Rí an Domhnaigh agus Balla,
Síos go Cnoc Néifinn agus a bhí uaigneach,
Nó gur thóg mé mo lóistín ins an gCarra,
Chaith mé cúig oíche i dteach geanúil Ó Maora,
Agus ag súil le bean óg ann a mhealladh,
Chruinnigh daoine agus confairt (ceannfoirt?) na tíre
Agus fuair mé ruaigeadh Sheáin Bhradaigh
Thart Droichead an Chláirín agus Cinn Mhara taobh thall de
Chuartód thart timpeall go Gaillimh
Siar Uachtar Ard fad is thabharfadh an lá mé
Cuartóidh mé Dinndur agus Camus -
Ach is ag Prompán Coill Sáile sea fuair mé romham faisnéis
Gur rógaire mná a thug chun bealaigh é
Bhéarfadh sí ar an gcaora ba bhradaigh san oíche
Agus ghoidfeadh sí an ghé agus an lacha,
Dheamhan sin tuar éadaigh as seo go Binn Éadair
Nár mhian léi cuid de a chaitheamh.
Chaith sí cúig lá ag goid uibheacha áil
Ach bhí a fhios agam féin nuair a bhéarfaí uirthi i ngéibheann
Go n-íocfadh sí gé bheite bhacach
Do chara agus do chuimhne, ná tabhair m'ainm síos leis.
Bhéarfaidh mé drár duit chomh maith leis
Ní tharraingeofar caol é agus beidh sé roinnt saolach

Mar tá fabhar na bhfígheadóirí agam
Cuir luach a dhéanta ina bhásta istigh fillte
Sin agus déan é go tapaidh agus tabharfaidh muid suas é go Seán Bacach
Ó Luaighairí
Mar is aige a bhí an seanchas fada
Chuala mé an Sairgint dá léamh sa bpáipéar
Go mbeadh margaidh mhóra anseo feasta
Go n-osclós an pánn atá thiar ag Coill Sáile
Atá dúnta suas le fada.
Tá an grafaíre agus an cábla ann
Tá mo dhrár ann agus is iomaí sin drár ann chomh maith leis
Ach coinnígí airdeall uirthi ag teacht na féile Pádraic
Goidfidh sí báinín feasta ach go dtige lá an tsléibhe
Gheobhaidh mé scéal go cé thug mo dhrár uaim chun bealaigh
Beidh na táinte agus céadta ag cruinniú fré chéile
Agus gach aon duine ar scanradh dá anam,
Tiocfaidh Mac Dé ag tabhairt breith ar an méid sin
Agus piocfaidh sé féin a chuid astu -
Nach ciotach an scéal é ag an mbean a thug mo dhrár uaim,
Cuirfear i ngéibheann í agus cuirfear glas uirthi.

*(S30: 237–9. Seán Ó Beaglach, 80, Coill Uachtair, Gort an Chalaidh, Gaillimh. Feilméara. 26 Iúil 1938.)*

## An Leipreachán [The Leprechaun] (P)

Leipreachán a chuaigh ar strae,
Is bhí sé amuigh i rith an lae,
Gan brúinín aráin ná cupán tae,
Is é a bhí go brónach.
Cé thiocfadh air is é ina luí
Go tuirseach tinn gan aon chorraí,
Ach buachaill beag a ghabh an tslí
Is thug dó bia a dhóthain.
D'ól sé tae is d'ith sé arán,
Is nuair a bhí a bhoilgín lán

211

D'fhág sé ag an ngasúr slán
Is thug sé corcán óir dó.

**TRANSLATION:**

A leprechaun who went astray,
And he was out all during the day,
Not even a crust to eat or a cup of tay,
and he was the sorry fellow.
Who should find him lying there,
Tired and sick, not moving a limb,
But a small boy who passed that way,
who filled him up with food.
He drank the tay and ate the bread,
and when his belly was full,
to the boy farewell he bade
and gave him a crock of gold.

*(S30: 456–7. Mairéad Ní Chomáin, 11, Cinn Uisce, Baile Cláir.*
*Fuaireas an scéal seo ó mo mháthair Sorcha Uí Chomáin.)*

# TOUNGE-TWISTER

### *An Dá Thadhg [The Two Tadhgs] (M)*

Bhí an dá Thadhg in aghaidh a chéile:
Do bhuail Tadhg Tadhg,
Is do bhuail Tadhg é;
Dá maródh Tadhg Tadhg,
Is murach gur mharaigh Tadhg Tadhg,
Do mharódh Tadhg é.

**TRANSLATION:**

The two Tadhgs were fighting:
Tadhg hit Tadhg,
And Tadhg hit him back;
If Tadhg had killed Tadhg,

Menlo school picture from the early 1920s.

And if Tadhg hadn't killed Tadhg,
Tadhg would have killed him.

*(S30: 127. No name.)*

# RIDDLES

### Tomhaiseannaí [Riddles] (B)

1. Luíonn sí go híseal, éiríonn sí go hard. Caitheann sí bróga ach níl aon bhróga aici? Liathróid.
2. Céard a fhásfas síos? Ruball.
3. Mo sheandeaide bocht agus a mhaide fána ucht agus é ag ól deoch i dtobar na féasóige? An bunsop.
4. Cé mhéid cos ar ocht muilt? Péire.
5. Chaith mé suas é chomh geal le scilling agus tháinig sé anuas chomh buí le gine? Ubh.
6. Tobairín uisce i lár an bhaile, boltaí iarainn agus postaí maide? Ceaig fuiscí.

7. Chomh bán le bainne, chomh hard le balla, chomh milis le mil agus chomh dearg le fuil? ÚII.

8. Chonaic beirt é, bhain cúigear é agus chogain dhá scór é? ÚII a chonaic do dhá shúil, bhain do chúig mhéar é agus chogain do chuid fiacla é.

9. Céard a bíos ag corraí is ag corraí agus nár chorraigh ariamh as a áit? Ruball na muice.

10. Chuartaíos agus fuaireas is b'fhurasta dom sin a fháil, rud nach bhfuair Dia is nach bhfaighidh go brách? Máistir.

11. Bíonn tú ag siúl agus bíonn rud agat agus níl aon mhaith duit ann agus ní féidir leat siúl gan é? Torann.

12. Thógfainn i mo ghlaic é agus ní chuirfeadh an rí gad air? Gaineamh.

13. Chuaigh triúr fear de mhuintir oró, ag baint slat lá ceo. An tslat nár bhaineadar, thugadar leo é agus an tslat a bhaineadar d'fhágadar ina ndiaidh? Triúr éan a chuaigh ag baint cluimhrí astu féin.

14. Siúd thall ort é. Ní ball de bhaill do choirp é agus tá sé ort ina dhiaidh sin? T'ainm.

15. Cén fáth a dtéann an chearc trasna an bhóthair? Mar bíonn sí ag iarraidh dul go dtí an taobh eile.

16. Cén fáth a mbreathnaíonn an bhó thar an mhóra? Mar ní féidir léi breathnú faoi.

17. Cén chéad rud a théann isteach den bhó san mbearna? A hanáil.

18. Seo é anall tríd an abhainn é, fear na coise caoile cruaidh agus mo léan ní fhéadaim rith? An Bás.

19. Céard atá cosúil leis an leath den ghealach? An leath eile.

20. Cailleach ins an gclúid agus bior ina súil? An tlú.

21. Cailleach ar an teach agus í ag caitheamh tobac? An simléar.

22. Rud beag bídeach ar mhullach an tí agus ní féidir leis an rí breith air? An ghrian.

23. Tá dhá chruach mhónadh amuigh ansin amuigh, ceann san oíche agus ceann sa lá? An ghrian agus an ghealach.

24. Trí chosa in airde, dhá chos ar an talamh, ceann duine beo i mbéal duine mhairbh? Pota ar cheann duine.

25. Bhreathnaigh mise amach tríd fhuinneog mo dheaideo agus chonaic mé an rud marbh ag iompar an rud beo? Fear a bhí ag imeacht ar rothar.

26. Pota óir agus é lán d'fheoil bheo? Méaracán.

27. Teachtaire beag ó theach go teach agus bíonn sé amuigh ins an oíche? Cosán.

28. Cén fhaid a ritheann an coinín isteach ins an gcoill? Leath bhealaigh.

29. Cén taobh a bhfuil an lámh ar an gcupán? Ar an taobh amuigh.

30. Capaillín boáilte donn; siúlann sí Éirinn is ní fhliuchann sí cos? Beach.

31. Droichead ar loch, gan maide ná cloch? Leac oighir.

32. Chuaigh mé suas an bóithrín, tháinig mé anuas an bóithrín agus thug mé an bóithrín ar mo dhroim? Dréimire.

33. Chuaigh mé suas an bóithrín agus tháinig mé anuas an bóithrín. Thug mé rud liom nach raibh mé á iarraidh agus shuigh mé síos is chuardaigh mé é. Is dá bhfaighinn é, ní thabharfainn liom é? Dealg.

34. Chuaigh mé suas an bóithrín agus casadh mo mháthair liom. Bhí méaracán óir uirthi is fáinneachaí airgid? Gunna.

**TRANSLATION:**

1. She lies down low and rises up high. She wears (wears out) shoes but has no shoes herself? A ball.

2. What grows down? A tail.

3. My poor old grandad with his stick beneath him, taking a drink in the bearded well? The eaves.

4. How many feet on eight wethers? A pair.

5. I threw it up as white as a shilling and down it came as yellow as a guinea? An egg.

6. A little well of water in the middle of the town, an iron bolt and wooden posts? A keg of whiskey.

7. As white as milk, as high as a wall, as sweet as honey and as red as blood? An apple.

8. Two saw it, five picked it, then two score chewed it? An apple your two eyes saw, your five fingers picked and your teeth chewed.

9. What is moving and moving and never moved out of its place at all? The pig's tail.

10. I searched and I found, and it was easy to do, a thing God never got and never will? A master.

11. As you walk along you have something that's no good to you, yet you can't walk without it? Noise.

12. I could pick it up in my fist but the king couldn't tie it? Sand.

13. Three men oró went cutting sticks one day. The stick they didn't pick, they took with them, and the stick they did pick they left behind them? Three birds picking their feathers.
14. It's on you. It's not one of your body parts but still it's on you? Your name.
15. Why does the hen cross the road? To get to the other side.
16. Why does the cow look over the hill? Because she can't look under it.
17. What's the first part of the cow to go into the gap? Her breath.
18. Down the river, here he comes to me, the man with the hard narrow foot, and alas I cannot run? Death.
19. What is like the half moon? The other half.
20. A hag in the corner and a pin in her eye? The tongs.
21. A hag on the house, smoking tobacco? The chimney.
22. A tiny little thing on top of the house and the king couldn't touch it? The sun.
23. Two stacks of turf out there, one at night and one in the day? The sun and the moon.
24. Three feet in the air, two feet on the ground, the head of a living person in the mouth of a dead one? A three-legged pot on a person's head.
25. I looked through my grandad's window and saw a dead thing carrying a living one? A man riding a bicycle.
26. A golden pot full of living flesh? A thimble.
27. A little messenger from house to house and it stays out at night? A path.
28. How far does the rabbit run into the wood? Halfway.
29. Which side on a cup is the handle on? On the outside.
30. A little striped horse; she travels the whole of Ireland and never wets her foot? A bee.
31. Bridge on a lough, without wood or stone? A sheet of ice.
32. I went up the road, I came down the road, then I took the road on my back? A ladder.
33. I went up the road and I came down the road. I took something with me I didn't want. I sat down and searched for it and if I could find it I'd throw it away? A thorn.
34. I went up the road and met my mother. She had a gold thimble and silver rings? A gun.

*(S31: 227–32. Fuair mé an t-eolas seo ó m'athair a tógadh ins an gCeathrún Rua.*
*Pádraig á Bhailís, 3 Sráid an Teampaill, Gaillimh.)*

# PROVERBS

## *Seanfhocail [Proverbs] (CGC)*
1. Nuair a bhíonn an t-ól istigh bíonn an chiall amuigh.
2. Níor dhóigh an seanchat é féin riamh.
3. Is mairg a bios gan charad agus é ina luí ar leabaidh an bháis.
4. Ualach ghiolla na leisce.
5. Ní náire an bochtanas.
6. Faigheann na ba bás ag fanacht leis an bhféar ag fás.
7. An té nach gcuirfidh san earrach, ní bhainfidh sé san bhfómhar.
8. 'Sé lá na gaoithe lá na scolb, ach ní hé an lá bheith dá lorg.
9. Nuair is cruaidh don chailleach, caithfidh sí rith.
10. Nuair a chríonnas an tslat is deacair a shníomh.
11. Lá an éigin a fheictear an caraid is fearr.
12. Ba mhinic ciúin ciontach.
13. Ba mhinic comhairle mhaith ag amadán.
14. Is namhaid an cheird gan í a fhoghlaim.
15. Is fearr ag marcaíocht ar ghabhar ná coisíocht dá fheabhas.
16. Is milis fíon ach is searbh a íoc.
17. Ní bhíonn tréan buan.
18. Ná díol do chearc lá fliuch.
19. Sceitheann fíon fírinne.
20. Rud a scríobhas an púca, léann sé féin é.
21. Coinnigh an cnámh i do láimh is beidh na madraí i gcónaí ag tafann.
22. Ní lúide an trócaire í a roinnt.
23. Bia agus deoch faoi Nollaig agus éadach nua na Cásca.
24. Ní maith sagart gan cléireach is ní maith fata gan péire.

**TRANSLATION:**
1. Drink in, sense out.
2. The old cat never burned itself.
3. Pity the person who has no friend and they on their death bed.

4. The lazy person's burden.
5. Poverty is no cause for shame.
6. Cows die waiting for the grass to grow.
7. The person who doesn't sow in spring won't reap in autumn.
8. The windy day is the day for *scolbs* [briars for fixing down thatch], but not the day to look for them.
9. When the old hag is getting it hard, she must run.
10. When the rod gets old, it's difficult to bend it.
11. On the needy day you know your best friend.
12. Still waters run deep.
13. A fool often gave good advice.
14. The biggest enemy to any craft is not to learn it properly.
15. Better to ride on a goat than go on foot, however good that is.
16. Wine is sweet, paying for it is bitter.
17. Strength does not last forever.
18. Don't sell your hen on a wet day.
19. Drink sets truth free.
20. The *púca* will read what he writes himself.
21. Keep the bone in your hand and the dogs will always be barking.
22. Compassion is not lessened by sharing it.
23. Food and drink for Christmas and new clothes for Easter.
24. A priest is no good without a clerk and one potato is no good without another.

*(S32: 20–5. Máirtín Mac Giollarnath, 60, Cathair Gabhann,*
*Baile Chláir na Gaillimhe agus daoine eile.)*

# 6

# LOCAL HISTORY

Ireton came to Galway in 1652 and demanded surrender. Galway yielded
after many months. Then Ireton's soldiers entered the city. It is believed that
the soldiers came near a Poor Clare convent, and they made the nuns flee
from the convent. The nuns entered the River Corrib. The soldiers thought that
these people would die, but their cloaks spread out in the water and the nuns
were carried to safety on the opposite bank. After this incident this place was
known as Nuns' Island.

A community's sense of place and identity, their understanding of themselves as a people, is expressed in their oral history, or '*seanchas*' as it is called
in Irish. These stories provide a living link with the past. They show how
the past is remembered in the collective consciousness, demonstrating which
events were considered important and who the important people were and
what impressions they made. The process of recalling the past involves
forgetting as well as remembering. Studying oral history allows us to discern
how the past is remembered and forgotten. As well as remembering and
forgetting, there is also 'disremembering', choosing not to remember that
which is perhaps too painful to be carried along on the river of memory.
There may also be exaggeration or minimalisation in respect of certain
details of the past. Placed beside the written record, oral history provides a
fascinating insight into the whole process of remembering that which has
gone before.

A great deal of the personal, intimate, local details of the community's
everyday lives was never formally written down and recorded for posterity.
Even in the written record, it is usually only the factual information which
is preserved. We often get little or no sense of the emotional aspect of a

particular time or event. In addition, many written accounts have been provided by outsiders, be they writers, journalists or government officials. Oral history presents history 'from the inside out'. It is a more democratic history, demonstrating how the whole community was involved in the weaving of their story up until the present.

The scope of oral history ranges far and wide, holding many disparate elements side by side in a chronicle of a community's past. Unlike documentary history, oral history is not strong on the exact dating of events, but it is very strong on the locations where events are believed to have taken place. So in the stories here, there are vivid memories of hedge schools, of the great snow storm when so much snow fell that the deer were able to walk out over the wall of the Deerpark in Athy, of places where gold was supposed to be buried to hide it from incoming marauders, how folk from the Claddagh used to sail across to Renville where each person had rented a rood of land to grow potatoes.

Reference to the Great Famine of the 1840s is muted. 'The potatoes rotted in the ground' and people could not pay their rent. Traumatic events like famine are often purposely forgotten by those who suffer them, to be recalled, if at all, in a quiet, almost dispassionate, tone. But the physical landscape retains the imprint. The ridges where the potatoes rotted can still be seen in the field in Athy – dumb testimony to a great tragedy. Landlords, good and bad, are recalled too, their legacy living long after themselves.

There are happy memories of the traditional fair days, a chance to go to town, sell or buy some animals, meet one's friends and neighbours, to break the tedium of everyday toil. The Galway fair would begin at three o'clock in the morning, but it was worth the early rise and the long walk, to participate in the great stir on Fair Hill. When money was not in great supply, people exchanged and bartered their wares, a score of eggs for a pound of tea, for example. Travelling hucksters brought small items for sale to people's homes – laces, rosaries, needles and thread. The travelling people would be given food and a bed for the night when the weather was bad. That too was changing. 'There are very few beggars going around now as the government is giving them all sorts of employment,' one account tells us.

The items here give us a chance to listen to the people of Galway telling their own story up until the 1930s, as they remembered it.

# OLD SCHOOLS

## *Seanscoileanna [Old Schools] (NB)*

Dúirt mo sheanathair liom go raibh mórán difríochtaí idir na scoileanna fadó agus na scoileanna nua anois. Bhí a athair féin ag insint scéil dó faoi.

Nuair a bhí sé óg bhí scoileanna scairte ann agus bhí múinteoirí ag múineadh na bpáistí in aice sceach i bpáirc éicint. Amuigh faoin aer a bhíodh siad agus ní bhíodh suíocháin faoi na leanaí. Níor ligeadh ainm mháistir amach mar bhí luach ar a gceann. Daoine ón gceantar a bhí iontu.

Bhí scoileanna ann agus istigh i stáblaí a bhíodar. Bhí scoileanna eile ann agus bhí iachall ar gach leanbh móin a thabhairt leis chun na scoile chun tine a chur ar lasadh in san ngeimhreadh.

Bhíodh scoil ann i dtithe na bhfeilméaraí agus bhíodh máistir ina chónaí i ngach teach a mbíodh sé ag múineadh ann, ar feadh lae nó seachtaine. Ní fhaigheadh sé ach scilling nó níos lú ó na daoine.

Bhíodh mar a déarfá na trí 'Rs' (á dteagasc ann): léamh, scríobh agus 'Voster'. Bhíodh Gaeilge go flúirseach ann ach tá difríocht mhór ann anois. Ní raibh aon leabhar ag na páistí mar ní raibh aon leabhar clóbhuailte an uair sin, agus fiú dá mbeadh, bhíodar go han-bhocht. Bhíodh slinnte ag cuid acu chun scríobh orthu, agus píosaí peann luaidhe slinne chomh maith.

Bhíodh binse fada amháin ann agus bhíodh ar na páistí suí air. Ní raibh léarscáil nó cóipleabhair in sna scoileanna. Shuíodh an máistir ar 'rostrum' agus stól aige. Bhí meas mór ag na daoine ar an máistir mar ba é an t-oideachas a chabhraigh leo slí bheatha a fháil.

**TRANSLATION:**

My grandfather told me there's a great difference between schools long ago and the new schools now. His own father used to tell him about it. When he was young there were hedge schools and teachers teaching the children beside a hedge in some field. They'd be outdoors and the children wouldn't have any seats to sit on. The master's name was kept secret because there was a price on his head. The teachers would be from the locality.

Some schools took place in a stable. Others required each child to bring turf to school to light a fire in winter.

There used to be a school in the farmers' houses and the master used to stay in whichever house he'd be teaching, for a day or a week. He'd only get a shilling or less [pay] from the people.

They taught, as you might say, the three Rs: reading, writing and 'Voster' [arithmetic]. Irish was very common then but things are greatly changed now. Children had no books because there were no printed books at the time, and even if there had been, people were very poor. Some had slates to write on and bits of slate pencils as well.

There was one long bench and the children had to sit on that. There were no maps or copybooks in the schools. The master sat on a stool at a rostrum. People had great respect for the master because education helped them get a living.

*(S31: 47–8. Pádraig Ó Dubhghaill. Fuair mé an scéal seo ó*
*Éamonn Ó Dubhghaill, Na Duganna, Gaillimh.)*

## Seanscoileanna [Old Schools] (NB)

Chuir na Quakers an tseanscoil atá in san gCladach suas. Chuir siad suas í sa bhliain 1801. An duine a thug an t-eolas seo dom, dúirt sé gurbh é an chéad mháistir a bhí ann ná Máistir Quoyle. Bhí na rudaí seo dá mhúineadh ann: scríobh, léamh agus áireamh. Bhí siad ag múineadh an chaoi le bád a sheoladh. Tá sé ag an Labour Exchange anois agus tá scoil nua tógtha i gCnoc an Diolúin.

**TRANSLATION:**

The Quakers built the old school in the Claddagh. They built it in the year 1801. The person who told me this said that the first master in the school was Master Quoyle. These subjects were taught: writing, reading and arithmetic. They taught how to sail a boat. The Labour Exchange has the building now and there's a new school in Cnoc an Diolúin.

*(S31: 48–9. Máirtín de Brún. Fuair mé an t-eolas seo ó*
*mo sheanmháthair, Cnoc an Diolúin, Gaillimh.)*

## Seanscoil [An Old School] (C'b)

Bhí scoil ag crosbhóthar Bhaile an Dubhlaoich. Cáin scoile an pháighe a bhíodh acu. *Primary Reading Made Easy* agus leabhar litrithe na leabhair a bhí acu. Thugadh na scoláirí fód móna leo. Chuireadh an máistir píosa maide thart ar mhuineál na scoláirí a mbíodh agachaí ann. 'Tally' an t-ainm a bhí air. Bheadh a fhios ag an máistir lá arna mhárach dá labhródh an scoláire focal Gaeilge. Chuireadh sé scoláire suas ar dhroim scoláire eile. Thugadh sé bualadh dó. Tá sin deich mbliana agus trí fichid ó shin. Bhí scoil eile i gCnoc Mhaoil Dris agus ceann eile ar an mBóthar Mór.

**TRANSLATION:**

There was a school at Ballindooly crossroads. The teachers would get paid from a small levy on the pupils. The books they used were *Primary Reading Made Easy* and a spelling book. The pupils used to take a sod of turf to school with them. The master would put a piece of wood with notches in it round the pupils' necks. It was called a 'Tally'. Next day, the master would know if the pupils had spoken a word of Irish. He'd put a pupil up on another pupil's back and hit him. That's seventy years go. There was another school in Knockmeeldrish and another at Bothermore.

*(S30: 168–9. Peaits Ó Fáthaigh, 65, Baile an Dubhlaoich. Feilméar. 5 Eanáir 1938.)*

# BAD WEATHER/STORMS

## The Night of the Great Storm/Oíche na Gaoithe Móire (O'm B)

There is a field in Renville called *Páirc Gharbh*. On the night of the big wind, 1840, the sea came into this field and up to the houses in Renville, a distance of approximately 400 yards further than the sea has ever been known to rise since. The tide was then in *Páirc Gharbh* and it was held here by the big hill. The field was covered for a full week. Then the people opened a drain and extended the drain to *Móinfhéir Mór*. The water was thus let flow into the sea again. When the tide had gone out of *Páirc Gharbh*, the people of the parish were picking fish for a week.

The field *Páirc Gharbh* is in the Athy property. Reindeer were enclosed nearby in Deerpark. One night, shortly after the Great Storm, there was a very heavy fall of snow. The snow was so high that it reached to the top of the high wall enclosing the deer. After a time, the deer walked out over the wall and they never returned.

*(S32: 437–8. Story taken down by Donnchadh Ó Treabhar from his mother.)*


### Doineann [Bad Weather] (NB)

Sa mbliain 1896 nó mar sin, i mí na Samhna, bhí stoirm throm ann in san dtír seo. Bhios an-óg an t-am sin agus bhí eagla mhór orm roimhe.

I dtosach an lae bhí calm ann agus bhí an éanlaith mara ag teacht isteach sa tír. Bhí scamaill dhubha ag teacht anuas orainn agus bhí a fhios ag na daoine a bhí ag iascaireacht go raibh stoirm ag teacht.

D'éirigh sé go hobann agus bhí an fharraige an-gharbh, briste suas. Bhí na tonntracha móra ag léimnigh suas in san spéir agus bhí an ghaoth ag séideadh go láidir.

Bhí eagla mhór ar na hiascairí agus rinneadar ar an bport chomh tapaidh agus ab 'fhéidir leo. Chuaigh mórán bád ar na carraigreacha agus cailleadh a lán daoine. Do bhí díon na dtithe sa mbaile briste suas agus rinneadh mórán díobhála freisin.

Chuala mé mo sheanathair ag insint scéalta faoi Oíche na Gaoithe Móire. Dúirt sé go raibh tintreach agus toirneach go flúirseach ann agus bhí eagla a gcroí ar gach éinne.

Do bhí báisteach throm agus tuile ann agus rinneadh mórán díobhála do na barraí agus na tithe amuigh faoin dtuath. Bhí cuid acu leagtha go talamh. Dúirt sé go raibh beithígh agus daoine báite in sna tuilte.

Bhí scéal ann go raibh tithe ann in san áit a bhfuil an pháirc in san gCladach. Do leagadh na tithe sin agus tháinig an gaineamh isteach agus cloiseadh an gaineamh ag bualadh in aghaidh na bhfuinneog. Nuair a stad an ghaoth ag séideadh ar fad, bhí an-mhórán díobhála déanta, agus d'fhág sé sin a lán daoine bocht. Cloiseann tú na seandaoine sa mbaile ag cur síos ar an ngaoth sin go minic.

**TRANSLATION:**

In 1896, or thereabouts, in November, there was a heavy storm in this country. I was very young then and I was terrified of it.

At the beginning of the day it was calm and the sea birds were coming inland. Dark clouds were coming down on us and the people who were fishing knew that a storm was coming.

It rose suddenly and the sea was rough and choppy. Huge waves were going up in the air and the wind was very strong. The fishermen were very scared and they made for port as fast as they could. Many boats went on the rocks and a lot of people were lost. The roofs of the houses in the town were broken up and it caused a lot of damage.

I heard my grandfather telling stories about the Night of the Big Wind. He said there was a lot of thunder and lightning and everyone was terrified. There was heavy rain and flooding and a lot of damage was done to the crops and the houses out in the country. Some were completely demolished. He said that people and animals were drowned in the floods.

The story goes that there used to be houses where the park is now in the Claddagh. Those houses were knocked down and the sand came in and they could hear it hitting against the windows. When the wind stopped blowing, much damage was done, and it left a lot of people in a poor state. You often hear the old people here talking about that wind.

*(S31: 44–5. Pádraig Ó Dubhghaill. Fuair mé an scéal seo ó*
*Bhean Uí Dhubhghaill, Na Duganna, Gaillimh.)*

## Doineann [Bad Weather] (NB)

Ar 13ú Samhain 1927, bhí stoirm ag séideadh. Bhí an spéir dubh dorcha agus mar gheall air sin, bhí a fhios ag na daoine go raibh stoirm mhór ag teacht. D'éirigh an stoirm sa lá ach ní raibh sé an-mhór ar chor ar bith, ach bhí sé an-mhór in san oíche.

In san tráthnóna, chuaigh fear as an gCladach go dtí Bóthar na Trá agus chonaic sé rud in san bhfarraige agus rith sé abhaile. Maidhm mhór a bhí ann agus tháinig an fear anuas go dtí an Cladach. Bhí go leor daoine ina gcodladh ach chuaigh an fear i mbád beag agus d'oscail sé gach doras agus chuir sé na daoine in san mbád.

**In the Claddagh, where old Irish customs and language persist.** *c.* **1901.**

Níor báthadh éinne ach leagadh ceithre theach agus seacht gcrann teileagraif. An t-ainm a bhí ar an mhaidhm seo 'Maidhm Trághal'.

In san oíche a raibh an mhaidhm sin ann, bhí toirneach agus tintreach ann freisin. Bhí glór garbh láidir a raibh bagairt agus uaigneas ann le cloisteáil ón trá.

**TRANSLATION:**

On the 23 November 1927, a storm was blowing. The sky was very black and so people knew a big storm was coming. The storm began during the day but it wasn't too bad. It got very bad at night.

In the evening, a Claddagh man went to Salthill. He saw something in the sea and ran home. It was a huge wave and the man came down to the Claddagh. Many people were asleep but he went in a small boat and opened every door and put the people into the boat.

No one was drowned but four houses were knocked down and five telegraph poles. The big wave was called *'Maidhm Trághal'*.

That night when the big wave was coming in, there was thunder and lightning too. A strong rough sound, threatening and lonely, was heard from the shore.

*(S31: 46. Pádraig Ó Dochartaigh. Fuair mé an scéal seo ó*
*Phádraig Ó Cuireáin, An Cladach, Gaillimh.)*

## DROWNINGS AND SHIPWRECKS

### A Shipwreck (NB)

Long ago, there used to be a lot of big steamers coming into Galway Bay. One day, as a ship was approaching the bay, it ran into a cliff of very big, big rocks. This ship was called the *Atoinatic*.

The sailors on board worked hard to save their lives and to save the ship. After some time, the ship went down and the people on board were killing one another to save their lives.

It didn't take very long for news of this disaster to spread throughout all Connaught.

The people put a pole where the ship sank and it is called the Magrita Pole.

*(S31: 41–2. Michael Cooke. I got this from James Colleran, Fairhill Rd., Galway.)*

### Báthadh Anach Chuain [The Anach Chuain Drownings] (C'b)

Bhí daoine as Anach Chuain ag dul ar aonach Chnoc an Diolláin uair amháin i mbád. Bhí aon fhear déag agus ochtar ban ann. Bhí go leor caoirigh acu freisin. Nuair a bhí siad píosa amach, chuir ceann de na caoirigh a cois amach tríd an bhád. Sháigh duine de na mná a haprún ins an bpoll agus séard a rinne sí ná an clár a chur amach, agus chuaigh an bád síos. Báthadh a raibh ann ach bean amháin as Anach Chuain ar ar tugadh Máire Lalaigh. Bhí fear amháin ann ar ar tugadh Tomás Uí Chosgair a bhí in ann snámh go maith agus tháinig sé isteach. Ach chuaigh sé amach arís ag sábháil bean, agus chruinnigh siad ar fad thart air agus báthadh ar fad iad. Bhí na caoirigh ar fad sábháilte mar bhí siad in ann snámh.

Tá Anach Chuain seacht míle ó Ghaillimh ar an taobh thuaidh, in aice Loch Coiribe. Tá Cnoc an Diolláin ins an gCladach taobh thiar de Ghaillimh.

**TRANSLATION:**
One time people from Anach Cuain were going to the fair in *Cnoc an Diolláin*, in a boat. There were eleven men and eight women on board. They had plenty of sheep too. When they were a little way out, one of the sheep put its foot out through the boat. One of the women stuck her apron in the hole but that caused the whole board to fall out. The boat went down and everyone on it was drowned, except for one woman from Anach Cuain who was called Máire Lally. There was one man called Thomas Coscar who was a good swimmer. He came in to land but went out again to save a woman. But they all gathered round him and all were drowned. All the sheep were saved because they could swim.

Anach Cuain is seven miles north of Galway, beside Lough Corrib. *Cnoc an Diolláin* is in the Claddagh, behind Galway city.

*(S30: 170–1. Micheál Mac Fhearáil, 50, Ceathrú an Bhrúnaigh, Gaillimh. Feilméara. 10 Eanáir 1937.)*


## The Russian Vessel (P)

About twenty-three years ago, shortly before the Great War, a sailing vessel was coming from Russia to Galway with a cargo of timber for Messrs. McDonagh. An Aran pilot took charge of her from Aran to Galway. Before he reached Galway harbour, he ran the vessel ashore on Mutton Island. The crew came safely ashore.

The vessel was heavily insured by its owner. The owner got his insurance and left the vessel there. Mr McDonagh bought the boat cheap. It was very picturesque on the Road Stead in Galway Bay. Three years ago it was sold to a Dublin foundry firm, who sent men to scrap it up. The iron, which was very valuable, was used for different purposes.

This Dublin firm exported most of the material to Sheffield and most of it was used for making knives. So this ends the history of the Russian vessel, which had the figurehead of a lady nine feet in length on its bow, which most ships carried in those days.

*(S30: 442. Written by Isobel O'Donnell, 11, New Docks, Galway.*
*I got this story from my father who heard it from his father.)*

# CROMWELL

### Ireton and the Poor Clares (NB)

The people of this district have an old story dealing with the middle of the seventeenth century.

When Cromwell left, his destination was England. He put Ireton in charge of his soldiers. Ireton came to Galway in 1652 and demanded surrender. Galway yielded after many months. Then Ireton's soldiers entered the city.

It is believed that the soldiers came near a Poor Clare convent, and they made the nuns flee from the convent. The nuns entered the River Corrib. The soldiers thought that these people would die, but their cloaks spread out in the water and the nuns were carried to safety on the opposite bank. After this incident this place was known as Nuns' Island.

*(S31: 149. Patrick Doyle from Mrs Doyle, New Docks,*
*Galway. 24 June 1938.)*

### Cromail i Roscam [Cromwell in Roscam] (O'm C)

Nuair a bhí Cromail ag teacht go Gaillimh chuaigh muintir Roscam taobh thiar de Dhroichead na Mine agus d'fhág siad a gcuid fataí agus a gcuid cruithneachta ina ndiaidh, mar bhí sé scríofa sa tairngreacht ag Naomh Mac Dara nach rachadh saighdiúirí Cromail níos faide siar na Droichead na Mine.

Nuair a bhí muintir Roscam taobh thiar de Dhroichead na Mine, chuaigh duine acu ar ais go dtí a mbaile dúchais chun na tithe agus an chruithneacht d'fheiceáil. Nuair a bhí sé ag an mbóthar an taobh seo den chathair, casadh arm Cromail air. Cheistigh an Caiptéin é.

'Cén t-ainm atá ortsa, nó cé as a dtáinig tú, agus cá bhfuil tú ag dul?' ar seisean.

'Sé an Breathnach an sloinneadh atá ormsa,' arsa'n fear.

'Ó tharla gurb 'in an t-ainm atá ort,' arsa an Caiptéin, 'scríobhfaidh mé ticéad anois agus taispeáin é d'aon duine a chuirfeas ceist ort. Táim 'gá thabhairt duit mar sé an t-ainm céanna atá ormsa is atá ort.'

Ghlac sé an ticéad agus ansin bhí saorchead aige dul trí'n arm. Nuair a tháinig sé féin agus a mhuintir go dtí Roscam, bhí na tithe lán de strainséirí agus bhí ceann na cruithneachta ite acu ag iarraidh iad féin a bheathadh.

Chuaigh sé ar ais arís ansin agus d'inis sé an scéal dá chomharsan. Ansin, ghlac siad misneach agus tháinig siad ar fad ar ais go dtí a mbaile féin san oíche. Cheap siad go mb'fhearr dóibh na tithe ar fad a dhó san oíche nó go mbeadh na strainséirí ann go brách. Níor cuireadh ceann ar na tithe sin ó shin.

**TRANSLATION:**

When Cromwell was coming to Galway, the people of Roscam went west beyond Mine Bridge and left their potatoes and wheat behind them because it was written in Saint Mac Dara's prophecy that Cromwell's soldiers wouldn't go past that bridge.

When the people were beyond the bridge, one person went back home to look at the houses and the wheat. When he was on the road this side of the city, he met Cromwell's army. The captain questioned him.

'What's your name, and where are you from, and where are you going to?' he said.

'My surname is Walsh,' answered the man.

'Since that's your name,' said the captain. 'I'll write you a pass now. Show it to anyone who'll question you. I'm giving it to you because you have the same name as myself.'

He took the pass and he got a free passage through the army. When he and his people came to Roscam, the houses were full of strangers and they had eaten the heads off the wheat to feed themselves.

The man went back and told the story to his neighbours. They took courage and returned to their home at night. They thought it'd be better to burn all the houses or there'd be strangers in them forever. Those houses were never roofed since that time.

*(S32: 504–5. No name given.)*

# STRONG MEN AND GIANTS

### *Giant Hugh and his Hound (O'm B)*

Many years ago there was a giant called Hugh living in Maree in the parish of Oranmore. The town land of Maree takes its name from this giant – *Machaire Aoidh* (Hugh's plain).

Aodh, or Hugh, was a member of the Fianna. He was said to be ten foot tall. He had been employed by the people to build a causeway from Ardfry to Middle Third. There are still traces of the causeway to be seen.

This giant Hugh had a great hound of which he was very proud. The hound was seven feet in length. One day Hugh tied the hound to a large rock. The hound was left here for some hours. When the tide came in, the dog barked in alarm. Unfortunately, no one heard him and the hound was drowned. When the tide went out, Hugh came and found the body of his hound. In anger and sorrow, he tore the large rock from the ground. He broke it into three pieces. One piece he threw into Ardfry. The second piece he threw into Cloch Fhada; this is the stone from which Cloch Fhada takes its name. He left the third piece in Kilcaimen.

The track of the giant's feet and the trace of the front paws of the hound are to be seen in Cloch Fhada. The hound was buried on the seashore and the shape of the hound can be traced in the grass which grows there.

*(S32:438–40. Taken down by Caomhghin Ó Treabhair, Rinn Mhíl.*
*He was told the story by his mother who in turn heard it from her uncle.)*

### *Réamonn an Cairéaraidhe (C'g)*

Réamonn an Cairéaraidhe lived about ninety years ago. He lived in Two-Mile-Ditch in this parish. The ruins of his house are to be seen opposite Fallons' now. It is situated in a field called *Garraí Réamoinn*.

He was 80 or 90 when he died. He was a very strong man. Raymond Jennings was his real name. He was called Réamonn an Cairéaraidhe because he used to work as a labourer for other farmers in this area and drew carts for them.

It was he who rolled the pillar stones to the Franciscan abbey in Galway with a crow bar. These stones were found in Larry Cooley's quarry beside the Merview Road in this parish. He had a young boy helping. When Réamonn would turn the pillar stone, the young boy would put another stone under it, so that Réamonnn could turn it again. The distance to the abbey was about a mile and a quarter. It took him about a month to lever each stone. It was on the Merview Road he levered them.

The largest stones are six feet in length and must have been three feet square at the base. The smallest are about a foot shorter and are about the same size as the others at the base.

One day, as he was levering one of the stones, Réamonn met a man at the bottom of the Merview hill. The man had a ton of Indian meal in a cart and his horse failed to draw it up the hill. Réamonn took the horse out from the cart and went under it himself and drew it up the hill.

Another day, when he was picking potatoes, his horse ran away. In the evening, Réamonn filled the cart with potatoes and drew it home himself.

*(S30: 27. Úna Ní Mhaoildhia, Cluain na gCáiníní, Gaillimh.*
*Ó Hanraoi Ó Griallais, 40, Caisleán Gearr, Gaillimh.)*


### Giants (NB)

A giant was once supposed to live near Loughatalia. He was able to throw large rocks about half a mile away. One time, another giant wanted to fight him and he was called Fiachail. They met and they had a great fight. The first giant put the second one, Fiachail, to flight and he was supposed to jump from Loughatalia to Renmore. That was known afterwards as the Giant's Leap.

This lake is so called because the seawater comes into the sea lake, Loughatalia, sometimes. That is the reason why it is given that name.

*(S31: 137. Patrick Doyle, from Mrs Doyle, 39, New Docks, Galway. 25 April 1938.)*


### Droim Dearg [Droim Dearg] (C'b)

Bhí Droim Dearg ina chónaí ar chreag Bhaile an Dubhlaoich. Bhí a chuid bróg sé throigh agus dhá orlach ar fhaid. Dhéanfadh siad cónra d'fhear ar bith sa tír. Bhí sé in ann crann mór a thógáil as an talamh le lámh amháin agus bhaineadh sé na géaga de agus dhéanadh sé maidí siúil díobh. Bhí sé ag caitheamh cloch mhór thar thithe na ndaoine fadó. Ritheadh sé tríd an dá dhoras ag breith ansin uirthi sula dtiteadh sí ar an talamh. Bhíodh sé ag goid chuile rud ó na daoine saibhir agus á thabhairt chuig na daoine bochta.

Tá creag Bhaile an Dubhlaoich taobh thiar den bhaile féin atá trí mhíle ó Ghaillimh ar bhóthar Áth Cinn.

**TRANSLATION:**

Droim Dearg lived on a stony crag in Ballindooly. His shoes were six feet and two inches long. They'd make a coffin for any man in the country. He could lift a big tree out of the ground with one hand. He'd take the branches off it and make walking sticks. Long ago he used to throw a big stone over the people's houses. He'd run through the house and catch the stone before it fell to the ground. He'd steal everything from the rich people and give it to the poor.

Ballindooly crag is behind the village itself, which is three miles from Galway on the Headford Road.

*(S30: 167. Máirtín Ó Ruaidhín, 63, Coill Uachtair, Gaillimh. Feilméara.*
*Fuair sé an scéal seo óna athair 30 bliain ó shin. 7 Nollaig 1938.)*

# HIDDEN TREASURE

## Ciste Óir i bhFolach [Hidden Gold] (B'p)

Bhí fear an-saibhir ina chónaí i dteach ins na Forbacha tráth. Bhí corcán d'ór na Spáinne aige. Bhí na péindlíthe i bhfeidhm ag an am seo agus bhí faitíos air go bhfaigheadh a namhaid é. Chuaigh sé amach lá agus thug sé leis an t-ór chun é a chur i bhfolach. Shiúil sé tuairim is leathmhíle go dtáinig sé chomh fada le cloch mhór. Cloch na Síóg a thugtar ar an áit agus chuir sé an t-ór i bhfolach faoin gcloch. D'fhág sé ansin é agus níor chorraigh sé é ná níor chorraigh aon duine eile é ach oiread. Díreach nuair a bhí sé ag fáil bháis, ghlaoigh sé ar cheann de na comharsana chuige agus thug sé an rún dó. Cailleadh an fear agus cuireadh é. Nuair a bhí sé seal curtha ansin, Seán Ó Loideáin, sin é an t-ainm a bhí ar an bhfear ar tugadh an rún dó, (labhair sé) le comharsa darbh ainm Seán Gabha fán rún. Bheartaíodar eatarthu féin go rachaidís ag lorg na háite an lá ina dhiaidh sin.

Lá arna mhárach, chuadar go dtí an áit. Chonaic Seán Ó Loideáin an chloch mhór agus rith sé chuige agus thosaigh sé ag cartadh faoi. Níorbh fhada go dtáinig sé chomh fada leis an ór agus ní raibh sé in ann labhairt le teann áthais. Ansin rinne sé comhartha le Seán Gabha teacht de chabhair air agus mo léan rinne sé amhlaidh. Nuair a tháinig Seán Gabha go dtí an áit ní raibh tásc ná tuairisc le fáil ar an ór agus gan le feiceáil ach leac bheag. Is dóigh nach raibh ceart ag Seán Ó Loideáin insint do neach beo fán ór agus gurbh shin é an fáth gur imigh sé as amharc nuair a tháinig an dara fear go dtí an áit.

**TRANSLATION:**

Once upon a time there was a very rich man living in a house in Furbo. He had a crock of Spanish gold. The penal laws were in force at the time and the man was afraid the enemy would get the gold. One day he went out and took the gold to hide it. He walked about half a mile until he came to a big stone. That place is called the Fairy Stone and he hid the gold under it. He left the gold there and never moved it, and no one else moved it either. Just as he was dying, he called one of his neighbours and told him the secret. He died and was buried. When he was a while buried, Seán Ó Loideáin (that's the name of the man who was given the secret) told a neighbour named Seán Gabha all about it. They decided they would go looking for the place next day.

Next day, they went to the place. Seán Ó Loideáin saw the big stone. He ran to it and began digging. It didn't take long to find the gold. He was so excited he couldn't speak. He signed to Seán Gabha to come and help him and, alas, he did just that. But when Seán Gabha came to the place, there was no gold at all, nothing to be seen but a small flagstone. Probably, Seán Ó Loideáin shouldn't have told anyone else about the gold and that's the reason it disappeared when the second man came to the place.

*(S30: 418. Máire Ní Chearra, Barr na Crannaighe, Gaillimh, a scríobh síos, Márta 1938. Fuair mé an scéal seo ó mo sheanuncail, Micheál Ó Flannnachadha, 72, feilméara, Barr na Crannaighe, Páirc na Sceach, Gaillimh. Tógadh sna Forbacha é agus fuair sé an scéal seo ó Pheadar Ó Flannachadha, 35 bliain ó shin.)*

## Ór i bhFolach [Hidden Gold] (NB)

Sa tseanaimsir do bhí mórán daoine ag iarraidh Éire a bhaint de na hÉire-annaigh. Do bhí a fhios acu go raibh mórán saibhris in sna coláistí agus in sna teampaill. Tháinig na Lochlannaigh agus do rinneadar dún mór sa taobh theas de Chondae na Gaillimhe ar bruach na Sionainne. Do bhíodar go láidir ann agus do rinne na Gaeil mórán iarrachta ar na Lochlannaigh do dhíbirt as an dtír.

Ní raibh aon mhaitheas ann ach do tháinig na Gaeil go léir le chéile in arm mór agus do bhí troid ann agus briseadh ar na Lochlannaigh. Bhí iachall orthu imeacht as an dtír ar fad. Do chuireadar ór agus airgead i bhfolach sa talamh. Do rinneadh mórán iarrachta ar an ór a fháil ar ais ach ní raibh aon mhaitheas ann. Deirtear go bhfuil mí-ádh ar na daoine a bhíonn dá lorg.

**TRANSLATION:**

In the olden days many people were trying to take Ireland from the Irish. They knew there were riches in the colleges and churches. The Vikings came and built a big fort in the south of County Galway, on the banks of the Shannon. They were a strong force and the Irish made many attempts to force them out.

Nothing was any good, until the Irish came together in one big army and the Vikings were defeated. They had to flee the country completely. They hid the gold and silver in the ground. Many attempts were made to retrieve that gold but it was no use. They say anyone who searches for it will have bad luck.

*(S31:23. Pádraig Ó Dubhghaill. Fuair mé an scéal seo ó*
*Éamonn Ó Dubhghaill, Na Duganna, Gaillimh.)*

## Ór i bhFolach [Hidden Gold] (NB)

Chuala mé na seandaoine á rá go minic go raibh pota óir i bhfolach faoi chrann a bhí in san reilig. Dúirt cuid de na seandaoine gur ór a bhí ann. Dúirt daoine eile gur coróin a bhí ann.

Tháinig na daoine óga ón áit agus chuaigh siad isteach sa reilig ag lorg an óir. Bhí sábh ag ceann de na fearaibh agus thosaigh sé ag gearradh an

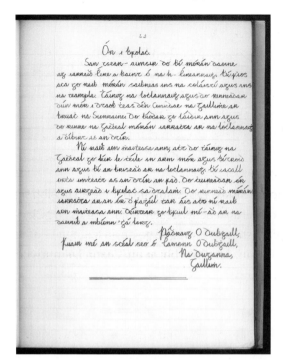

**'Ór i bhFolach' recalled by Éamonn Ó Dubhghaill of New Docks, Co. Galway, and recorded by Pádraig Ó Dubhghaill. The Schools' Collection, Volume 0031, Page 0023.**

chrainn. Ní raibh sé i bhfad ag obair nuair a fuair sé bás. Bhí an chaint sin ag dul ar aghaidh tríd an Chladach.

Tháinig fear eile leis an obair chéanna a dhéanamh agus fuair sé bás freisin. Tá an t-ór ann fós agus ní dheachaigh aon duine á lorg ón lá sin amach.

**TRANSLATION:**

I often heard the old people saying that there was a pot of gold hidden under a tree in the graveyard. Some of the old people said that it was gold was in it and others said it was a crown.

The local young people went into the graveyard to look for the gold. One man had a saw and he began to cut down the tree. He wasn't long working when he died. There was talk about that in the Claddagh.

Another man came to do the same work and he died too. The gold is still there but no one has gone to look for it since.

*(S31: 24. Máirtín de Brún. Fuair mé an scéal seo ó*
*Bhean de Brún, Cnoc an Diolláin, Gaillimh.)*

## Coróin Óir [A Golden Crown] (NB)

In san gCladach fadó, bhí rí agus banríon ina gcónaí. Chuala mé ó shean-bhean lá amháin go raibh ór le fáil in san gCladach agus gurb é an áit a bhfuil sé le fáil ná 'Ceann Láimhrighe'.

Nuair a bhí Cromail ag teacht isteach ar an trá, chuir na daoine as an gCladach an t-ór seo in san áit sin. Tháinig muintir an Chladaigh ó chlanna Spáinneacha agus mar gheall air sin bhí fáinne speisialta acu agus tugtar 'croí agus lámh' ar an bhfáinne sin.

Tá dealbh i dteampall Naomh Muire agus chuir na daoine an dealbh sin in san talamh nuair a bhí Cromail ag teacht isteach. Fuair fear as an gClad-ach an dealbh sin cúpla bliain ó shin agus thug sé go dtí an teampall é agus bhí coróin ar an dealbh sin freisin. An t-ór a bhí ar an 'Ceann Láimhrighe' b'fhiú seacht gcéad punt nó mar sin é.

**TRANSLATION:**

Long ago in the Claddagh, there lived a king and a queen. One day I heard from an old woman that there was gold in the Claddagh, in a place called *'Ceann Láimhrighe'*[?].

When Cromwell was coming into the country, the Claddagh people hid the gold there. Claddagh people came from Spanish families and because of that they had a special ring which was called 'hand and heart'.

There is a statue in St Mary's church and the people buried it when Cromwell was coming. A Claddagh man found the statue a couple of years ago and took it to the church. There was a crown on the statue too. The gold that was in *'Ceann Láimhrighe'* was worth around £700.

*(S31: 25. Pádraig Ó Dochartaigh. Fuair mé an scéal seo ó
Mhicheál Mac Cuaig, 80 Ardán Naomh Doiminic, Gaillimh.)*

## Scéal Fá Chiste [Story about Hidden Treasure] (CGB)

Bhí seanfhear sa tír seo fadó. Bhí go leor airgid aige. Ní raibh a fhios ag na daoine cá raibh an t-airgead (i dtaisce aige). Bhídís ag cuartú go leor áiteacha ach ní raibh sé le fáil acu. Fuair an fear seo bás agus bhíodh go leor spideoga sa teach. An oíche seo chuaigh fear a chodladh sa teach agus ag a dó a chloʊ san oíche dhúisiʊh ceann de na spideoga é agus rug sé ar lámh an fhir agus thug sé ʊo dtí an teallach é. D'ardaiʊh sé aníos an leac agus b'shin an áit a raibh an t-airʊead. Thug sé an t-airʊead don fhear agus bhí sé saibhir ʊo deo arís.

**TRANSLATION:**

An old man lived here long ago. He had plenty of money. People didn't know where he had the money hidden. They searched a lot of places but it couldn't be found. This man died and there were a lot of robins in the house. One night, a man went to sleep in the house. At two o'clock in the morning, one of the robins wakened him. He grabbed the man's hand and led him to the hearth. When he lifted up the flagstone the money was there. He gave it to the man, who was rich ever after that.

*(S32: 125. Tadhg Ó Dubhagáin, Móinteach, Baile Chláir na Gaillimhe.)*

# PENAL TIMES

### Relics of the Penal Days (C'g)

In front of the grandstand on the Galway race course, there are two big round flat stones. Beside the big one, there is a smaller one. The big one was used as an altar. The priest used to say Mass there. The wine, water and towel were placed on the other one. The people of Ballybane, Parkmore and the nearby villages attended Mass there. The large stone is called *Carraig an Aifrinn*.

When Tom Molloy of Cloonmacauneen was young, he heard his grandfather saying there was a little chapel about two hundred yards from his house. The priest used to say Mass there some Sundays. There was not enough place for all the people in the chapel, for it was only twelve feet long and eight feet broad, and so some of the people had to kneel on the grass outside. The people made a small well inside it. The ruins of the chapel are to be seen still. People go to the well and bless themselves with the water and pray there.

About 130 years ago, Mass used to be celebrated in a little house beside the road where Tom Hynes' shed now stands. It is about fifteen or twenty yards from our house.

Father Carolan from County Cavan was the priest who always celebrated Mass there. He celebrated it on Sundays, holidays and some weekdays. He lived in a house nearby. The people from Loughtavarna attended Mass there. A large flat stone was used as an altar. A smaller one was used as a table for the water and the wine. When all the people could not fit in the little house, some would kneel outside the door. Father Carolan always remained in this parish while he was a priest. The little house was situated between two hills.

Beside the transforming station in Galway, there is a crossroads and that spot is called the Old Gallows. The people say that in their youth there was a priest hanged there by the English soldiers.

*(S30: 67–8. Nóra Bhreathnach a scríobh síos ó Hanraoi Ó Griallais,*
*Caisleán Gearr, Gaillimh.)*

# FAMINE

### An Drochshaol a Bhí Amuigh Fadó [Famine Long Ago] (P)

Cúpla bliain ó shin, chuala mé seanfhear á rá go raibh a athair amuigh i mbliain an ghorta. Dúirt sé go raibh na daoine ag fáil bháis leis an ocras. Ní raibh rud ar bith le hithe acu, ach coirce agus cruithneacht nach raibh aibí. Ní fhéadfadh na feilméaraí rud ar bith a chur mar bheadh sé ite ag daoine nuair a bheadh sé os cionn an talaimh.

Bhí feilméara saibhir ann agus bhí scioból mór min choirce cruinnithe suas aige. Bhí na daoine ag dul thart ag iarraidh gráinne min choirce in ainm Dé.

Gach lá, bhí daoine caillte ar thaobh an bhóthair agus gach áit eile. Rinne na daoine poll dóibh agus cuireadh na céadta corp in aon pholl amháin. Ní raibh siad ag déanamh aon uaigh san am sin mar a dhéanann siad inniu.

Nuair a bhí an gorta thart, tháinig tinneas mór agus bhí beagnach gach duine buailte leis an tinneas. Fuair na daoine an galar sin ó na daoine a bhí caillte ar thaobh an bhóthair. Is iomaí lá a bhí cúpla duine caillte in aon teach amháin.

Dúirt an seanfhear freisin go raibh a athair amuigh Oíche na Gaoithe Móire. Dúirt sé go bhfaca sé na tithe ag imeacht trí nó ceithre mhíle ag an ghaoth. Chonaic sé an fharraige mhór ag teacht isteach agus báthadh leath den domhan, idir fhir, mhná agus pháistí. Is mór an trua an domhan an uair sin mar bhí cuid de na páistí gan aon athair nó máthair acu.

**TRANSLATION:**

A couple of years ago, I heard an old man saying his father was alive during the Famine. He said people were dying from hunger. They had nothing to eat, only unripe corn and wheat. The farmers couldn't plant anything because it'd be eaten as soon as the crop would break the ground.

There was a rich farmer who had gathered up a big barn of oatmeal. The people were going around begging for a little oatmeal in the name of God.

Every day, there'd be people dead on the side of the road and everywhere else. They dug a hole for them and hundreds were buried in one hole. That time, they weren't making a single grave for people as they do now.

When the Famine was over, a terrible sickness came and almost everyone was affected. They got the disease from the people who were dead on the roadside. Many days, a couple of people died in the same house.

The old man said too that his father was alive the Night of the Big Wind. He said his father saw houses transported three or four miles by the wind. He saw the sea coming in and half the world was drowned, men, women and children. It was a great pity for the world that time because some of the children had no mother or father.

*(S30: 438–9. Cáit Ní Ioláin, 14, Baile Cláir, Rang 8. Fuaireas an scéal seo ó Mhicheál Mac Cuimín, Cinn Uisce, Baile Cláir.)*

### *Ranna Céad/ Rinne Céad (O'm B)*

This is the name of a field in the townland of Renville in Oranmore parish. The field was formerly divided into one hundred and sixteen lots, each containing one rood. People came from the Claddagh in Galway by boat and rented the field, each taking a rood, and sowed potatoes here. The land belonged to the Athy family, descendants of one of the Galway tribes.

During the Famine, the potatoes rotted in the ridges. That year the Claddagh people were unable to pay the rent of their little holdings and the crop was allowed to remain in the ground. The ridges can still be seen in the field.

*(S32: 482. Written down by the teacher.)*

# LANDLORDS

### *The Landlord (B)*

About a hundred years ago, the terms on which tenantry were allowed to have holdings on the Roxboro estate were that they had to be available on the landlord's estate at any or every time he required them, sometimes without wages, with the exception of a shilling a day. But whether they were paid or not, they had to be available to report for duty on the estate when the tenantry bell rang.

At that time, Candlemas day was a holiday of obligation, but as the tenantry bell rang that morning the men had to go to work on the demesne and therefore could not hear or attend Mass. The parish priest noticed that the congregation was much smaller than usual and as a result of inquiries the following week he found out the cause of it. In his sermon the next Sunday, he complained bitterly about the members of his congregation who had missed Mass on the holiday and informed them very earnestly that on no account whatsoever were they to go to work on the next Sunday or on St Patrick's Day, which was the next holiday.

The tenantry bell rang as usual on St Patrick's Day, but no tenants arrived on the estate. They had gone to Mass. About eleven o'clock the landlord was walking on his estate and noticed that there was no work in progress. He made inquiries as to the cause from his steward who was a Scotchman and was told that it was a holiday. This made the landlord very angry and he told the steward to have the tenantry bell rung and if the tenants did not arrive, to get the horses and to go out and seize all the tenants' cows. As none of the tenants turned up, so the landlord's orders were carried out. They seized all the cows and put them into the pound.

When the tenants returned from Mass, they found what the landlord had done. So they went to the priest and told him the whole story. The priest went to the steward and asked him for the key of the pound, but he refused.

So the priest went over to the pound and prayed. Then he touched the gate and immediately it opened and the tenants got their cows back again. Shortly after, the landlord got a disease and the odour that was from him would hunt anyone away. No one could go near him with food or drink and so he died.

*(S31: 256–9. Seán Ó Fáthaigh, Scoil Bhreandáin, Gaillimh.*
*Fuair sé an scéal óna athair Éamonn Ó Fáthaigh, Barr an Chalaidh, Gaillimh.)*

### Na Tiarnaí Talún [Landlords] (F)

Ba iad na Blácaigh agus na Loingsigh na tiarnaí talún sa gceantar seo. Bhíodar ann ar feadh na gcéadta bliain. Nuair a cuireadh daoine as seilbh, chuadar go dtí a muintir féin.

Cuireadh triúr deartháireacha as an teach fadó. Bhí siad ina gcónaí i dteach beag i bhForamaoil, agus bhíodar go han-chompordach. Chuir na saighdiúirí amach iad lá fuar ins an ngeimhreadh.

Chuaigh siad ar an aonach seachtain roimhe sin agus dhíol siad bó agus d'ól siad a luach. Tháinig an fear i ndeireadh na seachtaine leis an chíos a fháil uathu. Ní raibh aon phingin ag na créatúir bhochta le tabhairt dó. An chéad lá eile tháinig ochtar de na saighdiúiribh agus leag siad an teach. Níor fhágadar an teach go ciúin. Tháinig na comharsanaí le cúnamh a thabhairt dóibh ach ní raibh aon mhaith dóibh ann. Ní raibh aon troid ann an lá sin ach mar sin féin ní rabhadar sásta an teach a fhágáil. Bhí beirt tógtha mar gheall orthu. D'imigh na daoine go dtí a muintir a bhí ina gcónaí i gConamara, agus níor tháinig siad ar ais go dtí an áit ina dhiaidh sin.

Fuair na tiarnaí talún píosaí móra den talamh ar dtús agus ansin thug siad amach na feilmeachaí do na tionóntaí. Nuair a thugadh siad acra de thalamh maith d'fheilméara amháin, thabharfadh siad acra go leith de dhrochthalamh d'fheilméara eile. Chuiridís an cíos céanna ar an mbeirt.

Bhí na tiarnaí talún go holc leis na daoine. Nuair a chífeadh na daoine na tiarnaí talún ag teacht, théadh siad i bhfolach agus d'fhanaidís ansin go mbeadh siad imithe as radharc.

Thugadh na daoine coirce, fataí, tuí agus móin do na tiarnaí talún gach bliain. Muna dtugaidís na rudaí sin, chuirtí i bpríosún iad.

**TRANSLATION:**

The Blakes and Lynches were the landlords in this area. They were here for hundreds of years. When people were evicted, they'd go to their own relatives.

Three brothers were evicted from their house a long time ago. They were living comfortably in a small house in Foramoile. The soldiers evicted them one cold winter day.

They had gone to the fair a week before that. They sold a cow and drank her price. A man came at the end of the week to collect the rent. The poor creatures hadn't a penny to give him. Next day, eight soldiers came and knocked down the house. They didn't leave the house quietly. The neighbours came to help them but it was no good. There was no fight that day but still they weren't happy to leave the house. Two people were arrested. They went to live with their relatives in Connemara and never returned to that place.

In the beginning, the landlords got large tracts of land and then they leased the farms to tenants. When they'd give an acre of good land to one farmer, they'd give an acre and a half of bad land to another. They'd charge them both the same rent.

The landlords were bad to the people. When people would see them coming, they'd hide and stay hidden until they'd gone.

People gave corn, potatoes, straw and turf to the landlords every year. If they didn't, they'd be put in prison.

*(S30: 278–81. Fuarthas an scéal seo ó Mháire Ní Iarnáin, 50,*
*Foramoile, Bearna. Feilméara.)*


### Tiarnaí Talún [Landlords] (B)

Bhí an tiarna Séamus de Bláca i gCaisleán na Creige in Anach Chuain. Ní raibh seisean go dona chor ar bith agus bhíodh go leor fearaibh ag obair dhó. Rinne Risteard Ó Ciarbhán an-mhaitheas. Thóg sé scoil do chlann na dtionóntaí. Bhí tiarna darbh ainm Gunning i gCill Rua in Áth Cinn. Bhí sé an-ghéar ar na tionóntaí. Dhíbir sé táilliúir bocht a dtugaidís Tadhg Bacach air as an teach uair amháin. Ní fhéadfadh sé aon bháille a fháil lena chur amach agus leag sé an teach air. Nuair a chuala sagart an pharóiste faoi, bhí sé ar buile agus d'iarr sé ar mhuintir an pharóiste teacht le chéile leis an teach a chur suas arís.

Tháinig siad aon lá amháin agus chuir siad suas an teach agus bhí tine ag an táilliúir ann agus chodail sé ann an oíche sin. Nuair a bhí an teach leathdhéanta an lá sin bhí seanGunning agus an báille ag teacht i mbéal an bhóthair le dhá chapall agus cóiste. Dúirt fear éicint leis an sagart go raibh siad ag teacht.

'Feicfidh muid má thagann,' arsa'n sagart.

Bhris srianta an chapaill ansin agus d'imigh an dá chapall abhaile agus d'fhág siad Gunning agus an báille i lár an bhóthair agus ón lá sin amach níor bhac sé le Tadhg Bacach.

Bhí tiarna talaimh darbh ainm Lampurt (recte: Lambert) i gCaisleán Lampurt lámh le Baile Átha an Rí agus bhí sé chomh holc leis an diabhal féin agus nuair a fuair sé bás ní tharraingeodh na capaill (a chónra). Bhí siad dá mbualadh agus ag iarraidh orthu siúl in ainm Dé agus ní shiúlfadh siad coiscéim. Bhí duine ann a bhí chomh holc le Lampurt féin agus d'iarr sé orthu siúl in ainm an diabhail agus rith siad leo chomh mear is a bhí ina gcosa agus is cosúil gur chuig an diabhal a thug siad é.

D'imigh na daoine a díbríodh go dtí tithe na mbocht, go hAmericeá agus isteach go dtí na bailte móra.

**TRANSLATION:**

The landlord James Blake was in Cregg Castle, Annaghdown. He wasn't bad at all and plenty of men used to work for him. Richard Kirwan did a lot of good. He built a school for the tenants' families. There was a landlord named Gunning in Cill Rua in Headford. He was very hard on the tenants. Once, he evicted a poor tailor they called Tadhg Bacach from his house. Gunning couldn't find any bailiff to throw him out so he knocked down the house. When the parish priest heard about it, he was furious and he asked the people of the parish to come together to build the house again.

One day they came and put up the house. The tailor had a fire lit and slept there that night. That day, when the house was half built, old Gunning and his bailiff were coming along the road in a carriage with two horses. Somebody told the priest they were coming.

'We'll see if they come,' said the priest.

The reins broke then and the two horses ran off home. They left Gunning and the bailiff in the middle of the road and from that day forward Gunning never bothered with Tadhg Bacach again.

There was a landlord called Lampurt (recte: Lambert) in Castle Lampurt beside Athenry and he was as bad as the devil himself. When he died the horses wouldn't pull his coffin. They were striking the horses and telling them to walk on in God's name, but they wouldn't take one step. There was a person there who was just as bad as Lampurt and he asked them to walk on in the name of the devil. They ran as fast as they could and it seems that it was to the devil they were taking him.

The people who were evicted went to the Poor Houses, to America and into the towns.

*(S3: 224–6. T. Mac Eochaidh)*

## Tiarnaí Talún [Landlords] (B)

Bhí tiarna talún ann fadó agus bhí sé an-saibhir agus d'fhostaigh sé tiarna eile os cionn an talaimh. Tharla go raibh bean an-bhocht san áit agus ní raibh sí in ann aon chíos a íoc agus bhí an tiarna seo ag dul dá cur amach as an teach an lá seo. Bhí an tiarna mór ag dul thart an lá seo agus tháinig slabhra ocrais air. Chuaigh sé isteach sa teach seo agus d'iarr sé béile ar an mbean. 'Chuirfinnse síos pota fataí duit ach cén mhaith duit iad gan aon bhlas orthu?' (a dúirt an bhean.) 'Tá an t-anlann agam féin,' a deir sé agus rug sé greim ar scian phóca a bhí ar an mbord agus sháigh sé an mhuc (a bhí ansin) agus dúirt sé léi a bheith ag ithe go mbeadh a sáith ite aici. Thug sé litir di nuair a bhí sé ag imeacht agus nuair a tháinig an tiarna talún eile thug sí an litir dó agus dúirt sé léi go raibh a cíos íoctha aici.

**TRANSLATION:**

There was a landlord a long time ago and he was very rich and he employed a land steward over his lands. There was a very poor woman in that place and she couldn't pay any rent. One day, the land steward was going to throw her out of her house. The landlord was going past and he was starving with hunger. He went into a house and asked the woman for a meal. 'I'd put down a pot of potatoes for you,' said the woman, 'but what use would that be to you, without something tasty to go with them?' 'I have the sauce myself,' said he. He took hold of a penknife that was on the table and stuck it into a pig that was there. He told the woman to eat till she had eaten her fill. When he was leaving, he gave her a letter and when the land steward came round she gave him that letter. He told her her rent was paid.

*(S31: 241. Pádraig Ó Bhailís, 3 Sráid an Teampaill, Gaillimh.*
*Fuair mé é seo ó m'athair a rugadh agus a tógadh ar an gCeathrú Rua.)*

# FACTION FIGHTING

### Faction Fighting (P)

About a hundred years ago, faction fighting was very common. The game was carried on with blackthorn sticks and ash plants. One faction challenged another faction to meet in their town. Then, when the sides were ready, the fight commenced. They lashed each other with ash plants and blackthorns and blood was often spilt. Then when the beaten party surrendered, they went home. The law put an end to this game, which is called faction fighting. The fights were carried out mostly on fair days and holidays.

*(S30: 451. Written by Bea Mangan, 12, Upper Salthill, Galway.*
*I got this story from my grandmother who got it from her father.)*

# BUYING AND SELLING

### Buying and Selling (NB)

Shops were very scarce in this district long ago. If the people wanted anything they had to go up the town for it. Every Sunday after Mass there'd be people with tents and they'd be selling everything. The money was very scarce in the old times. Men used to work for 10 pence a day. Instead of money, the people used to exchange a score of eggs for a pound of tea. The people used to work a day in exchange for some goods and they used never buy or sell anything on a Saturday. They considered it very unlucky. The days they bought anything were Monday or Friday. The market has never

A jolly group in the market place, Galway, *c.* 1902.

changed; the cattle fair was always held at Fair Hill for the last thirty of forty years. There used to be peddlers and jugglers going around. They used to sell bootlaces and rosary beads. They used to buy country chairs and sell them at a profit. If the people had no money they would exchange eggs or butter for what they wanted.

*(S31: 132–3. Martin Browne. I got his from Mrs Raftery, 78, Fair Hill, Galway. 12 April 1938.)*

Shop Street, Galway.

### Díol agus Ceannach [Buying and Selling] (CGC)

Ní bhíodh mórán siopaí san áit seo fadó. Tá go leor acu ann anois. B'éigean
do na daoine dul go Gaillimh chun na rudaí a bhí ag teastáil uathu a cheannach. B'éigean dóibh siúl siar agus aniar. Ní raibh aon ghluaisteán acu mar
atá anois. Ní raibh mórán airgid ag na daoine fadó, bhí siad an-bhocht.
Níor bhain siad mórán úsáide as airgead. Séard a bhí siad ag déanamh
ná ag tabhairt earraí eile dá chéile. Bhídís ag tabhairt beithíoch dá chéile,
caiple, caoraigh, muca, cearca.

**TRANSLATION:**
There weren't many shops in this area long ago. There are plenty now.
People had to go to Galway to get the things they needed. They had to
walk there and back. They didn't have cars as they do now. They didn't
have much money long ago; they were very poor. They didn't use money a

lot. They used to exchange goods with each other. They'd exchange cattle, horses, sheep, pigs and hens.

*(S32: 118. No name given.)*

## Aonaigh [Fairs] (C'g)

Tuairim is caoga bliain ó shin is i gCnoc an Diolúin dhá mhíle ón scoil seo agus in aice cathair na Gaillimhe a bhíodh an t-aonach ba ghaire dúinn. Faiche imeartha do mhuintir na Gaillimhe atá san áit anois agus ní bhíonn aon aonach ann. Sa bhFaiche Mhór a bios na haonaigh anois.

Maidin an aonaigh, bhíodh fear ina sheasamh ar an mbóthar ag Leacht an Bhearna sa bparóiste seo agus chaithfeadh gach duine go raibh stoc aige pingin nó dhá phingin a íoc leis sula ligtí isteach go dtí an t-aonach é. Thugadh sé an t-airgead sin do Chomhairle na Cathrach chun sráideanna na cathrach thart ar Chnoc an Diolúin a ghlanadh.

Cuireadh deireadh leis an aonach seo mar gheall ar dhá rud. Bhí an pháirc sin an-íseal fliuch agus bhíodh daoine agus stoc ag dul in abar ann dá mbeadh an aimsir go dona. Rud eile, ba mhaith le siopadóirí na cath-rach na haonaigh a bheith istigh i lár na cathrach acu, mar bhí a fhios acu go gcaithfeadh muintir na tuaithe cuid dá gcuid airgid ansin sula rachadh siad abhaile.

San am sin, bhíodh aonach mór amháin ann agus sheasadh sé trí lá, i mí Mheán Fómhair, ar an gcéad, an dara agus an tríú lá den mí. Aonach Chnoc an Diolúin a thugtaí ar an aonach seo. Capaill a bhíodh ann an chéad lá, muca an dara lá, caoirigh agus beithígh an tríú lá. D'fhan an t-ainm céanna ar an aonach mór a bhíonn anois sa bhFaiche Mhór san mí chéanna. Bíonn aonach mór eile anois ann i mBealtaine agus tugtar Aonach na Faiche Móire air.

Théadh ceannaitheoirí ó thigh go tigh faoin dtuath ag ceannach stoic agus déanann siad fós é freisin corruair.

Nuair a bhíonn fear ag tabhairt an stoic atá ceannaithe aige go dtí stad na traenach lá an aonaigh anois, caithfidh sé 'custom' a íoc le fear ar an mbóthar, ceithre phingin ar mhuc nó caora agus sé pingine ar bhó.

Le taispeáint go bhfuil an t-ainmhí díolta, cuireann an ceannaitheoir a mharc air le breasal má tá sé aige, nó gearrann sé cuid den fhionnadh le siosúr. Muna bhfuil siosúr nó breasal aige, déanann sé é le lathaigh ar bharr a mhaide.

Tugtar 'luck-penny' i gcónaí, tuairim is leathchoróin ar bheithíoch agus sé pingine ar mhuc nó ar chaoraigh.

Tugtar an ceannrach le capall nuair a dhíoltar é ach de ghnáth bíonn ar an gceannaitheoir é a chur ar ais go dtí an fear ar leis é. Téann muintir na háite seo go dtí aonaigh i nGaillimh, Áth Cinn, Baile an Rí, An Spidéal, agus an Turloch Mór, ach is é Gaillimh an gnáthcheann. Má bhíonn aistear fada rompu, tugaid capall agus carr leo ach siúlaid go Gaillimh de ghnáth. Tosaíonn aonach na Gaillimhe timpeall a trí a chlog ar maidin.

**TRANSLATION:**

About fifty years ago, the closest fair to us was held in Dillon's Hill [?], two miles from this school beside, Galway city. It is a playing field for Galway people now and no fair is held there. The fairs are held in Eyre Square now.

On the morning of the fair, a man stood on the road at Laghtavarna in this parish. Everyone who had stock had to pay him a penny or two before they were allowed to go to the fair. He used to give that money to the City Council to clean the city streets around Dillon's Hill.

At that time, there used to be one big fair. It'd last three days: on the 1, 2 and 3 September. This fair was called Dillon's Hill Fair. There'd be horses on the first day, pigs on the second, sheep and cattle on the third. The big fair in Eyre Square in the same month is still called by that name. Another big fair is held there now in May and it is called the Eyre Square fair.

Buyers used to go from house to house in the countryside, buying up stock, and they still do sometimes.

Now when a man is taking the stock he has bought to the railway station on the fair day, he must pay 'custom' to the man on the road, four pence for a pig or a sheep or six pence for a cow.

To show that an animal is sold, the buyer puts a mark on it with raddle if he has it, or he cuts a piece of its hair with scissors. If he doesn't have raddle or scissors, he marks it with mud on the tip of his stick.

A 'luck-penny' is always given: about half a crown for cattle or six pence for a pig or a sheep.

The halter is given with a horse when it is sold, but usually the buyer has to return the halter to the owner. Local people go to fairs in Galway, Headford, Athenry, Spiddle and Turloughmore, but Galway is the most usual place. If they have a long journey, they might use a horse and cart but they usually walk to Galway. Galway fair starts around three o'clock in the morning.

*(S30: 36–7. Nóra Bhreathnach. Ó Hanraoi Ó Griallais, 40, Caisleán Gearr, Gaillimh.)*

## An tAonach [The Fair] (NB)

… Tugtar 'eirnist' le gach beithíoch a dhíoltar san aonach. Tugtar 'ádh-phingin' nó 'bonn-sochair' ar airgead eile a íoctar ann. Tugann an díoltóir leathchoróin ar gach capall a dhíolann sé, scilling ar bhó, naoi bpingine ar mhuc, leathscilling nó mar sin, réalt, ar chaora, don cheannaitheoir nuair a bhíonn gach ré déanta acu. Sin an chaoi a íoctar 'ádh-phingin' nó 'bonn-sochair' chun ádh a chur ar an stoc.

Nuair a dhéantar margadh buaileann fear amháin a dhá bhos le chéile agus déanann an fear eile an ní sin freisin. Tugadh airgead don díoltóir i dtreo is nach bhféadfadh sé a fhocal a bhriseadh. Théadh siad go dtí an teach ósta agus bhíodh deoch acu leis an margadh a chríochnú.

Nuair a bhíonn na beithígh díolta acu, gearrann siad cuid gruaige na mbeithíoch le hiarann marcáilte agus ansin cuireann fear na mbó a ainm ar na beithígh le lagdhath dearg. Nuair a thriomaíonn an dath ní féidir le duine eile an beithíoch a dhíol arís.

**TRANSLATION:**

… An 'earnest' is given with every animal sold at the fair. The other money that's paid is called 'luck money'. The seller gives a half crown with every horse he sells, a shilling with a cow, nine pence with a pig, six pence or so with a sheep, to the buyer when they have everything settled up. The 'luck money' is paid to send luck with the stock.

When a bargain is struck, one man slaps his two palms together and so does the other. The seller is given money so that he cannot break his word. They used to go to the hotel and have a drink to finish the bargain.

When they have sold the animals, they cut some of the animal's hair with a marking iron and then the man who has bought the animals puts his name on them with a light red colour. When the colour dries, no one else can sell the animal again.

*(S31: 123–4. Pádraig Ó Dubhghaill. Fuaireas seo ó Bhean Uí Dhubhghaill, 39, Na Duganna, Gaillimh. 14 Márta 1938.)*

## Gombeen Money (P)

Gombeen money was loaned by a man in a village. The gombeen man used to charge about five shillings for the pound interest for this money. This was a common practice up to forty or fifty years ago.

*(S30: 452. Written by Bea Mangan, 12, Upper Salthill, Galway. I got this story from my uncle who heard it from his grandfather.)*

# TRAVELLERS

## Beggars (NB)

Up until recently a man named O'Reilly used to come around begging. He used to sell ballads for a penny. When the children saw him coming, they used to say, 'Up Tuam'. This made him very much annoyed.

Long ago, the people used to bring them (the travellers) in and make tea for them. During the bad weather, in the country, the people used to put them up for the night. When you give them alms, the travelling people bless you and your family and all the souls that ever left you. There are very few beggars going around now as the government is giving them all sorts of employment.

Up until recently, the country people came to Galway bare footed. They had to walk in and out and carry their own luggage. On a bad winter's night, the people would bring in the tinkers and give them a comfortable meal and a night's lodgings.

The neighbours around come in and listen to the tinker's stories. The women tinkers would be able to tell you your fortune.

*(S31: 89–90. Máirtín de Brún, Cnoc a Diolúin, Gaillimh.*
*I got this information frm Mrs Raftery whose age is 98.)*

# GAMES

### Games (NB)

There was a game of hurling in this district in times gone by. A team from Claregalway was playing a team from Castlegar. There were fifteen men on each side. The captains were Leahy and Flaherty. The men came from Claregalway and places near, and from Castlegar.

The game was played in the Sports Field. There were two parishes playing. Before a large crowd, Castlegar won by a small margin. The best players were Flaherty for Castlegar and Leahy and Quinn for Claregalway. Some of the players were hurt on the field.

The young men long ago used to play in what were called 'parish matches'. This was a game played between two parishes. They wore hurling caps and a colour represented each village. The people also wore jerseys when they played on either side.

They used to have a leather ball which used to be bigger than now and this was made by the shoemaker. The hurls then were larger than now and they were 'spliced'.

The other games they played in the open air were handball, rounders, bowls, throwing the hammer.

They played all these games at the crossroads and there were large crowds present at these gatherings. After the sports, they usually held crossroads dances.

*(S31: 128–9. Patrick Doyle. I got this story from Mrs Doyle, 44,*
*New Docks, Galway. 30 March 1938.)*

# AFTERWORD

Our family moved to Galway in 2009. It is an open, friendly place and people here are well used to receiving visitors and new citizens alike. All are welcomed and so it was with us. Still, I felt strange, as if I'd never get the measure of the place in all its exciting variation. Between old and new, there seemed to be too much to get a hold on. I couldn't find the heart of it.

Working with this material from the Schools' Collection has given me a way in. The children's handwritten accounts function as one layer of the palimpsest that is the story of Galway city and its surrounding areas. This research has forged a link with this beautiful city we now call home. I understand it better at every level: physical, historical, cultural, linguistic and emotional.

Such is the nature of oral tradition. It allows you to take the pulse of a people at a particular point in time – a pulse not always audible in written documents, or even in photographs. It has been a privilege and my hope is that readers, in Galway and further afield, will also feel something of the excitement of listening to these young voices, telling their own complex story in the 1930s.

Our gratitude goes to the founders of the Schools' Scheme, to the teachers and pupils who undertook the work, and to all the many local people who contributed lore to this memory archive. This culture-hoard can only become more valuable with the passing of time – *go gcúití Dia a saothar leo go léir*.

# NOTES

1   *Connacht Tribune*, 20 November 1937

2   http://portal.unesco.org/culture

3   S. Heaney, *North* (London, 1975)

4   See M. Briody, *The Irish Folklore Commission, 1935-1970: History, Methodology, Ideology* (Finland, 2007)

5   Séamas Ó Catháin, 'Súil Siar ar Scéim na Scol, 1937–1938', in *Sinsear* 5 (1988), pp. 19–30, and Séamas Ó Catháin, 'Scéim na Scol', in Margaret Farren and Mary Harkin (eds), *It's Us They're Talking About: Proceedings of the McGlinchey Summer School* (Clonmany, 1998)

6   An Roinn Oideachais, *Irish Folklore and Tradition* (Dublin, 1937)

7   See http://www.ucd.ie/irishfolklore/english_html/schools.htm.

8   Jonny Dillon, 'Folklore schools 1937–38', researchrepository.ucd.ie/.../ResearchPaper_FolkloreSchools1937–38.pdf. (2010)

9   Adrian Kelly, *Compulsory Irish, Language and Education in Ireland, 1870s–1970s* (Dublin, 2002)

10  Pádraig Ó Riagáin, 'The Galway Gaeltacht 1926–1981' in Gerard Moran and Raymond Gillespie (eds), *Galway, History & Society* (Dublin, 1996), pp. 651–80

11  Rialtas na hÉireann, *Gaeltacht Commission Report* (Dublin, 1926)

12  Rialtas na hÉireann, *Census of Population* (1926), vol. viii

13  Diarmaid Ferriter 'Ireland in the Twentieth Century', www.gov.ie/en/essays/twentieth.html

14  See: dublinopinion.com/.../the-irish-rural-working-class-and-1930s-ireland/

15  Peadar O'Dowd, *Old and New Galway* (Galway, 1985)

16  *Connacht Tribune*, 31 December 1938

17  *Connacht Tribune*, 3 December 1938

18    *Connacht Tribune*, 26 March 1938

19    *Connacht Tribune*, 15 October 1938

20    John Connolly, fisherman. Minutes of Evidence before Coimisiún na Gaeltachta, 31 August 1925, p. 7

21    *Connacht Tribune*, 12 February 1938

22    *Connacht Tribune*, 12 December 1937

23    *Connacht Tribune*, 1 January 1938

24    *Connacht Tribune*, 3 April 1937

25    *Connacht Tribune*, 15 October 1938

26    guh.hse.ie/About_Us/A_Little_History/

27    *Connacht Tribune*, 21 August 1937

28    *Connacht Tribune*, 25 June 1938

29    *Connacht Sentinel*, 12 October 1937

30    *Connacht Tribune*, 22 October 1937

31    *Connacht Tribune*, 6 November 1937

32    *Connacht Tribune*, 15 October 1938

33    *Connacht Sentinel*, 9 February 1937

34    *Connacht Tribune*, 31 December 1938

35    *Connacht Sentinel*, 9 February 1937

36    *Connacht Tribune*, 20 March 1937

37    *Connacht Tribune*, 31 December 1938

38    *Connacht Tribune*, 24 December 1938

39    *Galway Advertiser*, 30 December 2008

40    *Connacht Sentinel*, 12 January 1937

41    *Connacht Sentinel*, 20 April 1937

42    *Connacht Tribune*, 8 October 1938

43    *Connacht Tribune*, 10 December 1938

44    *Connacht Tribune*, 25 September 1937

45    Foreword in *Claregalway, Parish History: 750 Years* (Claregalway Historical and Cultural Society, 1999)

46    Caitríona Hastings, *Ag Bun na Cruaiche: Folklore and Folklife from the Foot of Croagh Patrick* (Dublin, 2009)